LADEN CHOIRS

LADEN CHOIRS

The Fiction of
PATRICK WHITE

Peter Wolfe

THE UNIVERSITY PRESS OF KENTUCKY

Copyright © 1983 by The University Press of Kentucky

Scholarly publisher for the Commonwealth,
serving Bellarmine College, Berea College, Centre
College of Kentucky, Eastern Kentucky University,
The Filson Club, Georgetown College, Kentucky
Historical Society, Kentucky State University,
Morehead State University, Murray State University
Northern Kentucky University, Transylvania University,
University of Kentucky, University of Louisville,
and Western Kentucky University.

Editorial and Sales Offices: Lexington, Kentucky 40506-0024

Library of Congress Cataloging in Publication Data

Wolfe, Peter, 1933–
    Laden choirs.

    Includes index.
    1. White, Patrick, 1912–   —Criticism and
interpretation. I. Title.
PR9619.3.W5Z95 1983   823   83–6831
ISBN 0-8131-1501-9

Contents

To Marla Schorr,
the Newby with the copper eyes,
and her blacklipped chum,
Captain Prewash

Acknowledgments

THE AUTHOR and publisher join in expressing their thanks for permission to quote copyrighted passages to the following: from *The Aunt's Story, The Burnt Ones, The Eye of the Storm, Flaws in the Glass, A Fringe of Leaves, The Living and the Dead, Riders in the Chariot, The Solid Mandala, The Tree of Man, The Twyborn Affair, The Vivisector,* and *Voss,* by permission of Patrick White, Curtis Brown (Australia), Ltd., Jonathan Cape, Ltd., and Viking Penguin, Inc.; from *Happy Valley,* by permission of Patrick White.

The time and energy of a number of people went into the preparation of this book. Special thanks are owed to Alan Lawson for his kind help with bibliographical problems; to Roland Champagne and Howard Schwartz for supplying rich background data; to Theresa Smythe for typing and proofreading the manuscript; and to the University of Missouri-St. Louis Graduate College for grants to cover expenses connected with researching the manuscript.

The combined help of the following people amounts to a major contribution: Jane Novak, Norman Simms, Buster Fulbright, Emil Sitka, Dennis Trent, Elmer Crow, Philip Wolfe, Jack Lowe, Gordon W. Jacobson, and Graham Pascoe.

A NOTE TO THE READER: All quotations from White's work are taken from the following editions; instances where an edition doesn't correspond to a work's first printing will be noted in the text:

The Aunt's Story. New York: Viking Press, 1948.
The Burnt Ones. New York: Viking Press, 1964.
The Cockatoos. New York: Viking Press, 1975.
The Eye of the Storm. New York: Viking Press, 1974.
Flaws in the Glass. New York: Viking Press, 1982.
A Fringe of Leaves. New York: Viking Press, 1977.
Four Plays. New York: Viking Press, 1966.
Happy Valley. London: Harrap, 1939.
The Living and the Dead. 1941; rpt., Middlesex: Penguin, 1967.
Riders in the Chariot. New York: Viking Press, 1961.
The Solid Mandala. New York: Viking Press, 1966.
The Tree of Man. New York: Viking Press, 1955.
The Twyborn Affair. New York: Viking Press, 1980.
The Vivisector. New York: Viking Press, 1970.
Voss. New York: Viking Press, 1957.

1. The Art
of the Copious

READERS HAVE started to feel that Patrick White is a good writer because he is Patrick White; they can admire one of his novels because if it weren't good he wouldn't have written it. They needn't look far to justify their admiration. White has the abundance of a major author who doesn't limit himself to one kind of book or restrict his range of experience. Although *The Tree of Man* (1955), *Voss* (1957), and *A Fringe of Leaves* (1976) convey the power and immensity of the wilderness, the setting of a White novel can also be urban. When he isn't returning to Australia's pioneer past, he will respond to our technological, pluralist society. That society needn't be Australian; parts of his best work take place in England, France, Germany, and Greece. Yet these locales are almost always seen through Australian eyes. Members of both the Australian colonial aristocracy and working class appear in all but one of his books, each of which gives a map of Australian society. Besides writing about artists and artisans, he portrays librarians, prostitutes, and soldiers. In *The Tree of Man, Riders in the Chariot* (1961), *The Vivisector* (1970), and *The Eye of the Storm* (1973), several important characters work in the homes of the rich.

Despite his awareness of social mobility in the industrial state, White rarely tries his hand at journalistic realism or institutional criticism. No social historian he. He doesn't show the expansion of cities and the growth of railways in Australia, nor does he chart the corresponding decline of sheep and cattle raising, gold mining, and grain growing. White offers visions, not programs. Grand in conception and strong in execution, his novels convey a fullness of statement, giving the impression that everything important about a subject has been said. This Victorian finality bypasses moral judgment. White belongs in the Flaubertian tradition of

the writer who disavows literature as a practical guide. No teacher or
prosecuting attorney, he doesn't want to lecture or to foment social and
political activity. Instead, he has carved out a system of deep-running
continuities by which we may be enriched. The process of enrichment isn't
always smooth; some of the action he describes is brutal, and some of his
insights make us wince. He would rather provoke than amuse. Perhaps he
provokes to excess. If entertainment stresses complexity of plot and serious fiction dwells on complexity of character, his delvings and nuances
reveal a jut-jawed rejection of the literary entertainer's role. He has wid-
ened the unfortunate twentieth-century split between serious art and
popular entertainment. His books, with their epigraphs and learned allusions, their foreign words and carefully honed ironies, display formal
splendor and linguistic cunning. They explore meaning itself, rather than
developing meaning through action, with most of what goes on happening
inside the characters' heads.

   White's slow-paced intensity builds from a relentless, probing technique. No literary playboy, he takes his work seriously. Indeed, his recent
practice of beginning his novels with three or four epigraphs smacks of
piety and uplift. The epigraphs add to the pored-over literary climate. They
state truths that the novel will explain, and besides serving as advance
notices of White's beliefs, they also prefigure his practice (another legacy
of the Joycean school of fiction writing) of killing several meanings at once.

   The centrality of artists in *Tree*, *Riders*, and *Vivisector* implies a unity
of impulse that a survey of motifs from his canon supports. Though
different, the novels all depend on each other. White sees life in the round,
yoking the depth and mystery of the human soul to the slapstick of
everyday existence. Often attacked for his plodding seriousness, he enjoys
verbal clowning as much as did his early mentor, James Joyce. *Voss*
includes a midwife named Mrs. Child, a Dr. Kilwinning who is notorious
for charging high fees, and a Mr. Plumpton, "whose name did not fit his
form" (p. 231). Again tuning his skills to a Joycean key, White displays his
anti-authoritarianism by giving a brothel-going policeman in *Riders* the
name McFaggott. This verbal fun can convey respect and admiration as
well as disdain; a saintly nurse in *Eye* is called Mary de Santis. White's
clowning freshens his perspective. If he failed to present the funny side of
his characters, he would be giving a foreshortened picture. We are all
laughable at times. In 1969 he discussed his art as a striving toward
wholeness, to which humor is essential: "I have the same idea with all my
books: an attempt to come closer to the core of reality, the structure of
reality, as opposed to the merely superficial . . . . A novel should heighten
life, should give an illuminating experience."[1] To disclose a deeper, more
vital side of a person, White bypasses convention, social duty, and the dead
shell of inhibition. "One of the things White often does well . . . is to make
us feel the significant weight of minutiae,"[2] said Peter Shrubb of his

instinct for the telling touch. White studies the pores of his characters' skin, the roots of their hair, and the fillings in their teeth. This scrutiny also serves wholeness. Without downgrading their thoughts, memories, and fantasies, he keeps reminding us of their physicality. Stubborn reality can intrude upon a character at any time, deflating long-windedness and thus preserving moral balance.

Part of White's ability to portray life in the round inheres in blocking the bogus drive to heroism with a well-selected detail. The length of *Eye* (over 600 pages) demands that the book not rush to climaxes, and it shows him several times lowering the intensity of a dramatic encounter in order to restore reason and balance. During a grave discussion a nurse worries about removing some cucumber seeds caught in her denture; a moment after voicing a lofty sentiment a lawyer sees one of his shirt buttons fly off; a bent nasal hair makes an actor sneeze away a purple fantasy. White's characters exist as solid bodies before they pronounce wisdom or doom. Physicality permeates all; the recurrence in the canon of toilets, trash, and excreta tones down pretense. Comic and thus anti-heroic in their ramifications, waste and decay depict the sordidness behind a pretty facade. What is more, this sordidness must be accepted, regular excretion being a function of good health.

This Whitmanesque touch tallies with White's 1969 self-description: "I am not a philosopher or an intellectual. Practically anything I have done of any worth I feel I have done through my intuition, not my mind."[3] Like a Romantic poet, he finds the rational, the institutional, and the deliberate both arbitrary and repressive. The level of being that interests him—the feeling, intuitive self—can encroach upon the visionary and the mystical. The stress he places upon feeling uncovers a civilizing point of view in White that can be described as feminist. Like many women writers, he finds value close to home. He enjoys describing domestic routines like baking and washing, and, aware that houses acquire souls along with their inhabitants, he sees to it that many of his major figures (the Parkers in *Tree*, the Brown brothers in *The Solid Mandala* [1965], Hurtle Duffield of *Vivisector*, and Elizabeth Hunter of *Eye*) live in the same house for many years. His psychological accuracy includes an instinct for atmosphere and other intangibles. When Laura Trevelyan of *Voss* is asked if her talk with a man told her anything important, she answers, "Not in words" (p. 104). This appreciation of subtext helps White impart the psychological undercurrents of an event. Often, a conversation will matter less than the feelings of those conversing. These feelings, usually unpredictable and rarely spoken, may have nothing to do with what is being said. The private region of self and the unlooked-for turns in experience leading to it comprise White's special turf. Particularly sensitive to the sharp changes of the inner life, he shows how spirits can brighten or darken without warning.

Which narrative mode best suits the surge of passion? White's own description of his fictional technique offers little help: "I feel that my novels are quite old fashioned and traditional—almost Nineteenth Century," he said in 1973, adding, "I've never thought of myself as an innovator."[4] The legacy from Victorian fiction shows in his seriousness of purpose, in the length of his novels (usually 400-600 pages), and in his thickly embroidered style. But even though his novels grind forward with a Victorian earnestness, they reject Victorian notions about property, social class, and narration. And they don't rely upon good storytelling and continuous plotting to make their points. Rather, their supple, granulated surfaces contain pores into which meaning and insight flow. This flexibility allows him to reify time and mood. The continuous sequential development created by a hard, logical plot structure tends to block analysis, introspection, and thematic growth. *Tree* refers several times to Shakespeare's *Hamlet;* the work also includes a glass which several characters hold up to nature. Rather than reproducing photographic replicas, the curving red glass that came from a church destroyed by flood reveals as it distorts, turning reality into a crimson miracle. The pounding rainstorm that floods the area where Amy and Stan Parker are homesteading turns up another miracle: the foundling who brings the fragment of glass into the book. The boy vanishes as mysteriously as he had materialized and is never heard from again. His piece of stained glass? Though left behind, it remains undiscovered for some forty years, until the Parkers' grandson finds it and sees in it inspiration for the "little bits of colored thought" (*Tree*, p. 499) that will shape the poem he wants to write.

The gulf of years between the two appearances of the glass and the young boys associated with it typifies White's art. Often the self doesn't form within our view, nor does White describe the events that lead to its formation. Vagueness can suit him more than precision. But it carries a penalty. Despite his remarkable skills, White has not ingratiated himself with the common reader. This failure (though White wouldn't see it as such) stems largely from problems created by his narrative construction. Dispensing with plot can indeed liberate and humanize, letting characters exist for themselves rather than serving a preordained narrative plan. That is, the characters aren't locked inside a restricting sequence of events; they can behave as they like. But the substitution of freedom for plot structure removes a reference point from which to view the action and blocks forward drive. The writer-reader partnership is wrenched. We feel adrift without the narrative aids and controls we have been trained to rely on to make our way through a long complex book.

White's refusal to concede to us aggravates our sense of disorientation. We don't complain about having to keep up with his performance: writers who put more into their work have always made us dig harder and longer to extract the goodness. What is said often turns the mind to what is unsaid; a sense of strength in reserve haunts his books. His scorn for niceties of narrative construction in some recent works both whets the intuition and goads the moral consciousness. A reviewer in the *Adelaide Advertiser* complained that the characters in *Vivisector* are driven by coincidence; Zulfikar Ghose called the technique of *Fringe* "appalling" and riddled by "cheap melodrama."[5] The frequent reliance upon coincidence and eavesdropping to sustain dramatic interest in *Eye* and *The Twyborn Affair* (1979), although outrageous, reveals White's ongoing commitment to complexities and nuances of motive beyond the reaches of conventional plotting. The last sentence of *Mandala* reads, "Then she [Mrs. Poulter] turned, to do the expected things, before re-entering her actual sphere of life" (p. 309). If the traditional novel in English studies man's development in society, Mrs. Poulter's retreat into self aligns White with a different literary convention. Like Eliot's Prufrock, who prowls the margins of *The Living and the Dead* (1941) and *Mandala*, White's people live their real lives in private, apart from people and approved social norms. "His work is haunted by the sense that some element in all experiences—perhaps the most important—must remain private, personal, and incommunicable,"[6] R.F. Brissenden has observed.

The wrenching of the traditional partnership between reader and writer echoes in the split between the individual and his surroundings; sometimes it even produces self-division in characters. White has rejected politics and technology in order to confront the interplay, in every human heart, of good and evil, courage and cowardice, wit and dullness. So balanced is this interplay that readers have wondered whether he sets up ideals and values simply to qualify them. Their puzzlement is justified; negativity, and even self-destructiveness, infiltrate all. The likeable Theodora Goodman kills the red-eyed hawk with whom she identifies in *The Aunt's Story* (1948). Mary Hare, who kills her pet goat in *Riders*, suspects that she embodies "something evil" (p. 83). Hurtle Duffield's artistic growth combines creativity and destructiveness. But the reverse also holds true. White's world isn't beset by moral squalor. If sympathetic figures can't suppress cruelty, evil ones will impress us with their insight and virtue. The cheap crook Ray Parker steals his elderly landlady's money from its hiding place in *The Tree of Man* in order to buy her a hot water bottle she needs but has resisted buying for herself; that he keeps the change from the purchase provides the humanizing touch that makes his caring act believable. The carping, snobbish Decima Scrimshaw, a paid ladies' companion in *Fringe*, voices a sentiment so touching that it makes the novel's heretofore indifferent heroine love her.

Heightened moments like this come without warning, in different guises and variations. J.R. Dyce's reading of the 1962 play *The Season at Sarsaparilla* notes how life in the work defies all logical formulations and

expectations: "The vitality of the play depends much on its inbuilt ironies . . . . The most feather-brained woman has clever children; the
woman most fit for motherhood has no children; and the teacher, an
accepted leader in the community, has nothing to offer; and his usefulness
is challenged by a little girl."[7] Ironies like these help White examine the
structure of reality. They also posit some new directions in which to
search. His novels either create an alternative reality or look for new ways
which would allow more vital interaction with the reality that is given.
White explores modes of interaction that, while socially prohibited and
morally outlawed, are possibly in tune with deeper needs. By violating
taboos like incest and cannibalism, transvestism and necrophilia, he is not
trying to outrage or shock. He knows that if these drives were less preva-
lent, our culture wouldn't need such strong taboos to keep them at bay.
Ellen Roxburgh's ordeal with her aboriginal captors in *Fringe* doesn't kill
her, as did Voss's. Rather, by giving her important information about
herself, the ordeal prepares her for her return to the British middle class.

Her preparations compensate for her pains; attainment comes by
accepting, not denying, the actual. Social life isn't disabling, but
nourishing and self-expanding. The negativism that marred much of
White's early work has mellowed in his maturity. Some of this mellowing
may come from his involvement in public causes. In the early 1970s he
began championing ecology and conservation. The 1980s have seen him
campaign for nuclear disarmament. This public activity has been accom-
panied by a ripening of imagination; the books published since he turned
sixty in 1972 (along with *Vivisector*, their immediate predecessor) outdo
their earlier counterparts in creative drive. Though somber and tormented,
these recent works fit into an ongoing pattern of acceptance that has
expanded with the years. White refers with less frequency and revulsion to
dentures, which, in *Riders* (1961), he would call "plastic teeth" and align
in pink symmetry, snapping and gnashing with all the malice of their
wearers. Yet *Riders* also reflects White's expanded morality. The faint
anti-Semitism smudging his description of Muriel Raphael in *Living and
Dead* and of the Bloch twins in *Aunt's Story* finds no parallel in either his
patient, loving portrayal of Professor Mordecai Himmelfarb or the creative flair he injects into the Kabbalism and Merkabah mysticism under-
girding Himmelfarb's piety. White's overcoming of his earlier impetuosity
also profits him elsewhere. The hastily sketched and summarily dismissed
prostitute Pearl Brawne in *Aunt's Story* ripens into the marvelous comic
creation Nancy Lightfoot in *Vivisector*. Finally, miles of vision and experience divide Stan Furlow, the thick-witted grazier and livestock owner of
The Happy Valley (1939), from his poetry-writing successor, Greg
Lushington, in *The Twyborn Affair*.

I

This growing affirmation channels into White's main subjects and themes. Any seriously told story will have moral and perhaps also metaphysical overtones. In White's work, the link between morals and metaphysics is neatly forged. The novels put forth definite philosophical views, even though these views are intuited rather than derived, and then give them metaphysical import. Viewing metaphysics traditionally, i.e., as the continuity between matter and spirit and also between the world of ultimate reality and that of appearances, Harry Heseltine sees White's style as metaphysical in origin: White's prose mixes abstraction and concreteness to convey the dialectic between physical and nonphysical experience.[8] Heseltine's insight explains more than verbal strategies. "Decay, even the putrid kind, did not necessarily mean an end" (*Riders*, p. 163), says Mary Hare. White agrees. He states his belief in the interconnectedness of matter and spirit by endorsing the fallible and the corrupt as the only sources of salvation. The mind needs the body; spirit runs to waste unless rooted in material reality. The prevalence in his later fiction of snot, phlegm, eye mucus, shit, and menstrual discharge shows that even the repulsive houses the divine. (Many of White's illuminati are physically ugly.) No Manichean, White affirms the goodness of matter. He also describes the process by which matter is redeemed—the interplay between birth and decay, attraction and aversion, and, finally, spirit and matter. "The seed can be sown in many ways" (*Riders*, p. 168), Himmelfarb learns, alluding to White's belief in the dynamism of interchange. Goodness needs its polar opposite, evil, to build the tension supporting all activity. Phrases like "the lovely colors of putrescence" (*Voss*, p. 382) and "the iridescence of slime" (*Riders*, p. 320) also serve to make the gross and the repellent an appropriate foundation of beauty. Rottenness nourishes. A character in *Aunt's Story* says of a *Monstera deliciosa*, an oozing, loose-leaved plant also called deadly nightshade, "Its fruit is eaten when black, and, one would say, almost putrid" (p. 213). A teenaged Hurtle Duffield is standing near a *Monstera deliciosa* when kissing Boo Hollingrake gives him an orgasm. Not only do Hurtle and Boo remain friends for life; fifty years after their first kiss, Boo sends him a telegram that reads, "All praise to the delicious monster" (*Vivisector*, p. 528).

Harshness is inescapable in our fallen world. To reject it is to reject reality itself and, with it, the Christian myth of redemption and resurrection. To accept it clears a path to God and helps us discover where we came from, what we are, and where we're heading. White recommends immersion and participation in the sensible world. The religious fervor Voss lends to his trek across the outback turns this stretch of dry, rocky terrain into a Promised Land. *Vivisector* teems with sticky, viscous matter. Only by accepting it does Hurtle become an artist and experience rebirth into an eternity. No ascetic, he faces the brutal and the sordid without flinching. His art thrives as a result. The events that help speed his development include seeing a model of a vivisected dog at a London taxidermist's, his sister's naked deformity, and the smashed body of his prostitute-lover. *Fringe* carries the argument forward: touching a suppurating wound with compassionate hands helps the healer more than the afflicted; Austin Roxburgh comes to love the weeping boil of a sailor because it opens his heart to suffering. Like White, he has learned to inquire into the why of things in order to get at the truth.

The dialectic observed in Austin's behavior irradiates White's novels. Rather than preempting each other, opposites like loss and gain or sanity and madness interact, shift places, and lend mutual support. Everything has a place in the mandala. Suffering underlies blessedness; physical impotence can signal intuitive fertility; social disgrace may promote moral goodness. Theodora Goodman's early years, the time normally connected with growth, feature a symbolic death, a near death, murder, suicide, and other subtractions from self. Parts Two and Three of *Aunt's Story*, which deal with Theodora's adult years, show her adding to her identity by merging with other selves and answering to new names. Stan Parker (*Tree*) and Elizabeth Hunter (*Eye*) both wither in the flesh while being reborn spiritually. The dialectic is explained by Holstius, a mentor imagined into life by Theodora: "True permanence is a state of multiplication and division" (*Aunt's Story*, p. 278), he claims, defining reality as process rather than a fixed state. This rhythm of spreading, molting, and merging sounds through all of White's writing. The leaking away of life in *Tree*, *Vivisector*, and *Eye* is matched by renewal and resurgence elsewhere. Arthur Brown both swells and shrivels as he dances his dance of the mandala. Hurtle Duffield's creativity lies dormant for years before bubbling into new channels. His first vision of the heavenly blue, the indigodd, comes to him during a stroke; his supreme vision comes at his death. Craving a fuller revelation himself, Mary Hare's father asks, "Who are the riders in the chariot, eh Mary? Who is ever to know?" (*Riders*, p. 25). He can't be answered in rational terms. Neither our minds nor our hearts can keep pace with the flow of experience; we don't understand why things happen. On the other hand, we do catch rare glimpses of life's unity; these intimations imply that everything hangs together, connected by myriad strings which lead to the hidden God. Necessity joins all things. White has discussed his use of correspondences and parallels to portray a divinely ordered universe moving toward a single goal: "Religion. Yes, that's behind all my books. What I am interested in is the relationship between the blundering human being and God . . . . God . . . made us and we got out of hand, a kind of Frankenstein monster. Everyone can make mistakes, including God. I believe God does intervene; I think there is a Divine Power, a Creator, who has influence on human beings if they are willing to be open to him."[9]

White gives many hints and clues of a transcendent reality beyond appearances. One such helper is a minor character in *Riders* known as the Dyer of Holunderthal, Himmelfarb's boyhood home in northern Germany. Stained and dyed by printer's ink, the shabby, malnourished dyer has an indelible influence on Himmelfarb. An occasional dinner guest of the Jew's parents, he idly suggests that Himmelfarb call upon a certain couple in the provincial town where he takes his first teaching job. His subsequent marriage to the couple's daughter makes good the inference set forth in Shakespeare's Sonnett 111: "And almost thence my nature is subdued/To what it works in, like the dyer's hand" (ll. 7-8). Certain truths can't be avoided or explained away. Once they touch us, they leave their mark, whether we like it or not. Nodding in the direction of Locke's doctrine of the *tabula rasa*, White describes the attainment of peace as an acceptance of the stains that experience prints up on us. The process can be involuntary. Mrs. Johnson returns the hat decorated with a black gauze rose that Theodora had deliberately left behind in *Aunt's Story*. Ellen Roxburgh tries in vain to suppress guilt over committing adultery with her husband's brother Garnet in *Fringe;* a garnet ring stolen from her finds its way back to her months later, and she wears a garnet dress (which, significantly, accidentally becomes stained soon after she dons it) on the ship returning her to British society. Her social reintegration will include her secret sin.

What applies to the individual often explains the whole, most metaphysicians agree. To see one's true self is to disclose the truth of the universe. All is one; God, the root fact of the universe, inhabits sky, water, and fire. Whatever is, is divine first. He energizes and controls all of creation. Reaching to the infinite, the mystery of unity comes forth in near-infinite variety. Some of White's pairings are funny; others are outrageous, like Eddie Twyborn's accidentally seeing his Australian mother three times in sprawling London. Such coincidences mesh with White's metaphysics. Life isn't a thought system; nor is reason the final measure of things, consciousness going beyond cognition. What baffles the mind may please the intuition or the soul. Our greatest insights happen unconsciously because, caught off guard, we yield to them. Overriding all dichotomies, these insights nullify thought. Arthur Brown and Mary Hare put their minds to sleep and then dissolve into the oneness of things. Content to be on a level with animals and insects, they strengthen themselves without trying to conquer or subdue. The humility and submissiveness underlying their mystical self-detachment finds voice in the contrast between

Theodora and her sister Fanny in *Aunt's Story*. Fanny recoils in disgust
from a grub she sees lodged between the petals of a rose in her parents'
garden. Theodora, whose appreciation has a wider sweep, "could not
subtract it [the grub] from the sum total of the garden" (p. 14). A wise
move: without its grubs, the garden would be incomplete; grubs and weeds
help complete the circuit of the garden's reality. They can't be removed
simply because of their ugliness. Worms are ugly, too, but their removal
would impoverish the soil and undermine the garden. Once begun, the
process of exclusion can claim all gardens, leaving us with nothing.
Theodora's acceptance of the grub, on the other hand, acknowledges it as a
source of meaning and strength. White will intrude such an unexpected
detail in order to show its broader relevance. It moves the interview
between Fanny and Theodora from the plane of social chatter to the deeper
recesses of the mind. In the process, logic becomes psychology, and intel-
lection becomes intuition. Theodora has intuited the organic continuity
between the self and the universe and between matter and spirit.

The unity of the world also declares itself in moments of stress, such as
Laura Trevelyan's delirium in *Voss*, Eddie Twyborn's nightmare, and the
dying visions of major characters at the ends of *Tree* and *Vivisector*.
Heated emotions melt differences in White's fiction, as they do in Romantic poetry. A Conradian scene in *Riders* makes the point well. The elderly
Mary Hare gets angry when her companion-housekeeper, Mrs. Jolley,
parodies a dance from the heyday of Xanadu, the Hares' now-decayed
mansion. She tries to stop Mrs. Jolley from dancing, but she is so caught up
in her purpose that she seems to be leading Mrs. Jolley instead of restrain-
ing her. The intensity of their struggle has swept away the issues that
prompted both the struggle and the motives of the strugglers. "You have
led me such a dance" (*Riders*, p. 89), says Mrs. Jolley after the gyrations
that she instigated have ended. Garnet Roxburgh voices similar dismay to
his would-be sexual toy, his sister-in-law Ellen, following their rut in a
forest clearing.

Most of these emotion-charged encounters are wordless. The perception that occurs on the inner planes of awareness has a finality and a
completeness that obviates talk. In fact, speechlessness will overtake
White's characters at their most heated moments; words can't pierce the
mystery of things. Amy Parker says little to Stan after he comes home from
rescuing people from a big flood. She is gripped by forces that can't be
articulated. "Most of White's novels depend upon a . . . sense of the terror
which underlies normal human existence,"[10] says Veronica Brady.
White's characters both take up and live out this preoccupation. Truth
comes in terror, not in fact, to Elizabeth Hunter of *Eye*. Being drenched
and pounded by a cyclone also prepares her to face any future ordeal. This
stroke of the dyer's hand puts her beyond the comprehension or control of

those close to her; it also lifts her above the dualities of cause and effect or of fulfillment and destruction. Neither reason nor ethics can encompass her. On the other hand, her nonduality, won from what the existentialists call a limit situation, tallies with some of the leading philosophical themes of our century. Nietzsche aspired to an order of being beyond distinctions of good and evil; Wittgenstein tuned his mind to data that revealed themselves but could not be spoken of or analyzed; Zen prizes bewilderment because it both takes the mind beyond reason and hints at the indivisibility or wholeness called the Buddha nature, which animates all. Reason and its handmaid, language, uncover little of worth in White. "Life isn't talking, it is living," notes Amy Parker (*Tree*, p. 416); "rational answers seldom do explain," concludes Laura Trevelyan (*Voss*, p. 439); Himmelfarb's reason for refusing a professorship at the close of World War II, "The intellect has failed us" (*Riders*, p. 211), voices his dismay with the scientific rationalism that led to two wars in his lifetime. Nor can the rigidities of language solve Holstius's paradox in *Aunt's Story*: "There is sometimes little to choose between the reality of illusion and the illusion of reality" (p. 272). Cartesian dualism has also resisted rational formulations. Only intuition can start to show where the mind ends and the body begins. It is not surprising that White's people feel closest to each other while silent. Words interfere. Often guilty of overstatement himself, White summarizes a character's vanity and narrowness with deft economy when he says, "Mrs. Jolley had experience of words" (*Riders*, p. 69).

But intuition can also fall short, unless prodded by terror to new heights of perception. Man has wandered so far from God that only by endangering himself can he see the truth, and even then his vision is screened. "Great truths are only half-grasped this side of sleep" (*Tree*, p. 289), asserts White. Certain life-enhancing experiences can't be shared, stated, or relived. They may even baffle the person to whom they are happening. Their value and meaning may thus never be fully known. "It is not outside, it is inside: wholly within," reads one of *Mandala*'s epigraphs, stating a proposition borne out frequently in White. Ruth Godbold, one of the chariot riders, enacts her creed of love but cannot explain it. Her pronouncement, "Everybody sees different. You must only see it for yourself" (*Riders*, p. 285), describes truth as relative, subjective, and situational—the network of division and multiplication noted by Holstius. Everyone must work out his salvation in private, and no one set of answers surpasses any other. Each rider interprets the chariot differently; the mandala absorbs light from many angles. Ellen Roxburgh can't explain her ordeal in the bush to the officer in charge of reporting the event to the colony's governor. Perhaps she will never understand it well enough to explain it to herself. Like Eddie Twyborn's homosexuality, it both wrings her and opens a door to new life.

The wringing always draws blood. White's world contains more pain than pleasure, and the pain, more keenly felt, is not gratuitous. Pain is the agency through which matter becomes spirit. Someone who can't feel pain can't feel anything else; someone who can't perceive ugliness will be blind to beauty. Hurtle Duffield complains that his paintings are dragged out of him "in torment and anguish, by a pair of forceps" (*Vivisector*, p. 235). Later, a drastic confrontation with terror—being stroked by God on a busy downtown street—gives him his first intimation of the indigodd. Illumination and breakdown also coincide for the Reverend Mr. Wakeman of *A Cheery Soul* (first produced, 1963); falling from the pulpit, he says, "Am I illuminated? I am blinded" (*Four Plays*, p. 260). White has always believed in the redemptive force of suffering, with the epigraph to his first novel, *Happy Valley*, from Mahatma Gandhi, affirming that pain can serve a higher end: "It is impossible to do away with the law of suffering, which is the one indispensable condition of our being. Progress is to be measured by the amount of suffering undergone . . . the purer the suffering, the greater is the progress." To clinch the point, a hand injury introduces Alys Browne to Dr. Oliver Halliday, with whom she will have the deepest relationship of her life. Suffering also furthers a deep engagement with life in *Vivisector*, where a character says of Rhoda Courtney, Hurtle's hunchbacked stepsister, "Miss Courtney . . . is *strong* and would carry us all on her back . . . to the end" (p. 563). The point of affliction has become the seat of strength and hope. And why not? Isn't a once-broken bone that has mended strongest at the point of the break? Rhoda's hump feels solid to Hurtle the one time he touches it as a youngster. This solidness is characteristic. Rhoda and White's other apostles have a tragic sense of life that goes against the safety of the world. They avoid making deals with society. To them, the means and the ends of life are knit; titles, bank accounts, and good addresses mean nothing. The sharpshooting Theodora doesn't collect her prize at the carnival shooting gallery, nor does the Aboriginal artist Alf Dubbo collect the money his paintings earn when his landlady sells them for him. The wise and the free (like White himself, who declined to keep the money that went with his Nobel Prize in 1973)[11] enjoy an inner peace that disregards the trophies of their competitive society.

Most of White's ugly, freakish, or deformed[12] apostles must make their way without the help of others; to love the afflicted takes more patience and imagination than most normal people can muster. One needs moral courage to carry a hump on one's back. On view all the time, making others uncomfortable, it can't be forgotten. Diane Arbus, who supplies one of the epigraphs to *Twyborn Affair*, prefaced a book of her photographs by saying, "Most people go through life dreading they'll have a traumatic experience. Freaks were born with their trauma. They've already passed their test in life. They're aristocrats."[13] Freaks are special to White, too. But he is less interested in positing an aristocracy of freakishness than in showing the steps by which the aristocracy is earned. Peter Beatson, one of White's best critics, views freakishness in White as an opportunity for spiritual growth: "Ugliness is not in itself a virtue, but those who possess it cannot take refuge on the surface, and must look for truth at deeper levels."[14] The search always wracks, making good Laura Trevelyan's words at the end of *Voss*: "Perhaps true knowledge only comes of death by torture in the country of the mind" (p. 440). Unlike those of Diane Arbus, White's freaks face constant struggle.

Whereas the unafflicted may follow their lights, the freaks in White must keep recreating and redefining themselves simply in order to exist. The sterner the limits imposed on them, the harder they must work. This test calls forth a heroism beyond the imagination of the unafflicted; it also widens the gap between the unafflicted and the freak. Life gains in drama for the person who can't lower his guard. "Eventually I shall discover what is at the center, if enough of me is peeled away" (*Riders*, p. 51), says Mary Hare, like an existential heroine bracing for a crisis. She and her kind must impose choice upon circumstance. And their working definition of circumstance differs from that of most people. They look foolish because they forage for value in places ignored by the safe and the socialized— Mary Hare and Arthur Brown impersonating animals, Rhoda Courtney keeping fifteen or twenty cats, Eddie Twyborn living like a woman for most of his adult life. These people are not trying to shock. Whereas it is easy to find wisdom and freedom in the realm of the socially approved, only a moral genius can wrest virtue from the despised and the repellent, especially when the attempt means peeling away layers of self. "Ugliness . . . points to a higher end,"[15] says Beatson, calling surface beauty an end in itself and therefore a brake to the imagination. By putting this moral limitation before us, the ugly make us stare at our meanness. We are angered. Since they are relatively defenseless, we strike out and smite them anew. A Himmelfarb must be crucified because he defines us negatively. The depth of this negation is sounded by Rhoda Courtney's belief: "Almost everybody carries a hump, not always visible, and not always of the same shape" (*Vivisector*, p. 429). The person with a visible hump rouses our deepest wrath. We see so much of ourselves in him that we avoid or oppress him, lest others compare us to him. Lest we compare ourselves to him as well? As is proved by the anguish of the onlookers to Himmelfarb's crucifixion, any attempt to drive the outsider further from us only shrinks the distance between ourselves and him and sharpens our guilt.

A system of metaphors describes the cleavage and collapse that accompany illumination. There is, first, Mary Hare's desire to pare away every-

thing around her animating core. This metaphor from Ibsen's *Peer Gynt*
(Ibsen is quoted in Norwegian in *Mandala*) occurs less often than one
borrowed from Yeats's "Byzantium," that of the refining flame, even
though they make the same point. The burning of impurities, like the
whittling of bark, leaves a quivering pulse. Disclosing the unawakened
in-dwelling spirit is the theme of Frank Le Mesurier's prose poems in *Voss;*
Laura, in the same book, dreams of winning gold from ashes and cinders.
The dangers of all truth-seeking come through most vividly in Voss's
expedition across the glaring desert. Selfhood emerges from the dust, grit,
and heat of the outback because, in breaking the pilgrims down physically,
the trek confronts them with their fears and phobias along with external
pressures. The confrontation weakens the body but hones the spirit;
"Privation, which had reduced the strength of his body, had increased his
vision and simplicity of mind" (*Voss*, p. 275), White says of the abrasive,
cleansing action of the desert's sand and grit upon one of the pilgrims.
Surrendering the ego makes the opaque luminous.

Yet the sand and grit break down the pilgrims, making vision only a
skimpy inference derived from something more immediate and insistent.
Suffering can blur the same ecstasy and revelation it brings about. If the
mandala is unified, its inner planes shouldn't refract light from surfaces
scratched and scored. Ignorance of the continuity between surface and
core misled Peer Gynt into peeling successive layers of an onion's skin in
search of the heart. In White, this self-division means that knowledge and
power can't fuse, and that the saved may be deluded into believing that
they are damned. Beatson's idea that "no emotion is intense or pure
enough"[16] to comprehend the hidden God rests on solid evidence. Doll
Quigley of *Tree*, Theodora, and Arthur Brown all have quick, responsive
hearts; all fail to profit from their vision, ending up in mental homes. The
blinding clarity of their wisdom has dimmed their wits. The human frame
buckles under the might of divine power in several other meetings between
the finite and the infinite. Those who break the bounds of reason and social
propriety must suffer, even though they reach a higher level of consciousness. As in Hegel, the secular law, however flawed, must be squared. It is
almost as if White is punishing his fool saints for arrogance. Furthermore,
his primitive justice has pre-Hegelian antecedents within the canon. The
Kabbalistic works that Himmelfarb reads in private teach him that
dwelling with God will exalt and expand the human soul. But the growth
will wrack the body in which it occurs because of the imbalance it creates;
spirit cannot thrive at the expense of flesh. Himmelfarb quickly learns that
a strong charge of the infinite can overwhelm the finite. The wisdom
contained in his esoteric books flattens him, sending him to his bed for two
weeks. Sometimes White varies the pattern of vision as privation. In his last
moments Hurtle reaches the point where creation and destruction merge,

just as Elizabeth Hunter undergoes blindness and illumination in one flaming instant of perception. Both die without sharing their wisdom with others.

The metaphysical overcoming of self always invites danger. Though less prideful than Himmelfarb, Hurtle, or Mrs. Hunter, Theodora is undone by her search for ultimate reality. A contingent being aspiring to the absolute, she is doomed. Her intimations of the noumenon lack permanence and continuity; she becomes a burnt one. The vision that elevates her has also scorched and wasted her. And it isn't clear that her pain has won the world a bargain. Eddie Twyborn reads a passage from Rochefoucauld that applies to her and her kind: *"Nos vertus ne sont pas le plus souvent que des vices dégisés"* (*Twyborn*, p., 136). The argument that our virtues are only disguised vices gains focus from one of the epigraphs to *Fringe*, Simone Weil's "If there is some good in man it can only be unknown to himself." The virtuous can't afford self-knowledge. One who appreciates his own virtue will be tempted to strut; giving in to such pride destroys virtue. Only humility can block the sin of pride, and only suffering can reinforce humility. Unless they felt goaded, the Theodoras and the Mary Hares would lose the edge that refines their spirits. "When man is truly humbled, when he has learned that he is not God, then he is nearest to becoming so. In the end, he may ascend" (*Voss*, p. 381), says Laura. Suffering reminds man of his separation from God: suffering is not a divine attribute; if God could suffer, He'd not have needed to send His Son to earth as the Redeemer. White's illuminati compel greater sympathy as fool saints (i.e., people gifted with second sight while lacking first sight or common sense) than they would as thoroughgoing paragons. Laura's forecast for the fool saint, "In the end, he may ascend" (*Voss*, p. 381), posits continued suffering. If suffering shows man his fallibility, it also gives him the privilege of being one with the crucified Christ. At the heart of the mandala writhes the stricken Redeemer.

The person who comes closest to bridging the gap between the contingent and the absolute—and who probably suffers most keenly for his pains—is the artist. Arthur Brown notes inwardly, while acting his tragedy of a cow, "Everybody had begun to share his agony, but that, surely, was what tragedy is for" (*Mandala*, p. 222). The tragedian confronts his apprehension of things by looking squarely at humanity's common heritage of pain. Shakespeare, the world's premier tragic poet, taps a common core of suffering in Stan and Amy Parker when a production of *Hamlet* reawakens their private agonies. Other figures in the canon would appreciate their plight. "I have sweated blood for every stroke of these" (*Tree*, p. 289), says Mrs. Gage of her dead husband's paintings. Her husband could have made the same claim; some of the blood sweated is the artist's own. Although the sight of one of his boyhood paintings horrifies Hurtle, he doesn't flinch. His unflattering self-portraits in later life show that that artist cannot relent if he wants to find the truth. Brissenden has summarized the contagion of cruelty bred by art: "Like the vivisector the artist has to carry out his work on living subjects—in his case on the body of humanity, in particular on the body of his own immediate community. Since he is a member of this community it means that he has to include himself in the vivisection: inevitably this must involve everyone, the artist and his fellows, in pain, discomfort, and suffering."[17] So ingrained and unstinting is the drive to create that, as Brissenden says, it goes against as humane a cause as anti-vivisection. Morals of any kind violate the artist's freedom, a freedom that sometimes violates the freedom of other living things. As a small boy, Hurtle tears a flower to pieces. Unlike Mary Hare of *Riders*, who serves living nature in all its forms, he must destroy things to see how they work. The destructiveness passes beyond painting into personality. His stoning of a cat, routing of a gang of larrikins, and (as an adult) driving two mistresses to suicide reflect his ongoing cruelty. This other self, or night side, belongs to everyone. Each nature has a negative pole. The self-defeating impulse that prods us all has already been seen in the destructiveness of White's most sympathetic figures; as Rhoda Courtney says, most of us carry some kind of hump on our backs. Her claim applies most strictly to artists. Hurtle looks ugly in his self-portraits; Alf Dubbo of *Riders* is sickly; the Parker's artist-neighbor, Mr. Gage, hangs himself. White sees the artist as a pathfinder in a dangerous wood. The sensitivity needed to chart imaginative terrain heretofore unexplored calls for ruthless self-honesty. The artist must bring *all* his energies to his work; cruelty can both feed and school the soul. He takes no shortcuts, brings no judgments, makes no exclusions. Seeing himself for what he is worth, he converts self-exploration into an upward journey.[18]

The journey's purpose is unity. To synthesize is to discover in the inmost life of things a common root of individuality. Hurtle wants "to dissect . . . down to the core, the nerves of matter" (*Vivisector*, p. 200). Only by probing the viscera of substances does the artist uncover the principle that gives them their reality. To make this discovery, he must first depersonalize himself. (Art dealers and collectors strike poses and put on airs in White's work; artists do not.) Willie Pringle of *Voss* is called "invertebrate" (*Voss*, p. 439) not because he is spineless, but because of his ability to assume different shapes. Like any other good artist, he has avoided hardening into a single identity or endorsing a received value system. So has Mr. Gage, White's first demonic artist-saint. Mr. Gage dramatizes his own fluidity. While staring at an ant, he nearly becomes the ant, "his arms . . . fixed to the ground at what appeared a permanent angle" (*Tree*, p. 103). Arthur Brown's letting himself go to probe the life activity of a cow or a dog reaps similar gains. Less an impersonation than a getting-into or a feeling-with, his enactments succeed so well artistically that they frighten their audience. This fear serves wholeness; because of it, Arthur enriches himself. Relaxing his grip on his individuality refreshes and renews him by helping him to discover new imaginative limits.

This kind of imaginative discovery brings most to light when undertaken with a minimum of baggage. The policy of traveling light has moral as well as aesthetic import for White, to whom simpicity is a function of strength, directness, and clarity. Himmelfarb's belief that "the simple acts we have learnt to perform daily are the best protection against evil" (*Riders*, p. 327) infers the goodness of simplicity. His mute soul clamoring with poetry, Stan Parker wants to "express the great simplicities in simple, luminous words for people to see" (*Tree*, p. 225). Although his artistic ambitions move from poetry to carpentry over the years, he always believes that great art wins goodness and beauty from simplicity. At his death, life's splendor and mystery flash before him as a host of simple, commonplace data. The knowledge that mind inhabits all lends both means and ends a new dignity.

Theodora Goodman confirms her belief in simple, honest reality by puncturing the grandiose. She will not presume. Asked if she believes in God, she says that she believes in a table and a pail of milk. Her more finely tuned counterpart, Mr. Gage, invokes simplicities—a child, an animal, or a stone (*Tree*, p. 104); the aspect of his painting that most touches Amy is its simplicity. Simplicity is the artist's watchword and standard; the main impulse behind art is the ability to wrest consequence from the seemingly trite. To say of Mr. Gage, "He would sit looking at an empty plate as if it were an object of importance" (*Tree*, p. 287), is to say that he takes his work seriously. Only those who have depth and richness of insight have his sense of purpose. Reflecting Mr. Gage's affinities, some of Hurtle's best paintings portray rocks, tables, and chairs. "There is a mysticism of objects" (*Tree*, p. 398), says White of the power of material things to grip us with their spiritual or psychic properties; again, mind inhabits all. Not only the artist, but everyone can intuit this finality and indisputability. The London landlord Will Lusty in *The Ham Funeral* (written 1947; first produced, 1961) has sensed the conjunction of mind and matter in things: "This table is love . . . if you can get to know it" (*Four Plays*, p. 27), he tells his wife. Miss Quodling's "Wonder if there's any life inside a rock" (*Four Plays*, p. 281), in *Night on Bald Mountain* (first produced, 1964), also questions the inwardness of matter. We share her bafflement. The serenity of objects suggests divinity. Self-contained and fully formed, objects live peacefully within their physical limits.

Some of White's characters seek this serenity. Curiously, their search weakens the integrity of White's vision. Theodora finds sanity only in tables and chairs; Sokolnikov, another character in *Aunt's Story*, expresses faith in a pail of milk. *Ham Funeral's* Will Lusty believes that a table is love, yet he dies early in the play. Sokolnikov and Theodora both go mad; Mary Hare disappears into the bush; Stan Parker dies within seconds of affirming his belief in life's oneness; both Alf Dubbo and his paintings vanish at the end of *Riders* without anyone feeling the loss. These depredations suggest that White doesn't understand the illumination he posits as the zenith of experience. Enlightenment doesn't add to the world's store of riches, happiness, or wisdom in White; her being whipped into the eye of a cyclone doesn't make Mrs. Hunter any kinder. As asserted reality with metaphysical trimmings, illumination lacks the force of enactment. G.A. Wilkes does well to note in *Tree of Man* "the tension between what the novel is apparently advocating and what it enacts."[19] Dorothy Green's disclaimer focuses the argument aesthetically: "White's gift for analysis is constantly at war with his dramatic gift; he seems unable to trust the reader sufficiently, and so subordinates the first to the second."[20] But laboring them doesn't carry White's beliefs into the realm of shared experience. As soon as he confers *satori* or enlightenment upon a character, he walls the character in—sending him to a mental institution or killing him off before he raises embarrassing questions with relatives and neighbors. Here is opacity and evasiveness peddled as mysticism. White's *donnée*, that the reason is the mind's most trifling activity, holds firm. The destruction of reason lets the intuition take over, just as the death of the body frees the soul. But frees the soul to do what? His failure to describe his beliefs drains their force. Little is communicated, still less is shared. White's meek and humble people don't inherit the earth—but neither does anyone else. Such irresolution and indeterminacy give offense. By sweeping the ethical and metaphysical problems he has raised into a net of pseudo-mysticism, White commits an act of literature.

The literary machine grinds on. In 1958 White said, "The state of simplicity and humility is the only desirable one for artist or for man."[21] His fiction shows the great difficulty of achieving the humility he prizes so highly, Laura Trevelyan standing as one of his very few characters who renounce pride and intellect in order to be humble. It should not surprise anybody that White chooses her to state his own beliefs in the power of humility: "A country does not develop through the prosperity of a few landowners and merchants, but out of the suffering of the humble" (*Voss*, p. 234). After great torment, Voss gains the humility to redeem his suffering, a sign of which is his rising to the stature of legend.

The value of Voss's elevation inheres in its Jamesian aura. As a literary touch, it dazzles, emitting sparks of dubiety within a cross-cultural framework. White cares less about the commonplace in practice than in principle. Writing from a standpoint of social and moral superiority, he equates eloquence with importance, and he sometimes presents his characters with condescension rather than with warmth. All this threatens to turn his novels into elaborate word games or literary structures, not bound by or answerable to life. The aesthetic shoulders aside the moral, making stamina and vitality secondary to style. Too often White crawls under the shadow of European literary culture. His long books, his heavy ideas, his use of foreign languages and settings, and his reliance upon Europe's leading minds all show him conquering the mother culture in order to submit to it.

Though best when he plays it straight with his material, his major preoccupations live as literary events, which is to say that they breathe stale air. One reviewer of *Voss* found no human content in the novel's main relationship: "The relation . . . between Voss and Laura Trevelyan is quite impossible," said the *Sydney Observer* reviewer. "This has nothing to do with men and women at all; it is merely some literary thing."[22] Rodney Mather has also complained that White's work is too literary, noting "the absence of a sense of the free, forward movement of the spirit. . . . Life is by no means absent; but neither is it the final arbiter; it subserves art."[23] Any writer sins who imposes his theories of life and language upon his characters. Elements in White annoy us because they are deliberate inventions, made up and put into the novels by auctorial fiat. By posing his characters in order to say something about them, White subordinates their freedom to his own. His refusal to let the action unfold naturally implies that they lack the vitality to hold our interest. Leonie Kramer's indictment, "White tries to make words do for experience,"[24] refers directly to character development. White has a fine sense of the point of things; he sees clearly, steadily and deeply. But he invents his characters in order to write about them. Rather than developing them along their own lines of force, he subjects them to the power of words. They take their preordained places in a Great Book. This denial of freedom paralyzes the works' vital centers of thought and feeling. Characters take meaning from White's artistic intent, not from each other or from themselves.

White has often won praise for his keen sensitivity to foibles. Marking his ability to distinguish the minute from the trivial, Beatson writes, "White records the private thoughts, secret trials, and intimate emotions of the inner life with almost frightening understanding and accuracy."[25] This power declines in direct ratio to the self-consciousness of the rhetorical performance taking place. The more heavily brocaded White's prose becomes, the shakier is his selection; the irrelevant blurs with the important in a gust of rhetoric. Perhaps his windiness bores and peeves White himself. Impatience would explain his frequent disparagement of his characters. "With *The Solid Mandala*, as with *Riders in the Chariot*, that White is rejecting is much clearer than what he is rejecting,"[26] complains Brian Kiernan. Negation permeates White's writing. Because it summons up his amazing verbal accuracy, no character or relationship is immune to it. "Harold Fazackerly made the noise with the mucus in his nose which his wife Evelyn [of forty years] deplored," says White in "A Woman's Hand" (first published in the August 1966 issue of *Australian Letters*); in *Eye*, Arnold Wyburd has been annoyed every day of his forty-year marriage by a pockmark next to his wife's nose.

Meaning and language part company here because these observations discount elements that have kept both marriages alive for forty years. The Lawrencean idea that love includes aversion as well as attraction runs through much of White; an appreciation of the ambiguities of love refines our consciousness, strenghtens the lifeline between people, and endows imperfection with redemptive force. This heightening, though, takes place in a literary climate, with White's strenuously contrived prose conferring fictive shape on nearly everything it touches. "There is . . . a sharp contrast between the kind of statement the novel makes, and in the way in which the statement is presented"[27] in *Tree*, says Leonie Kramer. Her observation can be extended. The belief that the imagination subserves rhetoric bridles White. The intrusion of an explicit stylistic aim produces an immediate faltering and wavering of focus. His descriptive genius restores immediacy, but by catching people at awkward moments. This device can offend the reader. Narrative focus has been sharpened at the expense of character and thus of theme. White's narrative flair, rather than expressing, denies the importance of virtues such as kindness and candor, which he always endorses in principle. Setting more store by straightforward talk would help him align his effects more smoothly with his meaning.

II

Would such straightforward talk sap the vigor and concentration of his prose? While White perceives life physically and intuitively, he writes about it intellectually. A cerebral writer in spite of himself, he often appears less committed to his characters than to the rhetorical materials he uses to make them live. But he can also transcend his intellectual enthusiasms. At such happy times, he doesn't so much relate experience as capture its sensation, vitality, and inner flow. These dramas bristle with vitality and mystery. So visceral are some of his effects that they uncover truths beyond the aim of most literary art. Much of White's heightened sense of purpose inheres in his attempt to capture things alive. At its best, his language lays bare essences. He expresses himself concretely when he lets his interest in the direct and the firsthand prevail over his intellectualism. Like Mr. Gage and Hurtle Duffield, he can make the most ordinary objects shimmer. Instead of worrying about abstractions and dialectical subtleties, he delves to the bottom of his data, where their living spirit dwells. His language takes on swiftness and force. Words embody worlds. Often tumescent and gnarled, his verbal effects assume a representational rather than a surrogate quality. Chapter 22 of *Tree* begins with one of the longest sentences in the canon. Tufted and tangled like the jungle mentioned in its opening phrase, that sentence merges the narrative self with the experiencing self. Other distinctions dissolve as the thickly overgrown bush presses upon us. Instead of organizing Amy Parker's gardening routine, White conveys the moist, green actuality of the plants and shrubs Amy tends. His long, aromatic, heavily cadenced sentence re-creates rather than reporting, explaining, or even describing. Here and elsewhere, the tactile values of his prose impart a strong physicality. This rhetorical strategy makes his work hard going, forcing us to attune ourselves sensually and intellectually. (White seems to have saved little of his oft-noted compassion for the reader.) The rigorous compression of his prose creates a Faulknerian intensity. Our eyes blink and our heads ache from the chore of extracting all the goodness packed into small spaces; our attention wanders. More than anything else, it is his practice of punching out a perception in every sentence that has made White a neglected classic.

Like other classics, his works are robust rather than mincing, having invited comparisons with Tolstoy and Lawrence. He follows these writers in his ability to shape and thus to control his creative energy. A hunger for huge themes and violent feelings tugs against a highly conscious artistry. While this tension can serve vitality, it can also give the impression that White is fighting something inside himself that distracts him from the business of telling a story. His prose has a determination that recalls Yeats's definition of rhetoric as the attempt of the will to do the work of the imagination. Rhetoric can indeed shove aside plot and character in White, making the play of language its own end. Such moments reveal the heavy-breathing author more as a performer than a creator. Unfortunately, they occur often enough to vex and confuse, as Alan Lawson observes: "The history of White criticism is full of utterly opposite, mutually exclusive thematic readings."[28] Stylistically, White poses the probem of qualitative extremes. When he's good he's unbeatable, but when he's bad his prolixity and his jarring rhythms approximate those in sociology textbooks. Though few writers delve as deeply into the psyche, his stiff, ornate sentences don't always make clean cuts. His style has angered critics from the start. One reviewer of *Happy Valley* found himself "antagonized and exasperated by his [White's] affectations"; A.D. Hope referred to the style of *Tree* as "pretentious and illiterate verbal sludge." Reviewing *Voss*, Ross Campbell complained of White, "My impression is that he has practically lost the power to write a plain, unaffected English sentence"; the reviewer for the *Sydney Observer* backed Campbell's indictment, adding his own flourish: "Reading the first hundred or so pages of *Voss* is like assisting at some weird rebirth of the English language."[29]

Other critics, noting that his style falls outside the mainstream of

English-language fiction, have judged White on friendlier terms. William
Walsh appreciates the intent underlying the bruising vividness of his prose:
"There is an almost Hopkins-like power in the way White outlines the
shapes and urgently communicates the intrinsic energy of *things*. The
novelist gives the impression of having . . . an almost molecular sense of
what is going on within objects." In a 1977 *New Yorker* review, George
Steiner praised *Fringe* as the work of "a master craftsman" and "a superb
technician."[30] Steiner and Walsh graze an important truth: that White
can make the language do nearly everything he asks of it. He is unafraid of
risks. Though not always in charge of his effects, he deals with areas of
psychic response too deep and too delicate to submit to narrative controls.
He also distorts language in order to arrive at truths which can be captured
intuitively but not logically. Thelma Herring and Brian Kiernan believe his
rhetorical strengths to be those connected with poetry, rather than with
fiction.[31] Many of White's gifts *are* more lyrical than narrative, an example being his power to show how ideas feel. Recounting layers of being that
he can't control, he also describes things in the process of transformation.
An image from the story "Down at the Dump" (*Meanjin*, June 1963),
wrings wonder out of the drab and the tawdry: "The sunlight . . . turned
the fluff in the corners of the room to gold." Such descriptions raze
barriers, confirming the parity of existence. White's is a thick, renewable
world full of exciting possibilities.

To say that he is often equal to the stringent and varied demands he
makes on language is to call White a super-realist. The term fits him. His
best insights strain the resources of a language and a fictional tradition
dominated by empiricism. Drawing mostly upon the internal matter of his
characters' lives, he recounts imaginative experience. A private mystery
may surface: "I have never told anyone about meself" (*Tree*, p. 299), says
the Parkers' drunken neighbor, Mick O'Dowd, of his artistic ambitions.
His secret longing comes from the buried life White can celebrate without
analyzing it or squeezing it into a system. Glimmers of buried gold light up
different corners. The phonetic properties of words, for instance, may
tease out a revelation better than the semantic ones. Describing the
crashing and shattering of a chandelier pelted by gunshot as "an excruciating crystal rain" (*Riders*, p. 32) recalls the brilliance of Robert Frost's
"crystal shells/Shattering and avalanching on the snow-crust" (ll. 10-11)
in "Birches."

Such purity and control, alas, occur rarely in White. All too often a
rush of images will assault us. His sentences aren't built to provide relief;
rarely is a perspective refreshed by a shift in voice or stance. Although his
technique of keeping us right against his data again recalls the immediacy
of poetry, good poets create immediacy without blitzing the reader.
White's blatant rhythm and color cries out for nuance and tone. Ironically,

he plays his materials false because he is too faithful to them. By forfeiting perspective, he fails to make artistic sense of his data. He could easily relieve our discomfort by calling more often upon the full range of his narrative skills. Restraint, though rarely invoked, can benefit him more than overstatement. "Then a fox ran screaming from the scrub, his fire fierier" (*Tree*, p. 171), he says, stressing similarity rather than trading on contrast. Repetition also describes, summarizes, and creates moral tone in *Eye*. Of the wraithlike Mrs. Hunter he says, "The lips suggested some lower form of life, a sea creature perhaps, extracting more than water from water" (pp. 22–23). Another look at Mrs. Hunter in the act of drinking— "Mrs. Hunter groped for and took the cup, her lips feeling for the lip" (p. 41)—endows old age with a pathos that puts her beyond blame. These images rivet us because of their economy and timing; their drama unfolds at sentence end, where the effects they depend on release their poetry. Nothing is forced, flamboyant, or overly explicit. The images develop from within, proving that poetic genius inheres not in the ability to dazzle but in the power to convey the wonder of everyday objects in natural language.

White best conveys his awareness of things outward and inward when he doesn't crowd us. Unfortunately, he forgets that rhythm and color can be subtly refracted. No aspect of his art is less consistent than his style. Some of his effects jar and bruise, while others emerge discreetly from hints, echoes, and intimations. This inconsistency has spread. Not only is there little agreement about his standing as a stylist; critics haven't even worked out a descriptive terminology that can be used to judge him. Herring speaks of "the tortured intensity of *Voss*" and "struggle and pressure in the prose of *The Tree of Man*"; disavowing this striving and stress, Mather believes that "White's is a relatively detached art. . . . Its language is cool, hard, brittle, noticeably . . . aloof."[32] Both critics are right. But both miss the point that White is as good as he lets himself be. Although he can make language do a great deal, he sometimes asks the wrong things of it. Most often he goes wrong because he doesn't know when to stop. A.D. Hope shows how his ingenuity trips him up when he says, "Mr. White has three disastrous faults as a novelist. He knows too much, he tells too much, and he talks too much."[33] Combinations in the same sentence such as "battering and nattering . . . slugged and glugged . . . hissed and pissed" (*Riders*, p. 212) interfere with the sentence's natural flow and emphasis. Not knowing when to stop can also trap White in a metaphor: "Swinging and bumping on the rope ladder, she was at the mercy of her own initiative, and that of the wind filling her skirts, making of her a mute bell which would have emitted a pathetic tinkle had it attempted to chime" (*Fringe*, p. 194). Woolen skirts don't chime; nor would a sea squall provoke chimes either from them or from their rain-soaked wearer. Instead of overworking his effect, White might have let us discover its merit for ourselves. "He is capable of perfection, but can rarely resist the temptation to improve on it,"[34] said a wise reviewer of *Mandala* in 1966.

Capable of spoiling an effect by overwriting, White can also undo himself by failing to work language hard enough. Instead of hammering the nail too hard, he sometimes taps it too lightly. *Mandala* contains at least two examples of this tendency: "Now at least he [Waldo Brown] was free, in fact, if not in fact" (p. 184) and "The carpet Jew had wrapped them (un)fortunately up" (p. 199). White's indecisiveness rankles the reader. Either Waldo is free or he is trapped; the Jew's wrapping job promotes either good or bad fortune. Had White wanted to define a middle ground, he should have rephrased the sentences, rather than resorting to parentheses or assigning the same word opposite meanings. If White's style is "a direct function of his deepest responses to life,"[35] as Heseltine says, it describes a psyche pitted with inconsistencies. *Mandala* isn't the only work in which White leaves jobs undone. The phrases "pianola linoleum" and "pianorolla on a pillion" (*Happy Valley*, p. 172) represent an easy way out. The repetition of sounds means nothing, developing neither character nor mood. The phonic associations of "A Maudie bawdie" (*Living and Dead*, p. 43), "Everyone agreed that Belle was the belle" (*Voss*, p. 76), and the Joycean "telly girl of the mellow-'cello voice" (*Eye*, p. 252) also sacrifice sense to sound.

White, justly praised for his "superb powers of evocation,"[36] has perpetrated still worse barbarisms: jawbreaking adverbs like "uglily," "brittlely," and "oilily" and the hiatus-ridden phrases "to imprint" (*Riders*, p. 487) and "the especial benefit" (*Voss*, p. 269). (White often uses "especial" for "special" and "masticate" instead of "chew.") Sometimes a wrong word will leak in, as in "He had even less [for fewer] clues to the whereabouts of Mrs. Julian Boileau" (*Vivisector*, p. 162). Clichés like "worn herself to a frazzle" (*Riders*, p. 261), "naked down to the soles of her feet" (*Vivisector*, p. 115), and "hit the nail on the head" (*Vivisector*, p. 329) cast further shadows on White's stylistic integrity. As these examples show, stylistic errors have dogged White into his maturity. *Fringe* contains the hissing "his mistress must resist" (p. 254), and *Twyborn* jangles sounds in "autographed photographs" (p. 333), later corrected to "signed photographs" (p. 357). A writer so prone to long sentences should also pay more attention to syntactic flow. The subject and main verb of the third complete sentence on page 12 of *Riders* are divided by thirty words, four commas, and a colon. In addition, problems in punctuation mar the novel: White needs four commas to stumble through a ten-word declarative sentence: "The fact was, Mordecai knew, his mother had, simply, died" (p. 123). The commas detract from the simplicity and dignity of the death.

Sentence engineering foils White again when he interposes a verb or even a verbal phrase between a relative pronoun and its antecedent: "Frank Le Mesurier was the worst, who had begun the soonest" (*Voss*, p. 263); "'You could get torn,' Mrs. Godbold warned, who had come up to the edge of the road" (*Riders*, pp. 3-4); "Mrs. Merivale was terrified, who had never, ever, been 'troubled'" (*Fringe*, p. 20). This mismanagement of relative pronouns invokes other violations of Coleridge's dictum that good writing rests on good judgment. White's assigning the phrase "in love with" some special but undivulged meaning recurs often enough to cast further doubt on his stylistic intent: "Turner was in love with the rich landowner [Ralph Angus]" (*Voss*, p. 248); the title figure in the December 1962 story from *Australian Letters*, "The Woman Who Wasn't Allowed to Keep Cats," was "in love with [her cat] Apricot." Clearly the phrase has a different meaning in each of these two examples[37]—and neither meaning tallies with the familiar one involving sexual passion. White's use of "in love with" betrays either carelessness or a tendency to endow language with private meaning. In either case, he smudges the line of communication between himself and the reader.

White's style remains a great imponderable. Capable of scaling rare heights of expression, he will allow the near at hand to slip through his fingers. Its lively imagery cannot hide the failure of "Dead Roses" to define feelings clearly enough: "Some of the women experienced a twinge on glimpsing the youthful situation which existed between the Mortlocks." "Which existed between" says nothing *about* the link joining the Mortlocks. Substituting "bound" would both define the link and save a word. "Youthful situation" causes a similar problem; it, too, lacks power and clarity. White often uses hollow nouns such as "experience," "nature," or "situation," relying on adjectives to deliver meaning. *Riders* includes the following phrases: "twilight situations" (p. 114), "innocent situations" (p. 124), "something of an irrational nature" (p. 126), and "some revelations of a personal kind" (p. 127). "Business of a confidential nature" (p. 168) and "of the embarrassing sort" (p. 145) puff out the contours of *Mandala*, while *Fringe* hobbles under the weight of "some revelation of a stunning nature" (p. 13) and "the married state" (p. 166).

These violations of verbal economy flaunt basic rules of sentence formation. Aggravating the problem, White prefers to use link verbs and subjective complements instead of action verbs which would convey the same idea. Instead of saying "the additional duty laid upon the mother was a source of embarrassment to the parents" (*Riders*, p. 107), he might have ended the sentence with the phrase "embarrassed the parents." Linking verbs also subdivide ideas and images, impairing coherence: "It streamed out of the holes of the anonymous woman's eyes. It was, it seemed, the pure abstraction of gentle grief" (*Riders*, p. 307) would stand more firmly as a single sentence, with a comma replacing the period after "eyes" and the next four words omitted. The following sentence from *Tree* makes us wish that White's admiration of simplicity had more forcibly affected his style: "There was a nervosity of fronds just twitching in a little breeze" (p. 328). Paring the sentence down to "Fronds twitched in a little breeze," would not only have shortened it, but also obviated the inconsistency which occurs later in the paragraph, when "nervosity" clashes with "this same smoothness and litheness." Twitching fronds make a good image. By interpreting it for us, White clutters his sentence and violates the unity of his images.

Some such violations are deliberate. Questioning the order of things, White breaks grammatical rules in order to redefine connections. His verbal dislocations question both the actuality of ordinary life and the intangibles underlying human conduct. One way in which White reveals the strangeness infusing the commonplace is by printing sentence fragments as complete sentences. The device sharpens the contours of the fragments, making them free-standing units of meaning. Like a musical chord, the fragment is witnessed on its own. But to what advantage? The effectiveness of freeing words from grammatical controls depends on the importance of those words. Including an idea or image in a grammatical action might weaken its punch. On the other hand, the free-standing image or idea achieves its impact at the cost of narrative flow. The sentence fragment will succeed artistically only if its chief component deserves special attention.

White often has both the audacity and the tact to fragment sentences effectively. For instance, the second paragraph of *Tree* ends with "The lip drooping on the sweaty horse" (p. 3). The image conveys the weariness of the horse after a long, hard pull, and, with it, the horse's sadness. Stan Parker, the rider of the cart the horse has been pulling, is about to make a first strike for civilization in the bush. Representing the nonhuman world, the horse droops; the hacking-down of trees to build fires and shelters for man makes Nature a victim. *Voss* also relies on a sentence fragment for a good start. Its second paragraph, "And stood breathing" (p. 3), exudes mystery, the white space after it supplying an element of foreboding. Prose usually extends to the right margin of a printed page. By leaving an expanse of white, White benefits from a resource of poetry. His next words—"What man?"—sustain the tension. White has drawn us into the action straightaway by forfeiting a grammatical nicety. If our balance and sense of rightness have both been affected, so have our souls. With no intellectual mediations, he has pierced the skin of reality; something immediate has come to the fore.

Such vividness isn't automatic. The effectiveness of any rhetorical device depends upon the skill with which it is used, and the impact of the sentence fragment varies inversely with its frequency. Lack of restraint leads to a sequence of three sentence fragments in *Riders*: "Which the latter mastered at astonishing speed. And began shortly to write phrases, and recite prayers. And grew vain" (p. 106). His not knowing when to stop spoils White's effect; intention has drowned in execution. The crude energy created by overriding grammatical controls runs to waste, and instead of dissolving, the authorial self obtrudes.

III

Self-conscious and hyper-rhetorical, White rarely communicates a love of writing—the sense of having a good time. He's sweating, and he wants as much from his readers as he's giving. His seriousness of purpose demands an equally serious response: this he doesn't let us forget. Aloof, he writes from a great height. Yet his overexplicitness (a function of authorial omniscience) suggests that he has a shaky foothold on his Olympian crag: he distrusts himself, the reader, and perhaps even language itself. (At least three critics have blamed an alleged failure upon his lack of self-confidence.)[38] His elevated tone has also kept him from inventing a poetic language rooted in Australia's youthful vigor. His elitist rhetoric floats miles above the egalitarian, wide-open land it refers to. Though he knows up-country codes and conventions, he finds them puzzling. His puzzlement has deepened in recent years, during which his art has also improved; the artist is thriving at the expense of the man, proving his own argument that vision is only born of pain.

Australia's rural heritage is outgrown, albeit with regrets, in *Twyborn;* in *Eye,* as in the American Midwest of F. Scott Fitzgerald's *Gatsby,* that heritage rejects those whose pseudo-chic once dismissed it as dowdy and quaint. Except for *Tree*, White either treats the Australian landscape historically or turns it into a symbol. Protective screens rise up throughout *Fringe*; his portrayal of Tasmania and Queensland in the 1830s owes as much to Victorian scene-painting as to Australian landscape. Most of the figures in *Eye* and *Twyborn* have lived their adult lives in Europe. (White spent more than half of *his* first thirty-five years away from Australia.[39]) What does this exile mean? White wants to be taken seriously as a writer, yet he doesn't write as an inheritor of an Australian cultural tradition. Literature is more a private matter for him than an expression of national self-consciousness or native themes. Gainsaying the social relevance of art, he has not tried to heal the split between philosophy and politics. Perhaps he regrets most of all that his countrymen's extroverted materialism has dulled their artistic sensibilities. But has he forgotten that material interests have always dominated Australia? In the nineteenth century, Australia's great age of migration and population growth, the mineral riches of the outback unleashed both the drive to practical action and the possessive impulse. The pioneer creed of staying alive and working hard to get rich starves the imagination. The gold rush of 1850 and the promise of the open prairie turned the capacity for wonder into materialist channels. Australia's soul has failed to keep pace with the middle-class creed of getting ahead. For all its primitive force, pioneer daring is very conservative and utilitarian. The swagman, the homesteader, and the gold prospector—all occupied with survival—had no energy left for vision. White's reproductions of Australian vernacular reflect this lack, expressing not frontier sinew but uncouthness. White often seems to be displaying it for the non-Australian reader, rather than employing its rough vigor toward more creative ends. He prefers its working-class speakers to middle-class suburbanites. But like an earlier Cantabridgian, E.M. Forster, he likes them all best when they keep their distance.

The consolations of distance tell little about White. Had he cut himself off from his fellow Australians, he would be less ambiguous. He does not dismiss his countrymen as apple-cheeked innocents, nor does he see his country ruled by mateship and the machine. His two most brilliant characters, Hurtle Duffield of *The Vivisector* and Elizabeth Hunter of *The Eye of the Storm*, stay in Australia, like White himself. Hurtle keeps developing his extraordinary skills to the end, while Mrs. Hunter dazzles and defeats her greedy Europe-based children with wiles normally associated with Old World sophistication. The frontier impulse, i.e., homesteading in the back country, gives Hurtle's art its Australian flavor, in addition to teaching him the endurance and the individualism that nourish his long artistic career. White admires pioneer energy enough to wish that he could admire it more. Life on the prairie needn't flatten and dry the spirit. Indeed, the wisdom Stan Parker acquires in his old age shows that rural living can speed the mind. He and several of his counterparts can be labeled by the adjectives that the historian Russel Ward uses to typify the Australian male: "tough, enduring, earthy; shrewd but not subtle or cultivated or over-scrupulous."[40] White doesn't rate urbanity so highly that he fails to see its shortcomings. Eddie Twyborn's disclaimer to his self-dramatizing Greek lover, "Oh, come off it, darling! My Australian arse won't take any more" (*Twyborn Affair*, p. 39), confronts pretense with common sense. In the novel Australian grit averts several crises caused by Old World hauteur. As is shown in White's own oversize works of unusual concentration, intricacy, and will power, Australians get jobs done. Though the pioneer legacy of mateship and materialism excludes finesse, it does help progress and relieve distress—all without fanfare. "I'll have a go" (*Tree of Man*, p. 179), says Stan Parker when asked to rescue a debutante from a fire. Arthur Brown voices the same modest willingness to face danger: "Remember when I cut my hand on the saw?" he asks his brother. "I'd try, though. Again I'd have a go" (*Mandala*, p. 21).[41]

White has had a go at Australian themes himself. One of the tasks of the Australian writer is to show Australia what constitutes Australianness, where it is to be sought, and how it can be strengthened. But the land of White's fathers is not intellectually the land of his choice. "Brought up to believe in the maxim, only the British can be right, I did accept this during the early part of my life,"[42] he said in 1958. Currents in his early work reveal that he has not shed this early conditioning. His most Australian novel, *The Tree of Man*, sounds, according to Jack Lindsay, as if it would rather be set somewhere else: its "lack of any organic Australian qualities"[43] gives the novel more of an American Midwestern than an Australian ambience. As he implies elsewhere in his essay, much of White's fiction is British in style and spirit, construction and characterization. While rejecting exile, White has disaffiliated himself from the main values and patterns of Australia. One of his problems as a non-exile with an already smothered sense of national identity has consisted of doing work his society discounts. His fiction has won few Australian friends because little in the Australian field of reality makes him relevant.

White has sought refuge in his detached mandarin style. No forerunner or fire-bringer of a new Australian idiom, he has by no means freed his nation's literature from European influences. Instead of creating a bold, fresh voice to match his nation's vastness, as Whitman did in the United States a century before him, he leans heavily on the ideas of Wordsworth, Browning, Lawrence, and Jung and on the techniques of Chekhov, James, and Joyce. His Australia drips *Kultur*. Because his style fails to set the nation off from other nations, it doesn't help Australians know who they are. His failure to define his homeland stylistically causes White to fret— perhaps needlessly. A so-called workers' paradise, Australia prizes leisure time much more than ideas. White is an intellectual. His English birth, his homosexuality, the fortune he inherited from his family's acreage, and his genius further divide him from the land of levelers[44] where he lives. But he has lived near Sydney since 1948, although the freedom provided by both his inheritance and his writing would enable him to live anywhere he might choose. White is less educated out of his instincts than out of touch with them. Although he can't take Australia, the "lucky country," on its own extroverted, nonintellectual terms, he clings to it. This self-division flickers over his work.

Perhaps the need for aesthetic distance demands that White play the outsider; the security of belonging could foster a complacency he can ill afford. He has flouted English grammar; he has varied it exquisitely; he writes about people who worry about their identities. That his recent work shows him confronting the problem of belonging spells out the depth of his preoccupation. Although married into the French peerage and fluent in the French language, Dorothy Hunter de Lascabanes of *Eye* never forgets her colonial origins; they haunt her because she hasn't shed them any more than White has thrown off his own boyhood worship of Britain. Rather than strengthening her, what remains of her heritage makes Dorothy feel Australian when in France and French when back in Australia. Ellen Gluyas Roxburgh of *Fringe* also feels pressure from two worlds, that of her childhood and of her adult life. In her case, though, the barriers are social, not geographical. Her first diary entry is revealingly datelined, "*At sea*" (*Fringe*, p. 69). Ellen keeps wavering, like a rolling ship, between the yeomanry of her Cornish girlhood and the squirearchy she has married into. After surviving terrible ordeals at sea and in the bush (symbolizing, for White, a civilized Briton's malaise among the unthinking?), she sets out at the end for her native England. Her ship is still hugging the Queensland coast at book's end; she is not seen reaching home. Whereas her lot remains to be at sea, Eddie Twyborn (who also crosses oceans) is beset by still graver self-doubts. Identity precedes belonging. Unable to decide whether he is a man or a woman, he lacks a self to fit into a country, social class, or family; ultimately he can't even apply for a British passport so that he can follow his mother back to Australia. He isn't alone in his alienation; all through the novel characters cross social lines, marry outside their religions, settle in foreign countries, perform jobs alien to their deepest needs, and pose as things they are not. Terms like "crypto-rich," "crypto-whore," and "pseudo-woman" pervade this novel of disguises and dis-locations. Like Pirandello, though, White knows that disguises or masks are real if they are worn with purpose. To accept a role is to feel and also to absorb its force. The sane man whose pretense of madness drives him mad haunts Western letters.

If not haunted, White is intensely self-absorbed. The dark brilliance of his mature work carries his self-absorption beyond questions of national-ity. In one of his rare winks to the reader, he makes one guest at Hurtle Duffield's retrospective exhibition say to another, "If you want me to tell you why you're a misfit, Patrick, it's because you hate everybody" (*Vivisector*, p. 532). The remark has import. For all the power of his vision, White rarely seems surprised, confused, or delighted by his characters. He is no comrade-teacher or lover-companion like Whitman. He doesn't rejoice over the human body; the act of sex is not a celebration but a vile animal act with sorry consequences. Lovemakers in *Vivisector* and *Fringe* look as if they're trying to hurt each other rather than give tenderness and joy; they couple in an animal's den. "Demanding the ultimate in depravity" (*Vivisector*, p. 318), Hurtle and Hero Pavloussi become stricken, moaning beasts whose "rooting" assumes "grotesque shapes" (p. 325). Like the Australian painter Norman Lindsay (1879-1970), whose canvas "The Dead Landlord" inspired White's play *The Ham Funeral* and who resembles Hurtle, White mingles strains of the sensualist and the puritan. The excessive brutality of his portrayals of sex shows the fear,

loathing, and envy of the outsider. White has not dealt with this fascina-
tion-revulsion; in recent novels he has sidestepped it altogether in favor of
describing its effects. Although central, Ellen Roxburgh's wantonness with
her husband's brother, Garnet, is glossed over. No explicit sex enters into
Twyborn, either; in the London brothel which becomes a metaphor for
England between the wars, sex occurs as a series of supervised acts nearly
religious in their ritual formality.

If heterosexual ties exude a rank animality, homosexual ones lack
energy, dignity, and purpose. White's homosexuals all face grief. Because
of his mediocrity in the pulpit, the Reverend Timothy Calderon of *Riders*
was posted in the baking northern outback. Weakness of character led this
Anglican minister to seduce his twelve-year-old Aboriginal ward, Alf
Dubbo. (The homosexual grocer Cecil Cutbush lives in disgrace after
seducing a boy of thirteen in *Vivisector*.) Later, after working his way
down to Sydney, Alf meets an art dealer named Norman Fussell whose
dainty walk, tightly rounded rump, and drag impersonations White sneers
at time and again. In *Vivisector* another art dealer, Maurice Caldicott, falls
in love with Hurtle, but White removes him from the action before his
feelings become a major issue. Does he remove him more cruelly than
necessary? When he says of Caldicott, "He had already developed the
yellow tinge which intensified toward his death" (*Vivisector*, p. 239),
White is indicating that he died of hepatitis B, an anally transmitted disease
common to gay males and involving one of the most uncomfortable
wastings-away imaginable. White also degrades and punishes Snow
Tunks, the bloated albino bus conductor in *Eye* whose lovers always
discard her. Snow is last seen spread-eagled on the sidewalk, too drunk to
walk. Her cousin Flora Manhood turns from her with the same disgust
that overcomes White. Eddie Twyborn can't run fast enough to flee
sorrow, presumably the fixed reality of his life.

Shot through with darkness, the canon includes many bleak reflections
on human nature. White's obsession with dentures (in "The Prodigal Son"
[1958] he said that "human teeth fall like autumn leaves"[45] in Australia),
which has diminished since the early 1960s, makes the wearing of false
teeth a badge of nastiness. They may fit poorly, cause discomfort, or stare
at the reader from a tumbler of water. Why should the wearing of dentures
receive the sting of White's satire? Some private sorrow drives him to
belittle his characters. Often the belittling detail, which he will reproduce
with devilish accuracy, involves eating. Like sex, which he also has problems accepting, eating sustains life. His discomfort with these life-
sustaining activities rests on the suspicion that life itself is tainted. His
apprehension keeps White on his guard. Disregarding intent, which can't
be proved, his practice of making his characters look ugly, foolish, or faded
has the effect of mocking human purpose. No sooner does he show

someone acting generously than he belittles him: "He showed his white teeth, on which a piece of dark fruit had stuck" (*Aunt's Story*, p. 265), he says of a man who has just offered a stranger a bed for the night.

The drive to denigrate can get out of hand. One brief scene in *Vivisector* describes a party given by a Sydney widow named Mrs. Mortimer. Not content to bestow upon the widow a philandering husband whose death has left her poor, White adds a goiter. A bit player in *Twyborn* is a nameless French domestic whose running sore has seeped through her knee bandage. Hurtle Duffield's reading of a friend's letter while on the toilet and then, having run out of toilet paper, wiping himself with it casts further doubt on White's ability to dispense simple humanity. The difference that has troubled critics between what White says and what he means has roots in his imagination; no less than Henry James, White sees life acrawl with "black merciless things." Even God makes mistakes, he said in 1969.[46] But negativity has not blanketed all his work; rather, men of good will have impressed him increasingly with the years. When a government surveyor says in *Fringe*, "I don't believe I've ever come across a fellow in whom I didn't find a fair measure of good" (p. 10), White is pleased—but skeptical; the old schooling reasserts itself quickly. His belief in the decency of both common objects and simple people sounds academic. Were this faith more than derived, he would not qualify it by ridiculing the virtuous and denying his characters satisfaction. An old tramp in "The Night the Prowler" (1974) can't enjoy the consolation of a comfortable last piss before he dies in a litter of debris. No one can say for sure whether White's having spent his college and university years in a country where he felt himself an outsider weakened his hold on life, but the effects of those years upon his psyche have turned his writing into a symbolic self-unfolding. Echoes from the past boom more loudly as time passes. The Lushingtons' first son, who died at the age of two months, was born on 28 May 1912 (*Twyborn*, p. 230), White's own birthday. Life doesn't thrive in White. Three of the four chariot riders, Theodora, the Brown and Roxburgh brothers, Hurtle, and Eddie Twyborn are all childless, like White himself; a miscarriage, a stillbirth, and infant deaths batter hearts in *Fringe* and *Twyborn*.

The germ of life shrinks and withers in White because it was planted in a sunless landscape. Reality itself seems to be protesting its gloominess. When seen from a ship, the New South Wales coast in *Fringe* looks "hog-backed, of a louring formal ugliness" (p. 163); the sea is a raking, lashing fury which "gargled hatred at its prospective victims" (p. 178). Just as falling into the malevolent sea clouds Pip's mind in *Moby-Dick*, the cabin boy in *Fringe*, Oswald Dignam, dies after a wave knocks him off a breakwater. It is germane that a survivor of the shipwrecked *Bristol Queen* vows never to sail again. But keeping to the land won't protect this ex-tar from evil, because the Brisbane River, earlier called "a vicious snake" (p. 319), irrigates the farmland whose crops he eats to stay alive.

Like the disguises pervading *Twyborn*, such touches say a great deal about White; the menacing river, sea, and coastline are all Australian. Is he downgrading realities that his early conditioning has prevented him from enjoying? Does disparagement constitute a mask he feels obliged to don before enjoying things that may be taken away from him, like his childhood home and homeland? A tendency to fight frontier anguish by throwing mud describes attack operating as a means of defense. This champion of endurance imposes upon long-suffering characters the burdens of his troubled past, not to mention those called forth by his gimlet eye. Perhaps White writes more of himself into his books than do most novelists. Because the man precedes the artist, the heartbeat of each of this moody genius's novels vibrates in tune with an ongoing psychodrama. White's is a soul in action. To study his works in chronological order will disclose the progress of his ongoing creative struggles. To place these struggles in their appropriate cultural milieu will generate a poetic vision both of our own time and of the state of fictional art.

2. Groping
in the Barrens

LIKE WHITE's first published book, a collection of verse entitled *The Ploughman and Other Poems* (1935), *Happy Valley* (1939) uses materials from Belltrees, his family's 220,000-acre homestead in the Upper Hunter Valley of New South Wales.[1] Also like *The Ploughman*, White's first novel offers faint hope amid a welter of wintry images, losses, and tears. Sometimes the hope is so faint as to seem nonexistent. Renewal always carries a surcharge of madness or grief. The speaker in a love poem called "Second Life," seeking ease from pain, finds hope (but not relief) in keener pain: "The Sun, in risen might,/Has burned pain deeper in my soul,/And ecstasy is come to me/When I sought mere delight."[2] The villagers in *Happy Valley* also try to break through their pain, but they are stopped by their environment. The community casts baleful shadows that are sometimes long enough to blot out individuality. Unlike Sinclair Lewis's *Main Street* (1920) or John Updike's *Couples* (1968), *Happy Valley* has no main character; instead we see stock figures such as the spoiled debutante, the local doctor, and the music mistress. Nor is the book controlled by an observer/narrator, like Sherwood Anderson's *Winesburg, Ohio* (1919) or Thornton Wilder's *Our Town* (1938). On the other hand, the book's large cast testifies to its young author's artistic readiness to distribute ideas and feelings over a cast of eight or ten important characters. What is more, White shows how one person's actions affect the welfare of others, some of whom may be unsuspecting and innocent.

The patterns formed by communal interdependence replace both a conventional plot and action. *Happy Valley* shows that, from the start of his writing career, White felt it wrong or cheap to tell a story. Though subtly and deeply joined, the characters keep their inmost lives private.

Most of what goes on consists of either small talk or unspoken hopes and dreams. Subtext, conveyed through interior monologues, carries the burden of the theme. Much of the interest comes from White's telling of the story, rather than from the story itself; what matters are the feelings leading to decisions, rather than the actions that conscious decision creates. White's skepticism about rural Australia touches every character and every commitment. *Happy Valley* deflates the myth of an idyllic community consisting of church steeples, a village green, and smiling families. His skepticism is historically valid: the golden age before the advent of cities, factories, and large-scale machine production probably never existed in either Australia or the United States. (Judging from the power of the uranium bloc in White's 1977 play, *Big Toys*, the future holds no place for that golden age, either.) The fresh territory ahead that beckons a Huck Finn or a Stan Parker also attracts forces that will corrupt it. Dealing with New South Wales squatters rather than with migrant workers in the torrid north, *Happy Valley* presents an Australia less rough, rugged, and brawling than that of its near contemporary, *Capricornia* (1938), by Xavier Herbert. *Happy Valley*'s main feature is its disconnectedness, both from the outside world and from itself. The English-born George Brown complains in *The Solid Mandala* that Australia has no shadows; because it lacks history, everything in it lives in the shrill present (p. 152). Oliver Halliday, Happy Valley's town doctor, would agree. After returning home from military service in France he notes, "At home everything was reversed. The people were young, adolescent, almost embryonic.... But the country was old, older than the forests of Fontainebleu. There was an underlying bitterness that had been scored deep and deep by time" (p. 19). Although *Happy Valley* does not confront the difference between Australia's ancient, brooding landscape and its uncaring white settlers, as Lawrence's *Kangaroo* (1923) and Herbert's *Seven Emus* (1959), its characters' failure to cope with the landscape deepens their alienation.

Missed connections abound in the novel. The enigmatic wisdom emanating from the earth influences no one except, perhaps, a Chinese family. Nor is there fellowship in Happy Valley; people exist in spite of each other, and most of them would rather be somewhere else. No believer in the moral superiority of rural life, White loads his characters with blocked impulses. Husbands and wives, parents and children, and members of different social classes and age groups can't communicate. The town's main link to the outside world, a dolt named Chuffy Chambers, drives the mail truck to and from nearby Moorang. His mentality reflects the self-defeating insularity of the villagers: communication with the outside world counts for so little that it can be entrusted to a halfwit. The villagers' relation to the stark, timeless landscape surrounding them supports this insularity. Whatever promise of distinction and uplift the area once held has ebbed and finally vanished. Happy Valley stands, or slouches, in the foothills of the Snowy Mountains in New South Wales's Monaro district. Extremes of weather plague the inhabitants. The soil grows dusty in the blazing, flyblown summer and it hardens in the winter; Oliver Halliday's wife calls the valley the coldest place in the world, and its heat stops the local schoolmaster, Ernest Moriarty, from sleeping. Counterweighing the movement and material progress boosting Australia in 1936-37, White sets his first novel in a faded, forgotten corner of a once-bustling area. The gold rush brought prospectors to Happy Valley some forty or fifty years earlier, but by the time of the novel the seams have been scooped clean and the ore carted away, leaving the place a drab backwater where obscure people lead uneventful lives. As can be expected, the town has grown boring, stuffy, and tame. The first signs of spring (and thus of renewal) exclude man; most of the action unfolds in winter and summer, the upleasant seasons. The absence of community spirit, conveyed by the interior monologues ending the first part of this two-part work, points up the town's irrelevance. Also emblematic of futility is the schoolmaster Moriarty, whose asthma, faithless wife, and low-paying job have sapped him. The sight of him lying immobilized in a sour-smelling room recalls Eliot's image of a sick society at the start of "Prufrock": "This was Happy Valley now, with Moriarty on a brass bedstead and the wash basin unemptied from the day before" (p. 122).

As these details suggest, White overcomes many of the handicaps caused by writing about a rude, inconvenient place where nothing much happens. His attitude toward Happy Valley controls his artistry throughout. No microcosm like Eliot's etherized patient, Happy Valley is a distant echo or pale reflection. Its dreariness and ignorance have put it outside the mainstream of reality as it is experienced elsewhere. Mind and heart languish in this drab, featureless waste, where the local School of Arts has grown dusty from neglect. People subsist. That Happy Valley offers a substitute for life, rather than life itself, shows in the malaise of its inhabitants. The wheezing cuckold Moriarty isn't the only local saddled with sickness; Hilda Halliday also has trouble breathing. And Alys Browne, who sews and teaches piano, keeps drawing her blood, with a paring knife and then on a rose thorn, because of her isolation; she is so lonely that she mortifies her flesh in order to create excitement. If her soul has lost its vitality, why shouldn't her body follow suit?

White moves with a convincing clarity of purpose amid this web of frustrations. He populates the town of Happy Valley, gives it a network of streets, shops, and homes, supplies a social hierarchy, and, with the foul weather, gives the inhabitants a common cause. Realistically, these inhabitants have spent different amounts of time in the area, and different reasons have brought them to it. Such variations add color to the background. Alys moved away for five years, but her father's death brought her back. Two younger characters who studied in Sydney, Sidney Furlow and Rodney Halliday, learned French from the same teacher. The lives of the villagers cross and knit in other ways. Besides depicting the sad comedown of Ernest Moriarty, the scenes at the local school show children of different backgrounds in a common setting. The actions of youngsters like Margaret Quong, Emily Schmidt, and Rodney Halliday comment wryly on those displayed by their parents in shops and pubs. When a setting provides an added emotional charge, like the annual Cup race or the dance preceding it, children and parents both act out of pride, greed, and envy, with White showing how easily the herd instinct can overtake a crowd. This fear of mass emotion and collective ethics will permeate all of his fiction.

I

The novel's cast of malcontents implies that White's fear of the masses reflects a similar disquiet with the individual, vindicating in part the *Sydney Morning Herald's* complaint that he peopled *Happy Valley* with "near-perverts, morons, neurotics, and defeatists."[3] In fairness to White, the negation and squalor are more effect than cause. Barry Argyle explains how milieu infects family life in *Happy Valley:* "None of the adults has found love, happiness, fulfillment in marriage, nor have the children in their parents. Instead they suffer, and they suffer each other."[4]

Disconnectedness in the home takes several forms. Ethel Quong's resentment of her roistering Chinese husband, Walter, sends their half-caste daughter, Margaret, to the home of her aunt and uncle for love. That Amy and Arthur Quong, Margaret's spiritual parents, are brother and sister rather than husband and wife calls into question the ability of the traditional nuclear family to promote well-being. The breakdown and bitterness gnawing at other families justifies this skepticism. Sidney Furlow discounts her parents, addressing them only to thwart them or to request gifts. Oliver Halliday can't please his son, Rodney. The apparent retardation of Rodney's younger brother, George, both suggests the loss of love in Oliver and Hilda's marriage and pinpoints a cause of it—the decline of Hilda. Six years her husband's senior, the whining, faded Hilda may have primed Oliver for the charms of the younger Alys by running out of energy.

Alys is as ready for an affair with Oliver as he is for one with her. Early in the novel she invests money from the sale of property inherited from her father, hoping to earn enough from the profits to leave Happy Valley. Oliver falls in love with her and agrees to take her to California. His obligation to Hilda, though, dampens his courage. Like Dickens's Oliver, he is punished when he asks for More by hoping to start life anew with Alys. In keeping with the book's niggardliness, he passes along the punishment. Alys resents him for igniting false hope in her. The new spirit he has created in her, besides making her miss him more, heightens her bitterness toward her prosaic routine. Ironically, he never learns the full extent of this deprivation. After hearing from him for the last time, Alys learns that the firm in which she has invested her money has failed, exploding her California dream. This loss pulls against the idea set forth in the novel's epigraph, from Gandhi, that moral growth and suffering go together: "the purer the suffering, the greater is the progress." Brissenden's objection to White's treatment of this morality applies to Alys: "The characters in *Happy Valley* suffer, but they do not in any clear sense progress; mainly because the pain they endure is brought about not so much by their own actions as by the random cruelty of life."[5] Alys's pain far outweighs what she gleans from her broken tie with Oliver; little or no progress accompanies it. But, leaning on an idea perhaps borrowed from Chekhov's *Three Sisters*, White may be saying that Alys's being stuck in Happy Valley will kindle adventurous impulses in her students that they will pass on to the next generation. By not going to California Alys may eventually enrich Happy Valley with the westering spirit. Her losing Oliver could have also created a surplus of love which will aid her students in more immediate ways.

Then there is Alys's piano, an important detail because music is perhaps the most ennobling of all activities for White. Music elevates the listener and especially the musician to a higher, richer plane of existence. The flute of Topp, a music teacher who lives in the same Sydney rooming house as Voss, gladdens the hearts of passersby; later Voss proposes to Laura Trevelyan right after thinking about her piano playing. In *Riders*, some organ music played at a cathedral in England's fen country (Ely?) puts Ruth Godbold in mind of heavenly scaffolding and ladders of gold. During the warm, penetrant strains of a waltz, Sidney Furlow becomes inflamed by Hagan. Oliver resolves to take Alys to the United States at the same annual dance. Although she is later left behind, the prospect of going away with him both sustains and encourages Alys for several happy months. Much of this glow comes from music. In *The Twyborn Affair*, Eddie Twyborn and Angelos Vatatzes, who perhaps enjoy the warmest sexual tie in the canon, play piano duets. By having Alys and Oliver play duets as well, White is infusing their relationship with some of the same warmth. Though heartbroken by her inability to carry this intimacy into the world beyond Happy Valley, Alys knows that Oliver still loves her. The comfort this knowledge provides will have to help her through the bleak winter ahead.

Her turncoat lover sorely needs the lyricism she represents. Futility has hemmed him in. First seen, characteristically, delivering a stillbirth, Oliver finds promise and hope crumbling around him. This breakdown worries him. He recalls deciding to become a poet and playwright as a youth while riding a ferry in Sydney Harbor. (Sydney's Hurtle Duffield of *Vivisector* will also enjoy a self-awakening as a ferry passenger.) But he has written nothing in years. Unlike the hawk circling Happy Valley in the opening chapters, Oliver doesn't soar. Instead, this overworked drudge, paunchy and graying at thirty-four, falls down in the snow after falling down in his all-night effort to deliver a live baby. Alys assuages some of his pain, but even as she restores him Hilda's nagging and sickness wear him down. His guilt compounds, weakening the moral fiber of his family. Hoping to prolong his fantasy of taking Alys to America, he delays telling Hilda about the letter inviting him to sunny Queensland, but tell her he does. Ironically, the strength Alys gives him works against her. Though her deep loving need for him at first keeps him by her side, it later encourages him to abandon her.

Oliver's nine-year-old son Rodney also knows the sweet sorrow of thwarted love with an unlikely person. Like his father's love for Alys, his love stems from need. Bullied by his schoolmates and unable to talk to his parents, Rodney turns to Margaret Quong. (His attraction to a girl four years his senior traces a pattern of heredity from Oliver, who married an older woman). He turns to her at a good time. Though the Quongs are the town's shopkeepers and creditors, they are scorned as Orientals; none of Margaret's fellow students will visit her. Rodney's friendly overture touches this poor little rich girl's heart. Besides ending her loneliness, friendship with another sensitive outsider will help her know her own feelings. When Rodney gives her a seashell on the way home from school shortly after they see a bull coupling with a cow, the giving takes on the force of a ceremony. Neither child is distracted or embarrassed. The shell's delicate tints, acoustical richness, and remote undersea origins all convey a magic unknown in Happy Valley. Margaret invites Rodney to her home later that day to see a litter of pups, affirming the vitality of her exchange with him.

With Rodney's help, Margaret grows more than any other person in the book. The onset of her first menstrual cramps near the end marks her emergence into womanhood. This new life doesn't daunt her. She has gained the maturity needed to deal with the loss created by Rodney's departure. Her decision to stop studying piano with Alys reflects her independence; her forgiving a frenzied Ernest Moriarty for beating her for a wrong she didn't commit warms this independence with a charity resembling mystical self-detachment. When White says that her new maturity has given her "a sort of superiority that would not be imposed upon" (p. 312), he speaks our very thoughts. And his words could mirror our ideas about her family, who also fight past privation to carry the day. Over the years the despised Quongs, who started with nothing, have become one of the town's richest families. The general store they operate provides their disdainful neighbors with staples; they also own land, a local car dealership and garage, and some race horses. The winning of the Cup race by one of these horses earns the Quongs still more wealth and power. If they lack the prestige to go along with their bonanza, they can console themselves by watching their domain grow. They have already eclipsed their townfolk. They run both the local movie house and the drinks concession at the annual Cup dance, not only feeding and clothing their narrow-minded neighbors, but also entertaining them. The victory of Arthur Quong's horse crowns the slow but steady process by which the family has taken Happy Valley on its own terms and prevailed over it. It is appropriate that they are the last local inhabitants the Hallidays see driving out of town.

Emblematic of the sweeping change they help bring about is Amy Quong's visit to the Moriarty home in the third chapter. Amy has come to collect a debt of £5. Her needing to dun the Moriartys implies that the debt is long overdue; that she can pry only a pound from Vic indicates the disrepair of their exchequer. The pressures on the Moriartys are more than financial. If the names Victoria and Ernest evoke Britain's great age of colonial expansion, then the Moriartys' tatty home is the last outpost of a sagging empire. Situated in a cold, empty place far from England, its supposed cultural center, the house reeks of asthma powder and rotten eggs; adultery takes place within its buckling walls; the loud ticking of its sitting room clock reminds its owners that time is running out. Victorian shibboleths such as duty and earnestness can't halt the invasion of pain and, finally, chaos. Ernest works for a low salary, teaching students who make fun of him. He can't fight their ridicule or condescension; because of his asthma, he can't fight the cold weather, either. But the transfer for which he keeps applying never comes through (unlike that of Oliver, a scientist in a science-dominated society). Vic, meanwhile, has grown tired of nursing him, of trying to manage the home on his low wage, and of remaining childless. She can thus put up no defenses against the sexual advances of Clem Hagan. On the night of the Cup race, Ernest finds them together, strangles her, and then, reeling with drunken grief, dies of a heart attack on a nearby road. The reversal foreshadowed by Vic's humiliating exchange with Amy Quong nearly a year before is complete. Arthur's winning of the Cup has made his family richer than ever. Both the Moriartys have died wasteful, pathetic deaths. The sordidness surrounding the deaths befits White's satire. The inverse analogy with the Quongs has run its inevitable course as the heartbeat of Victorian England comes to a long-overdue stop.

White's lead-in to the grisly finale shows as much skill as the finale itself. A few hours before the double death, while Vic is repairing his torn suspenders, or braces, Moriarty reads an anonymous letter explaining his wife's infidelity. He is literally bare-legged as he learns that he doesn't wear the pants in his home. Some ironic twists break the witty parallel. Moriarty's learning of his cuckolding while looking unmanly rouses a manly response he cannot sustain. Vic's suggestion that he spend the night in Moorang, where he is planning to read a paper on philately, has the reverse effect of sending him home. But so unsuited is he for marriage that he plays the outraged husband only long enough to kill Vic. His dying within minutes of her shows that despite his shortcomings as a husband, he can exist no other way. Without Vic—even a faithless Vic—to support him, he can't manage a natural function like maintaining a heartbeat. The man who couldn't control his wife or his students survives for a scant minute or two before the challenge of living on his own defeats him.

An object in the house associated with Moriarty is the brown mahogany sitting room clock. The clock was his to begin with. Furthermore, the order, system, and regularity that it represents express the masculine principle and, along with it, the inherited values on which Australia's male-dominated society rests. The mechanical innards of clocks and the use of the words "clock" and "ticker" as slang synonyms for the heart create a context for Moriarty's downfall. Usually flat and glassy on the surface, clocks symbolize a neat, composed existence Moriarty can never achieve. Their reasonable, practical operation connotes a moral standard elsewhere for White. In the outlandish Hôtel du Midi (*Aunt's Story*), where nothing answers to reason, the clocks all keep a different time. Clocks are also unreliable in Xanadu (*Riders*) because the mansion's sole occupant, Mary Hare, doesn't wind them. She has no need for clocks; though out of touch with the workaday world, she has attuned herself to natural cycle. Moriarty's clock also bespeaks an arbitrary mechanical system often slighted by those attuned to life's deeper rhythms. (When Vic reaches out to touch Hagan after sex, he tells her angrily that he's not a machine.) The values the clock imposes, while abstract, are also predictable. So is Moriarty's death. The last thing he does in his beleagured home is to smash the sitting room clock. He won't even let it wind down. The reality to which it refers, linear time, has proven to be a fraud and a mockery. Like his marriage, it both sustains and breaks him. To let it outlast him would be an abject confession of defeat. The clock has ordered his home no better than he has.

Another important symbol from the home is the pink cyclamen that sits on the center table. Although Vic's attentiveness to it makes the cyclamen her symbol, in a larger sense it encompasses and explains her marriage to Ernest. Its sprawling leaves reflect the house's disorder when Amy Quong comes to collect the money owed her. It lolls and droops during one of Ernest's asthma attacks. Vic fingers it nervously while entertaining Hagan for the first time. After her first night out with Hagan, it shows its disapproval by standing in prudish disdain: "The cyclamen stuck up straight. . . . Queer the antics of that flower. Anyone would think it had its ears back. Bitchiness in a flower" (p. 160). Argyle has noted that two of the book's leading female characters have male-sounding names:[6] the spoiled debutante Sidney Furlow and Vic Moriarty. No doubt the bitchiness Vic sees in the cyclamen applies more strictly to her than to the plant. She has just been kissing and locking pelvises with Hagan. Although the possibility that Ernest is sterile, even impotent, has made her desperate, that desperation can only defeat her. Her ascribing female traits to the erect cyclamen, a blatantly phallic symbol, together with her man's name, show that she is too self-divided to benefit from the androgynous vision so central to White's maturity.

A character with a stronger sense of himself is Vic's lover, Clem Hagan. But this hard-muscled ruffian has defined life so narrowly that his ideas about self and society hardly matter; in fact, they hardly exist. Unmoved by the Glen Marsh landscape, Hagan views it only as a source of material profit. His lack of imagination also involves denying other people any free-standing reality; twice, when characters tell him their names, he recoils in disbelief. Clem, or Clement, comes to town on the same inclement Monday on which Mrs. Chalker loses her baby, almost as if bringing the hard luck and the bad weather with him. His first hours in Happy Valley tell a good deal about him. He insults Chuffy Chambers, who had done him the favor of driving him into town; he wants to shoot the hawk that was wheeling over the town in the early chapters; he makes trouble in a local pub. This bony roustabout harbors aggression. Predictably, he relieves stress by dominating women, preferably married ones like Vic Moriarty who won't threaten his freedom. Sidney Furlow, on the other hand, makes him feel clumsy and slow; her sarcasm deflates his brawn and bluster. Or so he believes. Like several other important characters, he has a totem or leitmotif. Hair, often red, bristling on the backs of men's wrists, hands, and fingers (and sometimes their necks) symbolizes virility in White's fiction. Laura Trevelyan's sexual awakening to Voss, an amalgam of attraction and revulsion, occurs as she notices the wiry hairs covering his wrists. In *The Eye of the Storm,* Flora Manhood notices the hair on Basil Hunter's fingers the day she has sex with him. The thick, hairy wrists of Garnet Roxburgh in *A Fringe of Leaves* help mark *him* as an object of Ellen Roxburgh's lust and loathing. The homosexual Cecil Cutbush in *Vivisector* has hairless wrists. In *Happy Valley,* White treats the motif well. Right after mentioning the reddish hairs sprouting on Hagan's hands, he has the sensualist ask (sealing his cigarette with his tongue for good measure), "What about girls?" (p. 24). Women feel the force of his rank paws. Sidney Furlow accidentally brushes the back of his hand the first time she sees him; later, when Vic tries to coax him into bed, she tugs at the hair on his hands.

Ironically, he is more acted upon than active in the book's closing sections. The wayward, meandering structure sharpens in the last chapter with a courtroom scene and the return of the constricting effects of winter. This process began with the autumn race meeting, after which the cold sets in. Death takes over after the race, with winter bringing the loss of Alys Browne's money and dreams, the Halliday family's exodus, young Rodney's deathly intimations, and the downfall of the Moriartys. Figuring in the drift toward death is nineteen-year-old Sidney Furlow, the first of White's headstrong, horseback-riding socialites. If Sidney puzzles and frightens her parents, she also vexes herself. Belonging in the tradition of the bored, upper-class beauty which includes Ibsen's Hedda Gabler and Eliot's lady at the dressing table in *The Waste Land*, Sidney often sits at her own dressing table, feeling blocked. She ends an afternoon of riding with her anxious English suitor by locking her door and dragging her nails down her cheeks till they draw blood.

Her affinity with wire shows how her tendency to slice and slash recoils upon her. Wire has many uses: it conducts heat; it transmits electricity; it can be used for fencing; when properly tuned and strung, it will make music. Sidney promotes none of these civilizing benefits. Thin and skittish (Hagan can't remember having seen anyone so thin), she has a hard, cutting edge to her personality. She trembles so much that she seems to take no nourishment from her food. But, unlike a quivering violin string, she makes no music. Rather than seeking harmony, she serves discord and craves power, which she interprets as the opportunity to inflict pain. Her chief victim, aside from her parents, is the Wiltshire gentleman who wants to marry her. She ignores and mistreats Roger Kemble of Government House in Sydney, even though marrying him would lift her to "the topmost pinnacle" (p. 136) of Australian society. The joys of blasting the hopes of both her suitor and her social-climbing mother outweigh those of gaining an English establishment. Roger and her mother fuse in her mind as a composite victim. They also feel the sting of her cruelty. Just as she despises her mother for yielding to her, so she resents Roger for bringing out the worst in her. Included in this worst is the refusal to communicate. The brat who shuts her door in her mother's face also ignores Roger's marriage proposal and destroys his unread letters. By siding with Hagan, a bigoted roughneck who she thinks murdered his mistress, she makes another calculated attack on her parents. She hates herself, and she knows she can't change. So who merits her malice more than those who have always loved her? Marriage to Hagan appeals to her power fetish. It will disgrace her parents socially; it will relieve her own tedium; it will be undertaken on terms unfavorable to Hagan. Only if he agrees to marry her will she testify in court that she was with him during the Moriarty debacle. The value of her alibi? In a conservative town where everyone knew of his affair with Vic, he could never avoid a conviction without her testimony.

Agreeing to Sidney's proposal wins Hagan only marginal freedom. What *she* has won with her blackmail is entrapment and grief for two people. Hagan is not the passionate inferno she believes, even though he could have gone to jail for Vic's murder. He keeps his hat on in her presence out of ignorance, not out of defiance or class anger. He reacts from the loins, not from the heart or the mind, let alone the social conscience. His only imaginable tie with a woman is sexual. This brutishness serves Sidney's purposes, satisfying her craving to be soiled. She is still a virgin. A sexual pirate of thirty-one, her bridegroom-to-be lacks patience, tenderness, and imagination. It will be a wonder if their marriage survives the honeymoon in Java, that volcanic island, let alone thrives on the Scone farm that her father has given them. Marjorie Bernard's statement that "The field is possessed by the strong and the insensitive. . . . Only the ruthless survive"[7] misses the irony of White's justice. Sidney and Hagan have *not* triumphed. Their mutual overthrow, though not described, is inevitable. They have gotten what they want and what they deserve. Their world will shatter with a sound many times louder than that produced by Moriarty's cough or the solo strains of Alys Browne's piano.

White's speeding of the action toward the end to invite issues that go beyond the final pages shows real maturity. Though *Happy Valley* is no murder story, murder does focus and unify the action. By forging a destructive bond and destroying a hopeful one, i.e., that of Alys and Oliver, the deaths of the Moriartys block renewal. What is more, Alys's affair with Oliver intersects with that of Vic and Hagan, the demise of the one sinking the other. The collapse comes suddenly. Oliver has packed his gear and started to drive out of Happy Valley with Alys on Cup night. Finding Ernest's corpse in the road first delays the lovers' getaway and then stops it. Like poor Ern, the lovers do not pass the outskirts of town. Oliver learns from Ernest both the futility of rebellion and the depth of his duty to Hilda, another deceived spouse trammeled by poor health. This identification convinces Oliver that, without him, Hilda could come to the same grief as Ern. His estimate rings truer than he knows. His actions reveal no moral difference between him and the other timid, ineffectual men who people White's early fiction.[8] His sense of duty and his love for Alys both look cheap. Had he trusted his heart, he'd not have worried about the wreckage love can cause. Like Ern, Hilda's opposite number, Oliver's love for Hilda is dead. Yet he lets it prevail over the promise conveyed by Alys and California. He has lost faith in himself. Happy Valley pulls him back only long enough to fetch his family and take them to Queensland; he ignores the welfare of his neighbors, and he writes Alys a letter of explanation instead of conveying his decision in person. As befits a man whose sense of respectability outpaces any drive to self-being, he lacks the moral courage to explain himself in a personal interview. (Interview, ironically, is the name of the winning horse in the Cup race.) He claims to be making a stand for sanity, but by yielding to his whining wife he is merely showing off to himself at Alys's expense.

II

White multiplies the connections between the two adulteries. Ern's thinking of "loops of telephone wire cutting right into the throat" (p. 271) while strangling Vic invokes the destructive Sidney. The murder scene includes other invocations. After strangling Vic, Ern cuts his hand on the vase containing the cyclamen. The bloodshed caused by the breaking of the vase describes the death of both the marriage and the death-dealer, catching Ern both literally and figuratively red handed. It also refers back to the hand injury that sent Alys to Oliver's clinic nearly a year before. The links joining the characters are deep, obscure, and tight. They are also richly expressive of the characters. The pool of blood forming from Ern's cut recalls a similar stain on Alys's kitchen table in chapter 4. This pool of blood, in turn, harks back to the ominous puddle of water left by Amy Quong's umbrella in the Moriartys' front room in chapter 3. The Moriarty house is haunted by the image of life leaking away. (Ironically, no loss of blood leads to either Moriarty death.) Repetition of different kinds both controls the many-sided plot and teases out the mystery of unity. That the various lives in Happy Valley are acausally linked doesn't cloud the impression of unity. The repetitions not only join the various lives, but also criticize them. Mrs. Chalkers' stillbirth in chapter 1 hangs over the Moriartys, with Vic having some dried egg on her blouse when she first sees Hagan and Ern being accidentally served a rotten egg on the day he dies. The network of interlocking motives and fortunes is further tightened by White's chapter arrangement. Chapter 27 ends with Oliver phoning the police to report the Moriartys' deaths. The first sentence of chapter 28 shows Sidney climbing out of bed, as if Oliver's phone call had awakened *her* and thereby endowed her with official police powers. The tension created by the double death holds; like the Moriartys, Sidney seems headed for a sexual calamity in which Hagan will play a big part.

The book's two-part structure, suggesting opposition without the resolution or synthesis evident in three-part works (such as *The Aunt's Story* and *The Twyborn Affair*), posits the same grimness. Like the first part of *Eye*, the first part of *Happy Valley* covers one day, the winter Monday of Mrs. Chalker's stillbirth, Alys's hand injury, and Hagan's arrival in town. The action continues to unfold in terrible weather in Part Two, which White divides into two time periods. Six months have passed since the end of Part One. Baking heat is enervating most of the locals, while infecting some with midsummer madness. In chapter 18, the action moves ahead to late fall. Nearly everyone fears the advent of winter, whose frosts they lack the inner warmth to repel; only Hilda Halliday, sickly as she is, welcomes the cold, since its onset will deliver her from Happy Valley. The winter *is* fearsome, but because White portrayed its icy grip in Part One, he need only mention it in Part Two. Like the book's first ten chapters, its last ten take place on one day—the dripping, raw day of the Cup race. Cup Day marks the end of mellow autumn and the coming of ice and snow. Everyone dreads winter; the Hallidays leave lest its gusts lash them as they did the Moriartys. The approaching winter threatens to be particularly fierce, judging from the events of chapters 14 and 15, which, took place in summer, the season of planting. Chapter 14 showed Hagan grinding against Vic; in the next chapter, this provocation is consummated as Oliver and Alys declare their love for each other and then make love during a rainstorm. From this point on infidelity moves the plot, with most of the book's actions and ideas referring to at least one of the two adulteries. No wonder the locals are bracing against the cold; their healer and their intellectual leader have deserted them, both fixated upon arrangements made the foregoing summer.

III

The only flaw in the neat structure appears in the last paragraphs of each part, where, discrediting the work's ability to convey its own meaning, White waxes magisterial. His blanketing the closely perceived action with moral abstractions causes regret. But not surprises; first novelists often have more trouble concluding than do more experienced hands. In White's case the first novelist's worries extend to that other problem spot, the beginning. *Happy Valley* starts shakily. Its third sentence introduces a hawk riding a bank of white winter air. Though the hawk "happens to be in the sky in a necessary spot at a necessary moment" (p. 9), the necessity is White's alone. He needs a unifying device. Like the bells of Big Ben in Virginia Woolf's *Mrs. Dalloway* (1925), the cruising hawk allows the author to shift settings and bring in new characters while keeping a fixed point of reference. The hawk does the job much less effectively than Woolf's tolling bells, partly because White does not control it. He says that the hawk is "magnetized" by some private aim. Then he writes, "But that is beside the point. In fact, the hawk has none but a vaguely geographical significance" (p. 9). How has necessity paled so within a few sentences? And how private is the hawk's aim? White should have picked a weaker adjective than "magnetized" if he wanted to scuttle the hawk so quickly.

The scuttling of the hawk also makes us ask why he didn't choose a device or image more closely bound up with his own aim.

More inconsistency follows. The same paragraph which can't make up its mind about the hawk also tells of a railway line dribbling through the morning mists. This image, too, fights itself, the idea of dribbling train tracks clashing with the urgency of a magnetic field. If White's hawk knows of a connection between the two images, he keeps his own counsel. White then cuts to his first dramatized scene, the labor and delivery of Rita Chalker. But the scene occurs, contrary to expectation, in Moorang, not in Happy Valley, and the baby is born dead. The snow covering the area seems to have frozen White, who acts as if he might trip on a sheet of ice. Having dismissed his hawk, he wavers between "We," "I," and "You" while groping for a safe foothold. Narrative stance keeps shifting unpredictably. The author effaces himself but then moves to the fore, breaking into the action in order to criticize it: "Men who work a lot in the open, especially those who work with sheep, have a habit of repeating things" (p. 25). He generalizes, "Mauve is a dangerous color" (p. 38). His own opinions needn't intrude. He can impress the reader with his technical skills: his interweaving of motifs to show the interdependence between the book's two adulteries shows real distinction; likewise, his interior monologues are splintered and discontinuous in cadence, yet ordered by both the consciousness and the speaking style of the character to whom they refer. The author intrudes again when a search for the telling image prevents him from letting theme dictate style. Of Hagan's sensuality he says, "This . . . meant a good steak with juice running out of the sides and blonde girls with comfortable busts" (p. 26). The authorial stance bothers him. While giving an overview of Happy Valley or recounting the private life of one of its residents, he adopts a genial, even folksy, tone out of keeping with the sophistication he shows elsewhere: "Well, it had happened like this" (pp. 90-91), he says, prior to describing the meeting and courtship of Ethel and Walter Quong.

These lapses are regrettable because, for the most part, the style of *Happy Valley* tempers its inventiveness with good sense. Its compact, subdued voice contrasts admirably with White's bolder effects—the violent image of Ern yanking at Vic's tongue after strangling her to death, and the foreboding sentence logic introducing Sidney's entry into the action, "She had a very red mouth and had been to a finishing school" (p. 42). The book is filled with telling insights on subjects ranging from impressionist art to sheep ranching or investment. Such insights lend the book authority. What is even better, White doesn't pad their force by overexplicitness. A light touch helps join his definition of wealth to the town's richest family: "Mrs. Furlow had paid a lot, not so much for the sake of the fur as for the privilege of paying a lot" (p. 280).

This careful phrasing is wedded to a deft organization. Recovering from its shaky start, the book gathers strength and conviction through the middle sections. The sexuality of chapters 14 and 15 sets the tone for Ern's attack on Margaret Quong in chapter 16. This violence sluices into chapter 17, the book's middle chapter, and energizes the book's most violent figure. Appropriately, that chapter belongs to Sidney, who emerges from it with new control and strength. Her cruelty holds the action together. Each event in the chapter feeds it, starting with her destruction of Roger Kemble's letters. Her urge to punish those who love her calls forth the memory of a local fire which, to her regret, went out before destroying her parents' property. Cruelty continues to goad her. Angrily she whips her horse, who stands for the instincts which have misled her. Her frustration and self-contempt are both at their peak when she happens upon Hagan in her father's paddocks. After a conversation bristling with sexual innuendos, they see a snake—which Hagan kills, to her great glee. Inflamed by both his violence and the symbolism called forth by the dead snake, she keeps prodding Hagan. The snake's death has left her the only devil in the field, and her new power warms her with satanic pride. But she freezes when Hagan kisses her. She can only relate destructively to a suitor or would-be lover. Her craving to be defiled by Hagan, and thus put out of the reach of Roger Kemble's smooth English hands, gives way to loathing. She lashes Hagan's face with her wire-like riding crop, bringing to two the number of stallions stung by her cruelty. This destructiveness spills into the second half of the book, where, amid bucketing autumn rains, a tide of wild emotions drowns reason and order. Madness calls the tune when the villagers dance to Chuffy Chambers's harmonica, when the Moriartys die, and when Oliver forsakes Alys for Hilda.

White uses Joycean motifs other than stream of consciousness to shape this chaos. Like Father Dolan, the sadistic prefect in *A Portrait of the Artist*, Ern punishes a student unjustly; the student in each book responds to the punishment with unusual detachment. White's next model, another scurvy educator, is Stephen Dedalus's mentor, Mr. Garrett Deasy of the "Nestor" episode of *Ulysses*. But whereas Deasy writes about cattle, the ineffectual Ern reads about them. The "Aeolus" episode of *Ulysses* supplies the references to journalism and the oft-repeated act of falling just short of one's goals ("almosting it"). Some echoes ring more softly than others. In "Scylla and Charybdis," AE or George Russell mentions Mallarmé, whom Sidney reads in her bedroom; Hagan knew a tart in Sydney named Bella, no doubt named by White for the title figure in "Circe." White also refers to episodes in *Ulysses* in order to criticize his characters. On the day when they first have sex, Molly Tweedy pushes a piece of chewed seedcake from her mouth into Bloom's. Vic's licking a postage stamp after Ern lacks this rich sensuality—as it is meant to; their marriage is weaker than that of the Blooms. No idolater, White shapes other borrowings from *Ulysses* to his own narrative intent. Just as the Ascot Gold Cup race is won by an outsider in *Ulysses*, so an underdog wins the Cup in *Happy Valley*. But Happy Valley's Cup doesn't represent renewal in the form of the chalice or female vessel, as it does in Joyce. Rather, it signals the overthrow of Saxon supremacy and the onset of winter, both within a resoundingly Australian context supplied by the turf. Australians have always loved horse racing. Writing in 1883, a French visitor, Edmond Marin La Meslée, said of Australia's great annual sporting event, "Cup Day is Melbourne's *Mardi Gras*. The city is deserted and the whole world flocks to the race course. Shops, banks, government offices, establishments of every kind, shut their doors."[9] This festiveness chills to desperation amid the cold rain, mud, and disappointment that grip Happy Valley on Cup Day.

Recording lost hopes and some new entrenchments, *Happy Valley* opens the door to White's novelistic career with craft and verve. Its subject, the heart racing inside a static, commonplace exterior, will provide the bipolar tension energizing the mandala. As is shown in the clash between the monotonous outback and the fierce idealism with which Voss faces this wasteland, and again in the withered frames of geniuses like Hurtle Duffield and Elizabeth Hunter, the dialectic set forth in *Happy Valley* will power White's future explorations of the moral and metaphysical orders.

3. Silhouettes
on a Glass Box

The Living and the Dead (1941) poses technical challenges beyond those facing the freshman novelist of *Happy Valley*. Set mainly in England, the book includes important scenes which take place in Germany and France. Though using a smaller cast than its predecessor, it delves deeper into its characters' lives. Its time scheme also displays a new sophistication. Not only does the work swathe three generations; it also shifts time, repeats events from different points of view, and, perhaps most boldly, ends only hours after it begins. On the other hand, it is written with the mind's eye rather than with a keen visual sense. The White of *Living and Dead* doesn't transcribe material data with the same accuracy and sharp particularity he brought to *Happy Valley;* he traces moods, sifts feelings, and evokes atmospheres, rather than conveying the sensation of physical experience. Subjectivity presses into all. The act of observing a phenomenon will count more than the phenomenon itself, the expressive and evocative qualities of images overriding the representational ones. This practice of synthesizing, internalizing, and abstracting experience, rather than copying it, means that nothing much happens. *Living and Dead* may be White's flattest and most trivial work. Teasing out motive and nuance with a Jamesian fussiness, he works harder at establishing himself as a serious writer than he does at creating characters who touch our hearts. His people are seen piecemeal, stumbling toward each other in dim corridors or being stunned by the glare of the urban inferno. They rarely communicate, preferring instead to pore over the residue of desire and memory. If this immobility saddens them, it numbs us. Their regretting their mistakes, their lost chances, and their wasted time robs the work of amiability and attack.

The book speaks so indistinctly and moves so slowly because it has to slice through a fogbelt of literary allusions, borrowings, and private myths. Like Joyce, White celebrates memorable personal experiences by using them in his fiction. Two 1928 poems concerning his sister, "Long Ago: a Reminiscence" and "Susan," from the privately published *Thirteen Poems* (1930) by P.V.M. White, refer to events that reappear transformed in *Living and Dead*.[1] White uses a different sort of interface to deal with his bad days at Cheltenham School, Gloucester,[2] out of which his adolescent verse was written. Although the book's most derided character, Connie Tiarks, lives in Cheltenham, she ultimately agrees to marry a Staffordshire man named Allgood; her coming marriage, the hope conveyed by her fiancé's name, and her leaving Cheltenham (where Ellen Roxburgh of *Fringe* will also live as a victim) all speak well for White's personal outlook as a budding novelist. The treatment of other autobiographical data tells less about White. Elyot Standish spends a year in Germany at age sixteen before attending Cambridge University. White also lived there, both before and during his Cambridge student days, some of the 1932-33 poems in *Ploughman* bearing a German dateline. (A minor figure, Norman Maynard, also studied at Cambridge.) Finally, the action centers on a house in Ebury Street, near London's Victoria Station, presumably because, besides liking the symbolism called forth by the street's name, White, too, lived on Ebury Street after leaving Cambridge.[3]

The intellectual ferment of the day, especially London-Oxbridge politics and aesthetics, influences the novel nearly as much as does White's personal life. The Marxism, working-class sympathy, and endorsement of the Loyalist cause in the Spanish Civil War that saturates much of Orwell also trickles through *Living and Dead*. From the Auden circle comes the imagery of sexual desire blossoming in the shadow of industrial desolation. But White lacks his older contemporaries' Marxist faith in social progress and class equality. Elyot's sister Eden kisses her working-class lover, Joe Barnett, near a gasworks. The ugly factory and the carcass of a dead dog the lovers happen upon appear as grim portents. The love between Eden and Joe doesn't stand a dog's chance, and Joe dies only weeks after that scene. What is more, his death proves nothing. The gasworks still spew out noxious waste that pollutes the nearby stream; the blasted loyalty symbolized by the dog's carcass enjoys no rebirth. Joe would have served justice better by staying home and marrying Eden than by fighting Franco in Spain. The social barriers he razes are rebuilt quickly when his aunt, Julia Fallon, refuses to mourn with Eden, even though she has worked for the Standishes for some twenty-five years. The working class, too, respects and enforces barriers. Although she remembers wheeling Eden in a pram as a baby, Julia will not share her grief.

I

Splits open elsewhere as well. None of the book's main characters, the Standishes of Ebury Street, can integrate mind and body or thought and action. As a girl, the self-divided Kitty Goose, who later becomes Catherine Standish, is warned by her father, "You forget there's a belly as well as a soul" (p. 24). Her maturity finds her correcting this imbalance by overcompensating—fixating upon physical appetite at the expense of principle and idea. Also worried by his failure to strike a moral balance, her bystanderish son Elyot feels uneasy about dismissing the noises and the faces confronting him on the street. His sister Eden solves the problem by reaching into the proletariat for Joe with his yeomanry vigor and skill with wood. This solution doesn't originate with her. Throughout the Standish family, parents and even grandparents are revealed in their children. From her grandfather, a Norwich socialist, Eden inherited a disposition toward leftist politics. Her gentle-born grandmother's marriage to this harness-maker provided the model for Eden's social descent in search of sexual love; though she lacks her grandfather's craftsmanship, she admires it in others. From her mother comes the tendency to love unwisely, a pattern of behavior enforced by White's sending both women on a holiday with a man across the English Channel to Dieppe. Dieppe's coastline is where Catherine sees her foundering marriage break up. Some twenty years later, Eden feels estranged from Norman Maynard in Dieppe, despite his prob-ably having impregnated her during their weekend there; all their other liasions took place in "the sterile. . . area of Maynard's room" (p. 155).

Elyot spurns, rather than follows, his parent's sexual example. No timid wooer of women, the ex-army Captain Willy Standish had an affair with one of Catherine's friends while Catherine was carrying Elyot. The sorrow caused by his father's philandering here and elsewhere has made Elyot hesitant, awkward, and withdrawn with women. His rejection of three women, German, English, and Jewish, bespeaks his inability to open his heart. Although he grows both morally and aesthetically by renouncing literary criticism for imaginative art, he still cannot commit himself sexu-ally. His fear of hurting women results ironically in his causing at least as much grief as Willy did. It also raises questions about his art. He dismisses Hildegarde Fiesel because her overheated sexuality offends his Stand(off)-ish soul; he never warms to Connie Tiarks because she is too submissive; Muriel Raphael is too calculating. Who can please him? Finding reasons to dismiss women as different as the three who flock around him, Elyot wears a self-protective shell that also blocks the flow of his imagination. Until he learns that Muriel's heart is as calcified as his own, he continues sleeping with her. Each of the three Standishes discovers sexual love at the same time; each picks a lover of a different background; each meets grief. White seems to side emotionally with their defiance of Engish social convention while condemning it intellectually. Though he never defends the class system, he punishes those who flout it.

Manhandled worst by White's uneasy toryism is Catherine Standish. She augers in a minor way the Australian matron who outlasts her decent plodder of a husband. More complex than her amiable, accommodating mate, she can imagine a life beyond marriage. In *Tree, Eye,* and *Fringe* she commits adultery; she makes love to another woman in *Twyborn;* in *Mandala* she turns to the bottle during her widowhood. The dangers of living alone after years of being protected by a man show through vividly in "Dead Roses," from *The Burnt Ones.* The deaths of her father and her husband within a short time free this story's heroine to take a holiday, during which like Theodora Goodman before her and Elizabeth Hunter after her, a trauma both shatters and remakes her. Catherine fares less well than these other heroines. *Living and Dead* at first appears to be shaping up as a domestic novel of marriage, childrearing, and social history, but Catherine's pregnancy disjoints the pattern by frightening Willy. He starts going out alone, which leads to his affair with one of her friends; a business setback lowers the Standishes' income to the point where Catherine and Willy have to lease their house's ground floor in order to meet expenses. Giving up his final responsibility, the one to himself, Willy renounces painting in favor of drink. He can't function without the regimentation that drove him from the army. Freedom has foiled this self-divided man as a husband, a father, and an artist. That Catherine names their daughter Eden (who was conceived during a marital crisis, perhaps even in Dieppe, where *she* later conceived her own child), charts the gulf between her dream of Paradise and the bleak reality. Willy is one of the walking dead. Luckily, the outbreak of World War I gives him the chance to restructure his life. But he only partakes briefly of the hated military routine that sustained him while wearing him down before his marriage. As Catherine tells her children, he dies in combat.

Catherine's repeating of prior experiences expresses her entrapment, too. The repetition can be funny, at least on the surface. Though years intervene, she replaces a husband named Willy with a lover named Wally. Just as Willy keeps her waiting in a Paris restaurant, so Wally's tardiness forces her to spend time alone in a London bistro. People take advantage of her because; ashamed of her socialist father, she refuses to face the world fully. Like White's characters of the 1970s, Dorothy Hunter de Lascabanes, Ellen Gluyas Roxburgh, and Eddie Twyborn, Catherine suppresses a vital side of herself. Catherine Standish the London matron disclaims the provincial schoolteacher Kitty Goose. This denial, along with her rejection of her father and the guilt issuing therefrom, detracts so much from her that Willy seeks companionship and love outside the home. To deny one's background is to deny oneself. Catherine's suppression of her Norwich past casts fierce shadows. Had she accepted her doughty, working-class intellectuality, she would not only have strengthened her marriage; she would also have known how to nourish the trait when it returned somewhat thinned out in Elyot, and she would have removed Eden's need to find a blue-collar lover to restore a lost continuity.

In place of the intellectuality she rejects because of its common origins, Catherine substitutes carnality. She lives in the flesh her father had chided her for neglecting. Her figure holds firm well into middle age. She treats nervous stress with doses of physical contact. Within minutes after her husband walks out on her she invites her five-year-old son to share her bed, making the idea sound as if it came from him. Flesh rules her to the end. On her deathbed she sees a crocus bulb on her windowsill as a "little golden phallus pressing at the air" (p. 334). Since physicality governs her, the steps in her life are clearly marked. Her overthrow begins when she rejects the marriage proposal of a rich, well-bred friend of many years' standing in favor of casual sex with Wally Collins, a meaty-looking jazz saxophonist with an American accent. She revels in her choice. "To cling to this was essential, to avoid the shadowy ways of introspection" (p. 287), she says of her sexual tie with Wally. Wally unintentionally denies more than he fulfills in her. She ignores her social breeding (which he admires), allowing the flesh to claim her more and more. During their relationship Catherine sleeps till eleven o'clock in the morning, dresses self-consciously, and makes herself up heavily. Her spirit hardly protests. The extent to which her sensuality gnaws at her nearly quiescent morality shows clearly in her last outing with Wally, which, significantly, also marks her last recorded sortie outside the home. At a party in north London's Maida Vale, she meets a young parody of herself named Kay (Kitty-Catherine-Kay), who upsets her and makes her drink too much. "And you're Mrs. Standish" (p. 319), Kay says straightaway, needing no introduction. The dynamism of the encounter shows Catherine the difference between her gaudy, oversexed present self and the youthful promise she once knew. The recognition crushes her: she passes out from drink and dies a week later. The vanity underlying the last words she says within our hearing, a day before her death ("I wonder . . . is my hair tidy?" [p. 333]), shows how little she has learned. White denies her any kind of final vision because she has offended his sense of proper moral relationships. Having condemned Elyot for failing to let himself go sexually, he also blames Catherine for abandoning herself too readily. His basis of judgment goes beyond mere sex: Catherine is punished for consorting with a mongrel.

And is her mongrel punished as well? A parson's granddaughter with grown children should never have fallen for Wally's cartoon sensuality. White associates Wally with neon-lit cabarets, dirty linen, and cheap lodgings in run-down neighborhoods. The associations occur quickly,

White characterizing Wally with a swiftness and a floridness rare in the canon. These fast brushstrokes answer a need more aesthetic than moral. Because the novel is two-thirds finished by the time Wally appears, White needs to pair him off quickly with Catherine, which means that their relationship has to be physical. Likewise, the need to characterize Wally before pairing him off calls for some high-color sketching. As crudely as Wally is protrayed, he has enough Dickensian bounce to pass muster—but then White smudges the impression by patronizing him, dressing him in an ill-fitting mauve suit, putting a toothpick in his mouth, and denying him the ability to speak correctly. White also disapproves of Wally's saxophone music, calling it "a sweet sticky fluid" (p. 258), even though Wally's ability to lose himself in his music ranks him among the living. White doesn't know him or his music well enough to smooth him into his narrative pattern. So concerned is he with reminding the reader that Wally belongs on the fringes of a serious novel that, in presenting him, he disjoints his living-dead dualism.

The crossing of class lines by sex in *Living and Dead* reflects the changes sweeping England during the mid-1930s. This sexual mobility worries White, exposing his fear of both lower-class energy and domineering women. Women initiate all of the affairs centering on the Standishes' Ebury Street home. In no case does the sexual tie last long; in each case the intruder is left reeling. The non-establishment figures who grow in importance as the novel progesses all drop out suddenly. Either White can't dramatize his theoretical fondness for them, or he never talks himself into believing in social democracy. The compassionate, protective Julia Fallon serves the Standishes for twenty-five years. Scornful of subtlety and indirection, she regulates her life by simple truths (White associates her with decent, forthright substances like bread and cheese). Yet, despite her ripe wisdom, she starts little. Connie Tiarks is another person whom White endows with wisdom and then ignores, like Julia. Eden and Elyot meet Connie as small children, when all three are living in Somerset during the 1914-18 war. Connie's lumpy face framed by fine, pale hair contrasts with Eden's sharp features and dark, abundant curls. Connie's yearning to give and receive love also sharpens Eden's bullying greed. When Connie leaves Somerset, Eden, without ever having said a word about answering the letters Connie had offered to write, screams to her, "Goodbye. . . . Send me some postcards as well as the letters" (p. 108). Much of this greed comes from Eden's taking advantage of Connie's wish to please and to belong; Connie tries too hard, taking purpose away from Eden and Elyot. By putting herself at a disadvantage she has alienated those whose love she wants so much to win. Voicing damp pieties as an adult like "It's so, it's so *complete*," upon seeing a famous painting (p. 179) shows her performing for others rather than relaxing and enjoying herself.

Connie's drive to please others came early in life. Sent by her parents to

a Somerset family and then forced to sleep on the couch because Eden
wouldn't share her bed, she learned rejection at the age of four or five.
Much of her time in Somerset she spent alone in dark places because she
wasn't allowed to share the sunshine. In a war game, Eden and Elyot take
her prisoner and stow her in a toolshed. War has aggravated the darkness.
While their seniors discuss the war against Germany, the Standish children
force war games on her. She always loses, just as she lost the battle for
territory and equality centering on Eden's bed. She becomes so frightened,
nervous, and unhappy that she wets the couch in her sleep. The following
exchange shows her accepting persecution as the price of inclusion. When
Eden tells her, "We're going to put you in prison" (p. 100), Connie stays
calm. Eden and Elyot have already made her their victim. Though sent by
her parents to Arcadian Somerset, she can't escape the war or effect her
own armistice. Rather, she paticipates in a conflict which has adopted
cruelty to the defenseless as a basic working principle (after *Living and
Dead*, White began the sensible practice of setting off dialogue with
quotation marks):

> Let's play at war, Eden said.
> It made Connie quail.
> I'll be the English, Elyot said.
> No, said Eden. I'll be the English.
> All right, he said. I'll be the French.
> Wasps were heavy in the trees. . . .
> Who'll be the Germans? Eden asked.
> As if she didn't already know. . . .
> I'll be the Germans, Connie sighed.
> Her hands became green, twisting grass.
> Will you, Connie? Eden said. All right, then, Connie's the
> Germans. Now you must run away and hide. Before the French
> and English attack. [pp. 99-100]

The passage of years changes neither the game nor the players. Connie
sympathizes with the suffering in Spain. Eden makes her moist-eyed compassion look ineffectual by taking positive action; she works in a leftist
book shop and then goes to Spain, while Connie commiserates from a safe
distance. On another level, Connie, like Alys Browne in *Happy Valley*,
serves as a companion to the elderly. Hard, glinting Eden lacks both the
patience and the kindness needed to companion anybody. Her going to
Spain to fly warplanes merely carries forward a wish she had voiced as a
small child. In Somerset she loved war games; whereas the news of the
Armistice gladdened the others, it left her unmoved. She would have
invented her own war if she hadn't had one ready made.
Her opposite number, Connie, symbolizes peace, wholeness, and love.

She writes to the Standish children even after being savaged by them; White reprints some of her letters without, significantly, displaying any responses she might have received. Then she seeks out the family in London, spending at least one Sunday a month with them for several years. War frames the lives of Connie, Eden, and Elyot, as it does their lopsided friendship. All three characters attain consciousness during World War I. All become adults during the Spanish Civil War. Only Connie sheds this legacy of cruelty and death. Whereas Eden remains riveted by war and Elyot, going to the opposite extreme, stays passive and uncommitted, Connie plans to marry. It is a brave choice. She has had to overcome a great deal of negative conditioning in order to accept the love of Harry Allgood. Although at first she resists, watching him wince, her agreeing to marry him lifts her outside the pecking order begun some twenty years before in Somerset. She refuses to transfer to this likeable, pipe-smoking physician the misery heaped on her by the Standishes.

A less sympathetic interloper in Ebury Street is the varnished, coiffed Muriel Raphael. The scurvy handling accorded art dealers in *Riders* and *Vivisector* implies that White dislikes them all, perhaps for trading on the self-lacerating labors of their imaginative superiors. Muriel, who runs an expensive gallery, can do no right. Hers is one of the twisted hearts in the novel. "A Mozart symphony left Muriel clear-eyed, satisfied. It was, she felt, a triumph of accomplished intellect" (p. 292), says White of her calculation and control. Still attacking her bloodless self-sufficiency, this future booster of environmental reform sneers at her for eating vegetables, raw salad, and carrot juice. Is he not sneering at good sense and self-restraint? Does he not both misjudge and mistreat her by splashing her with perfume and making her wear a garish dress with a sequined scarlet nipple? This unfairness violates the consistency of his character sketch; few devotees of health food would sport the gaudy rags in which White dresses Muriel. Perhaps he extends too little imagination to her and too much to her Saxon counterparts. Perhaps, too, he lashes out so intemperately because Elyot can't resist her, and because he, White, can't punish him for slumming sexually the way he punished Catherine; 1941 was a bad time to risk being called an anti-Semite. Besides, being a writer is punishment enough, implies White in a self-dramatizing flourish. Elyot's writing hasn't made women like him. The Jewish Muriel chooses Elyot as a lover for reasons unflattering to him: she doesn't want her neatly arranged life to be skewed by a man; better for Elyot to bore her than for someone more exciting to upset her. Her insult doesn't rouse him to action. Though repelled by her "cold, answering sexuality" (p. 214), he can't dismiss her. Her sexuality is "answering" because it mirrors the dryness and remoteness of his own. Rather than confronting her, he ignores her, hoping, along with White, that she won't press him for explanations.

A character less predatory and thus more amiable than Muriel is Joe

Barnett, the high-principled carpenter Eden falls in love with. Yet, because he has been willed into existence by a stroke of the author's Audenesque faith in the working class rather than by conviction, Joe must suffer like his fellow intruders in Ebury Street. No matter that he does his job well, has a keen social conscience, and follows instincts as noble as those of any other character in the book: "Joe Barnett like to believe. He was born with a faith in faith. . . . He moved in a world of images and facts, propelled by his own conviction that, even if something had gone wrong, man in himself was right enough" (p. 192). No matter either that Eden seeks *him* out, after seeing him at some political meetings, as Mag Bosanquet will later do with Terry Legge, a Sydney labor leader in *Big Toys* (first produced, 1977). Joe is punished more harshly than the most egregious social climber in the canon. Given a prod by White, who doubts the press agentry he lavishes on Joe, Eden fills him with the political idealism that later sends him to his death in Spain.

Like Catherine Standish, Joe quivers intensely but too briefly to be numbered among the living. His lover, Eden, merits exclusion for different reasons. As with Joe, the rhetoric surrounding her clashes with the facts. Eden supports the political left because, in her view, it favors action and commitment over apathy and fence-straddling. Her conduct, however, opposes this selfless vigor. As full of bottled-up nervous energy as Sidney Furlow of *Happy Valley*, Eden doesn't need to learn the importance of action. She is so hyperactive already that she exudes death. Life has no chance with her prowling around. Her father died when she was small; ten years after her abortion, her mother dies; her aggressiveness has made her brother one of the walking dead. Can we be surprised that her lover dies, too? Or that she seems to be following him to the grave? She had brought him to life just long enough so he could die for a cause he didn't understand. Though love affects her differently, it yields the same sad results. It does quiet her stridency; her embrace with Joe gives a soft glow to the "barren marsh . . . and the black line of a canal" (p. 276) where they declare their love. But her will can't stay quiescent for long. As a child, she grew excited ("Eden's eyes were bright. . . . The blood was jerking into her cheeks" [p. 100]) when she caught Connie and took her prisoner in their war game. At the train station where Elyot sees her off twenty years later, the fingertip of one of her black gloves reveals a hole, as if her grabbing both tore the glove and gave it death's color. By contrast, when she is not clutching or pushing, she grows bored; she only commits herself when she can be boss. Her affair with Norman Maynard, for example, fails to move her because its emptiness leaves her nothing to manage. White conveys her indifference technically. A page after entering the action, Maynard propositions her without much ceremony. She accepts his offer with the same deadpan casualness and, after having sex, leaves him immediately, showing more verve in her departure than in the surrender of her virginity. Ten years later, when Elyot remarks inwardly that he doesn't expect to see her again after she leaves for Spain, he can be trusted. She has become a burnt one, scorched by heat she can't control. Whereas Joe died fighting to regain the freshness and the goodness misleadingly conveyed by her name, she goes to her death because she sees that her wilfullness has brought only negation. She has no talent for living, nor do others thrive in her presence. Elyot's feeling no emotion at her departure indicates that, however long she stays away, he won't miss her.

II

It is clear why Elyot Standish gets more of White's attention than any other character in the book. He is a bachelor with a sister; he writes; he is as puzzled by the new egalitarianism sweeping London as White must have been after arriving from Cambridge to live in the city. When his mother says, "His manner was perpetually sideways" (p. 139), she is referring to his inherited tendency to show but a thin edge of himself. The cautious, withdrawn Elyot doesn't face people directly. His self-estimate, "He had no actual life of his own" (p. 12), reflects White's view of the between-wars London intellectual as "that most sterile of beings."[4] He doesn't ripen into wisdom because he doesn't shape up. Typically, the books's first scene shows him being left behind, whereas the more adventurous Eden has already visited France and Switzerland. The leavetaking reinforces a pattern of futility which haunts him. He never tries to dissuade Eden from going to Spain, despite his belief that she will die there. Then a drunken, nondescript figure wearing a mackintosh (the uniform of the drifter in Joyce and Greene) reels into a path of a moving bus. Not only does Elyot fail to save him; he also leaves the scene of the accident before learning whether the victim survived.

Richly revealing of Elyot is his conduct toward Connie Tiarks. At Somerset, where he first meets Connie, he finds himself, at age six, caught in a pecking order between a headstrong female and a timid one. One day, when Eden has a dental appointment, Connie and Elyot are left to themselves. When Connie asks him to play with her, he responds in a way that he wouldn't have dared to had Eden been there: "Let's play at murders," he says, adding, "I'll be your murderer. . . . I'll tie you up in rope and strangle you" (p. 104). Connie's reply—"Can't I just be with you?" (p. 104)—shames him. Her appeal wouldn't have fazed Eden. But the more complex Elyot has a conscience. Still resenting Connie for blocking his drive to cruelty, he suggests climbing a mulberry tree, an activity only slightly less dangerous to her than being strangled. Again she makes him blanch. Though she had never before climbed the tree, she overcomes her fear, a torn knee, and some scratches on her face, neither complaining nor retreating. But she never makes it to the top, which the graceless Elyot has attained without waiting for her. What happens after her fall from the tree tells more about him than about her: "He slithered from the tree" (p. 105), White says of this mini-Satan who believes that Connie fell deliberately to plague him. The response is typical. As was borne out in the scene involving the drunk and the London bus, another person's need paralyzes him. As *will* subsequently be borne out in his behavior with Hildegarde and Muriel, he arouses in females needs that he can't fulfill. At the foot of the mulberry tree he orders Connie to be quiet, rather than comforting her.

The episode brings out his cowardice, dishonesty, and failure to cope. Helpless when faced by the unforeseen, he promises to give her his knife if she gets up and stops crying. When she does recover, she hears straight-away that he never intended to hand over the knife. Then he goes off by himself, leaving her alone, even though she didn't try to use the moral advantage his lie bestowed upon her. He continues to discount her. In Germany he tears her letter to pieces and flushes it down the toilet, as if dismembering and disposing of *her*. Years later, when she offers to marry him in a last, desperate overture, he dismisses her again. The style of his dismissal explains as much about him as did his panic during the mulberry tree incident years before: he tells Connie that she deserves more than he can give her. His words are meanly self-protective, albeit true. Of his own feelings he say nothing. He ignores his heart because he can't deal with it. Treating Connie's love as if it had never been offered allows him to disregard it, as he does his own feelings. Connie's telephoning Harry Allgood within an hour after being rebuffed by Elyot constitutes a recognition of the fate his rebuff has spared her. A life spent with someone incapable of caring is no life at all.

Elyot needs a breakthrough. His work reflects both self-absorption and self-denial. He disparages his literary criticism, terming himself "a raker of dust, a rattler of bones" (p. 176) whose parched preserve is "the literary achievements of the dead" (p. 17). Too dry and self-critical to become an artist in his own right, he turns to criticism, keeping a foothold in the arts to compensate for his father's failure as a painter. Though he is a critic and not a creator, a worker with words rather than with paint, he nonetheless maintains an artistic stance. The novel's closing scenes provoke in him a recognition as powerful as Connie's. He decides to transform artistically the energies displayed by his family and social circle. In a sense, he decides to write *The Living and the Dead*. Perhaps any final interpreta-tion of the novel entails reading it as coming from Elyot's hand, rather than from White's. White invites such an interpretation. The next-to-last chap-ter repeats both Elyot's parting from Eden at Victoria Station and his solitary homecoming from chapter 1. White repeats these earlier events not to launch Elyot into a frenzy of artistic creation, but, more cautiously, to show him pondering their meaning. Like the isolation caused by the departures of Eden and Connie, the sensitivity and purpose activated by his intellectual groping help develop the climate conducive to artistic endeavor.

Thelma Herring believes that Elyot is too cautious and self-immersed to produce art: "Elyot, it is implied, genuinely chooses life. . . . The trouble is that Elyot's choice is stated rather than demonstrated: we don't see him *experiencing* this intense form of living, and nothing in the novel leads us to believe him capable of it."[5] Herring expects more from Elyot than does White, who, knowing him better, never claims for him the honor of becoming an imaginative artist. What *does* he claim for Elyot? He wouldn't have brought the novel full circle merely to convey Elyot's futility, for Elyot has already depicted that futility on his own for twenty chapters. Nor does he leave Elyot alone in the empty house where his mother died. The brief epilogue shows Elyot, who used to cover his ears to shut out street noises, going into the streets. The recurring image of the Chinese box in the closing pages symbolizes the idea of the artist's mind containing the minds of his characters. But that symbol doesn't yet pertain to Elyot. He is still drifting. Although other Londoners are taking buses to their destinations, he has no place to go; nobody awaits him. The novel ends with a recognition, rather than a resolve. More contemplative than dramatic or demonstrative, its next-to-last paragraph lifts him from the limits of "time . . . place . . . and the tyranny of a personal routine" (p. 358). He is content to drift, now that his imagination has been awakened. Amid a litter of waste, his creativity is born. Death has illuminated his moral darkness by giving insight into his dead mother, the death of his friendship with Connie, and the awaited death of his sister. If readers like Herring remain unimpressed by the depths to which his soul has moved, let them note that Joyce's Stephen Dedalus, too, stands far from *his* goal of becoming a creative writer at the end of *A Portrait of the Artist*. To censure White for the book's tentative ending is to ignore both Elyot's defensiveness and the literary tradition to which Elyot belongs. Years may lapse before his touch, like that of Michelangelo's God on the inner dome of Rome's Sistine Chapel, creates life. In the meantime, previously dark corners of his psyche glow. No one can predict the size of the imaginative fire this spark will ignite. No one, therefore, can gauge the worth of his illumination. What matters is that both Elyot and White are content with the glow his illumination emits, neither author nor character chafing to convert it into artistic capital.

III

Elyot's disconnectedness from those around him reflects the brokenness of the action. *The Living and the Dead* is full of unspoken feelings, inchoate dialogues, and inconclusive scenes. Communication scarcely exists; the more important the issue, the less the characters have to say about it. Joe neglects to tell Eden goodbye before leaving for Spain; ironically, she learns of his departure to this warm Latin country from her cold, withdrawn brother while the two of them are listening to music of the Norwegian composer Grieg. White continues to drain Joe's Spanish adventure of dramatic color. Joe's death is reported by a fellow soldier on a postcard. Julia, who learns of the death from Joe's mother, relays it to Eden with wooden terseness: "We had a postcard telling us. Just that he was killed" (p. 350). Seconds later, she leaves Eden's bedroom to go and make coffee.

Symbolizing the lack of communication in the novel is the opacity of the glass box Connie buys for Elyot in chapter 12. On her way to deliver the box, she stops at a fruiterer's, where the juicy roundness of the oranges distracts her, evoking her sexual frustration. She leaves without the box, but it is soon found where she had forgotten it by Wally Collins, who meets Catherine Standish when he delivers it to Ebury Street. The milky planes of the box shut out light, hiding the contents. But nothing lies inside; this cold, flat object is empty. No Pandora's box that lets trouble escape as soon as it is opened, Connie's dubious gift only hastens or aggravates trouble that already exists. Though it introduces Wally to Catherine, it doesn't send Catherine to the nightclub where Wally is performing or prompt her to ask him to lunch. Its cloudiness conveys Elyot's already blurred vision. Believing that it came from Muriel, Elyot overrates her generosity and wastes himself on her, neglecting Connie, its true donor. His mistaken view of it shows him to be boxed in by insensitivity. But since he always underrated Connie, the misunderstanding about the box creates no big change or climax. "It was the clearness that revolted, that you didn't want to see" (p. 302), he observes one night, coming out of a nightmare. Connie's box didn't trouble his sleep, nor does it generate much drama after the day of its purchase. The sexual relationships of the Standishes fail to reinforce or mesh with each other, like the ones in *Happy Valley*, even though they occur simultaneously. The function of the glass box is as opaque as its surface. To believe in its effectiveness as a symbol entails believing that confusion is best depicted by confused writing.

This maladroitness smears most of the book's poetic effects. White's images often sing and leap when brief but sag and look forced when extended. The images in the following sentence fight each other, the tensions they exert eventually capsizing the sentence, even though they are shrewdly arranged in different parts of speech. Adjectives like gummy and orchidaceous don't belong in the same sentence with a noun like thunder or verbs like pressed, rustled, and struck. The variety that recommends the sentence finally sinks it. It is stuffed with more material of different shapes, colors, sizes, and textures than it can house: "And the music pressed, pressed, the sad and gummy tendrils of the saxophones, a rattle of sultry thunder in the drums, great clusters of orchidaceous light stirred in the tonal undergrowth that rustled round the legs, that struck an answering note from sequin or from tulle, or the taut black cloth covering the expectant calves" (p. 256). On the other hand, a more economical effect like "the smell of leather and the flash of buckles" (p. 21) quickly captures the spirit of a harness shop. A still happier stroke, because unexpected, owing to White's usual avoidance of cosmopolitan glitter, comes in a nightclub in chapter 14. The cabaret song sung by the entertainer Ruby May swaggers with a banal cynicism that recalls similar turns in Auden and Isherwood's *Ascent of F6* and Greene's *Brighton Rock*. The theme voiced at the song's outset, "No more love, / I've lost the art of crying" (p. 262), refers to Elyot and Muriel. Ironically, this couple, who quail at the pangs caused by sexual love, eat quail while hearing the cabaret tune of desolation.

Irony also helps narrative structure. Part One of *Living and Dead* ends with Eden's abortion. Its last sentence, "These [Elyot's slippers] were easy to the feet" (p. 172), prefigures a sinking of both fortune and spirit. The mood of Part Two is sullen. Much of the action takes place on a series of Sunday afternoons, that stuffiest of times in genteel, between-wars London. Rather than conversing, the characters gaze out windows, as if the answers to their problems will come walking down the street. From this idleness comes the impression that their vigor is muffled inside the damp flannel atmosphere of Ebury Street; they can't solve their own problems. The character who suffers most, losing her reputation and self-respect along with her life, is Catherine, who rebels most stormily against Ebury Street's stifling gentility. A member of the older generation dominates the book's second half. In most novels of family life, like Bennett's *Old Wives' Tale* and Lawrence's *Sons and Lovers*, the children shoulder their parents aside as the action unfolds. Catherine Standish, Stan Parker, and Elizabeth Hunter show that White's people face their greatest challenges in their maturity. White accepts the technical problems coming from this view of age. The passage of time that most writers of chronicle fiction achieve by moving from the older to the younger generation, often killing off the elders in the process, happens differently in *Living and Dead*. The outbreak of the Spanish Civil War and the appearance of Wally Collins give the action a realistic temporal flow. White also conveys the psychological effects of time by shifting both pace and point of view. Chapter 2 ends with a quarrel between Catherine and Willy. Chapter 3 focuses on the same scene, repeating some of the dialogue verbatim. But the point of view has switched to Elyot, who was disturbed by the quarrel while trying to sleep in the next room. White shifts perspectives to show how children protect themselves from the carelessness and cruelty of adults. He also tallies the cost of that protection, for the children's defenses are sometimes misjudged: Elyot learns to insulate himself all too well; the foolhardy Eden, who needs protection from the dangers she courts, has abandoned caution; Connie Tiarks suffers keenly, but at the hands of her contemporaries rather than at those of adults. Mood varies, along with the characters' problems. A good example of effective cinematic cutting comes between chapters 9 and 10. Whereas chapter 9 dealt largely with blue-collar people and ended in a carpenter's workshop, chapter 10 cuts to a chic bohemian dinner party. The bright chatter overheard at the party contrasts, in turn, with the uncouthness of Wally's friends at the Maida Vale party where Catherine later meets grief.

Balance occurs again with the two deaths at the end. Whereas Catherine is a mature, well-to-do woman who dies at home, the much younger Joe Barnett, who must work to support himself, stands with the working class and dies in distant Spain. These deaths crown the book's investigation of innocence and experience. Already pondered have been Eden; Eaton (sometimes pronounced Eden?) Place, which adjoins Ebury Street; a figurative fall in the name of Julia Fallon; a real one in Connie's mulberry tree mishap; Elyot's snakelike slithering down the tree when he discovers the mishap; and a girl named Eve whom Elyot befriends as a boy of ten. This elaborate symbolic machinery functions in a near void. As often happens in this novel about disjointed lives, White disjoints narrative elements rather than seeing them through. The effect created by the disjunctures is usually unsettling. Like the deaths of the Moriartys in *Happy Valley*, those of Catherine and Joe redeem nothing, their careful balance cancelling them out. Except for Connie and Elyot, who are only seen peeping from their cocoons, the others stay inside their boxes and under their eiderdowns, cut off from fresh air and the busy hum of the streets. Patricia Morley, puzzled by the title of *The Living and the Dead*, complains, "The novel deals with two groups of people, the spiritually living and the living dead, but it leaves the two groups unrelated to each other."[6] Disregarding the validity of the mind-body split she presumes, we can grant Morley's confusion. The book's title is a misnomer. Passion kills. The living, who assert their vitality physically rather than spiritually, thrive only briefly, leaving Ebury Street more of a burial ground than a fashionable address.

Lack of control accounts for other excesses and miscalculations. For instance, White allows manner to overtake matter. In chapter 8 Catherine invites Elyot to join her in soup. He notes of her invitation, "The voice glanced. It was not the glance of diffidence. It definitely implied a disparagement of soup" (p. 173). The soup doesn't deserve this flourish. Distractions become obsessions, and large issues drown in minutiae when a minor character like Gerald Blenkinsop gets more exposition than his small role in the book warrants. White misleads the reader by lingering too long with descriptions of minor elements. Besides choking narrative flow, these descriptions detract from character development, making the people in *Living and Dead* hard to sympathize and indentify with. Nor do the people attain enough autonomy to move the action. Had White blocked them out more naturalistically and thought less about his Jamesian stance, he might have won the reader's confidence. But he lacked the patience to get the reader on his side, thereby forfeiting a receptive audience for his tonal effects. Self-consciousness spoils *The Living and the Dead*. Its characters are flat, its dialogue wooden, its style overripe and derivative. White's imposing a literary climax on this all-too-literary work has created an unintended irony. His calling *Living and Dead* in 1969 "the book I like least"[7] might well stem from his having ended it in a way that accentuates its artificiality.

Marjorie Bernard's complaint about the book's inability to carry into the everyday world refers again to manner: "It's an inside-out book. Every object . . . becomes a symbol of an inner life. The characters look out of windows and see their own desolation. The weather is never good."[8] White's attitude both conveys and controls the book's resolution, as Bernard implies. Elyot holds the stage by himself at the end because his counterparts, lacking literary ambitions, have all departed. "It is an un-happy book; all the characters are lost or frustrated or decadent so that it is difficult to know who are the living and who are the dead,"[9] she adds, feeling as let down by the novel's title as Morley did. White has defined life so cerebrally that his people either explode or refine themselves out of it. A scowling puritanism rules *Living and Dead*. Sexual, social, and military activity fends off the void only temporarily. And aesthetic activity? Will it, too, run to waste? White ends the novel before opening himself to the charge of either nihilism or elitism. Continuing the action would only have worsened an already bad book. His well-judged restraint fails to make up for other faults which, cumulatively, label *The Living and the Dead* a misfire.

4. Pieces of Self

THE STILL, SLACK neutrality of *The Living and the Dead* leaves us unprepared for the sensual gusto, verbal invention, and humor of *The Aunt's Story* (1948), a work that engages our hearts and minds from start to finish. Rightly judged as White's first serious look at the linkages joining self to universe, the work also moves gracefully, avoiding the solemnity and ponderousness that can make his later, longer works such heavy going. The art of *Aunt's Story* relies on a severe economy of means. White's sketch of a successful meatpacker in a passenger train speeding through America's corn belt reveals a prototypical rags-to-riches businessman who enjoys explaining how he overcame humble beginnings, how he remembers his mother, how deftly he has furnished his home, and how his love of foreign travel has lifted him above his philistine counterparts. What is more, White manages this cameo sketch in a single page. He also unifies it several pages later with a detail so small that it could easily go unnoticed: "The train rocked the track. The man in the laundered shirt stirred. He was having trouble with his groin" (p. 254). Even the Protestant work ethic has pitfalls: a career of striving and achieving has given this nameless practitioner of New World energy a hernia that, presumably, he hasn't the time to notice, let alone to have repaired.

But if White saw America crawling with Babbitts, he'd not have lived there as a young man or thought of becoming an American citizen.[1] Other Americans extend friendship and kindness to Theodora Goodman, the book's main figure, without trying to impress her. One tells her where to find lodgings when she gets off the train that bears the herniated meatpacker; her son would have driven Theodora to the guest house had she not walked away from his truck. Next a family of decent, rugged homesteaders takes her in, feeds her, and offers her a bed for the night. When she disappears again, they look for her, bring her food, and, rightly perceiving her painful disorientation, arrange for her to be taken to a mental home.

The reader learns of Theodora's need for help before the Johnsons, her would-be host and hostess, do. White confirms our knowledge of her madness in a scene richly expressive of the novel's art. Theodora intuits the continuity swathing the Johnsons and their possessions while rocking in their rocking chair. Again White's metaphysics generate mirth. Typifying the book's self-correcting moral vision is the image of Theodora sitting in a rocking chair and appreciating how everything in the Johnson house rocks in unison while she herself is off her rocker. Such a union of imagery and moral balance can only strengthen White's comedy.

As the union implies, several things can happen at once in the robust world of *Aunt's Story*. White organizes space, rather than leaving it empty or merely using it as a static receptacle for dramatic action. Objects impart rhythm and texture. In her interview with Miss Spofforth, director of the girls' finishing school she attends, Theodora stands "caught in the wide spaces between the bookcase and the fire" (p. 55). In the following description of a rabbit hunt, White avoids saying that Theodora's shot hit its mark. Instead, he shows the drama unfolding as it would in real life, describing its effect upon Theodora and Frank Parrott and, through it, restructuring the time-space-motion continuum: "Frank shot. He missed. There was no subtraction from the scrambling of the rabbit scuts. Theodora took aim. Then they watched the tumbling uncontrol of fur. For a moment time had been put off its course. The fur subsided on the earth. The silence trembled, ticked, ran. It had begun again." (p. 62). Elsewhere, as well, White avoids merely re-creating objects to help the reader picture them. His sudden transitions, one-line paragraphs, and explosive imagery give the book a physical urgency that encroaches upon fantasy. In Part Two, in fact, it becomes fantasy, as the difference between illusion and reality blurs. His internalizing of external experience here carries the work beyond normal fictional limits. Not content with merely reporting an event, he instead tries to include in his description all the states of being affecting it: weather, time of day, and the feelings of the people involved.

Two of the book's outstanding stylistic effects disclose the brilliance of his verbal performance. One, extended and elaborate, describes a struggle between two people for a nautilus shell; it ends with the shell slipping out of anxious fingers and falling to the floor. White's repetition of the stressed monosyllable "hands" conveys the futility of the empty-handed strugglers as they watch the nautilus shatter at their feet. Hands and only hands are what remain of the fantasies and physical energies causing the struggle: "And the nautilus became a desperate thing of hands. Theodora heard the crack of bones. Hands were knotting the air. Then, hands were hands" (p. 208). The comma after the first word in this last sentence, though grammatically unnecessary, creates a pause in which the strugglers face, with diminishing disbelief, the smashing of their hopes.

The second stylistic effect, a more ambitious triumph of perception and integration, opens Part Three. Having left Europe (the setting for Part Two), Theodora is sitting next to the herniated meatpacker as their train heads west. White sees to it that the shift in setting to America's heartland doesn't escape us: "All through the middle of America there was a trumpeting of corn. Its full, yellow, tremendous notes pressed close to the swelling sky. There were whole acres of time in which the yellow corn blared as if for a judgment. It had taken up and swallowed all other themes, whether belting iron, or subtler, insinuating steel, or the frail human reed. Inside the movement of corn the train complained. The train complained of the frustration of distance, that resists, that resists. Distance trumpeted with corn" (p. 249). Rarely in modern fiction has a new chapter or section of a novel opened so stunningly. Phrasing like "whole acres of time" and "distance trumpeted with corn" violate logic and sequence in order to intensify the pressure conveyed by adjectives such as "swelling" and "belting." The shrewd deployment of verbs adds to this concentration, White bombarding and engulfing our senses with "pressed," "blared," and "swelled." Instead of arguing or concluding, the highly figured language portrays the fact of profusion. White wants us both to hear and to feel the corn growing, and he succeeds. "Distance trumpeted with corn," the simple declarative sentence ending the paragraph, brings the pattern of sounds full circle. Like the effects preceding it, the pealing clarity of this sentence sounds the difference between the vibrancy of *Aunt's Story* and the stodge of *Living and Dead*.

Such effects create a rhythm, the force of which Theodora feels but never understands. Although life hangs together, it never reveals its connecting principle. Miss Spofforth, the headmistress, knowing that Theodora is special, foresees for her "moments of passing affection, through which the opaque world will become transparent" (p. 56). Theodora tries to solidify and extend these luminous moments, but because reality is perceived through undulating veils of different thickness, she fails.

The dangers of defining life too closely are conveyed poetically. A Sydney baker named Jack Frost kills his sleeping wife and three daughters in order to arrest the joys of family life; seeing his happy family preparing Sunday tea elated him so much that he wanted to preserve the moment. Though the episode covers only a page, it captures the book's meaning: the attempt to fix impermanence or to wed the personal to the universal brings death. The quest for certainty in a doubt-ridden world must be resisted. If White conceived of Theodora as a Romantic heroine,[2] he punishes her for violating the neoclassical virtues of moderation and balance. His morality resembles that of Augustan satire, except for its nonsocial impulse. Theodora's is one of the hearts that yearn to pierce the infinite, and her pride must be put down, even though it expresses itself in humble, self-effacing acts. We live amid appearances, White insists; though ultimate reality keeps tempting us, it also stays out of reach. No supervening value can be grasped. The two expatriate pretenders to social eminence, the American Madame Rapallo and the Russian General Sokolnikov, have been seen clutching at the nautilus shell whose pearly beauty and acoustical richness suggest the prize of Europe. But because the graces of civilization can't be forced, the nautilus breaks. Theodora learns a similar lesson in America. Running her fingers over the face of a marble clock, she encounters flatness, not the indwelling reality of time or even time's passage. This innocent muscular reflex invokes another comparison. Her groping fingers are playing the same deathlike tune performed in a major key by her fellow Sydneysider, Jack Frost. Nor does she shut her ears to the echoes put out by the tune, imagining herself as capable as the baker Jack Frost was of murdering from love. Her tour of France, where Jack Frost had served with the military, helps sharpen their resemblance.

Others beside Theodora share Frost's propensity for loving murder; proof of this comes from their walking around Sydney after having eaten his cakes. Though they may refer defensively to being "left high and dry" by the "chord of mass hysteria" (p. 91) sounded by Frost's multiple murder, their clichés can't wipe the torment from their hearts. Their inability to suppress their kinship with the baker gives his townsfolk nightmares, along with indigestion. None need feel singled out for chastisement. As is shown in Theodora's failure to penetrate the workings of time and in the expatriate pretenders' defiance of time's changes, we all seek permanence; stability brings comfort, shielding us from accident. But because it also blinds us to life's fluidity, it misleads. Now the novel's symbol for art, which, like ritual, tries to protect the contingent, is the mirror; a character calls the English poet Wetherby "the original interpreter of mirrors" (p. 217). By repeating and multiplying an image, mirrors extend, enchance, and lend depth. But by trying to ward of accident, art lies. Like the images born of facing mirrors, it springs from our rage for order and stability, not from the material world. Mirrors create nothing new. Hard, brittle surfaces, they foster self-entrapment while overlooking sensible, three-dimensional reality.

Aunt's Story is itself an artifact or pseudo-statement. How does *it* avoid falsifying, distorting, and misleading? Included in any answer must be the freshness and inclusiveness of White's prose. To refer to a "dark green shiny silence" (p. 39) is to impart color, texture, and mental properties to the intangible without encouraging false hopes. Rather than denying change or accident, the phrase uncovers hidden possibilities coexisting in the finite. Through it all, White refuses to strike poses or take authorial liberties. He doesn't pretend to know what is on his characters' minds all the time, nor does he schematize the varied action of the book.

The very title, *The Aunt's Story*, has a modesty of purpose that implies respect for Theodora. White would rather err in the direction of contingency than toward determinism; thus he shifts setting, time, and voice in each of the novel's three sections, sustaining only the moral ambiguity around his main character. On the other hand, *The Aunt's Story* has structure; the numerous repetitions, the letters written to and from characters who have left the action, and a central figure who remains always in view shape the action without straitjacketing it. Finally, there is the controlling medium of pace. Cecil Hadgraft has shown how the book's rising tempo both focuses and bolsters the action as it moves forward: "This astonishing novel, White's most perfect if not his greatest, is tripartite, and the sections grow shorter and more freighted, as though pressing in an urgency to their predestined conclusion."[3]

I

This urgency makes for ambiguity because Theodora occupies such an ambiguous, anomalous slot—that of an aunt. White's calling aunthood an institution (p. 4) connects with his presentation of it as an official designation, rather than as a solid reality with reliable guidelines and expectations. Because the children she loves belong to other people, Theodora's being an aunt confers no intimacies. It isn't surprising that she calls herself both a companion and a governess. Her niece Lou is the only one of her sister's three children with whom she communicates, and their communication occurs mainly in letters. This same uneasy mixture of proximity and remoteness touches her relationships with the surrogate nieces and nephews she adopts in her travels; she enjoys little first-hand contact with the children she loves. Deprivation carries into her relationship with Lou's parents, who see her as both an insider and an outsider, a burden and an attraction. Though she's called upon by Frank and Fanny when they need help, she is rarely invited as a guest; she is never seen being entertained in her sister's home. The Parrotts don't know how to act toward her without a family emergency like death to structure their responses. They see no purpose in knowing her for herself. She is a woman in a male-dominated world; she belongs to no profession and has no special skill; a spinster, she walks alone in a society of couples. Her steps lead to darkness and isolation. She lacks a job, a lover, and, now that her mother is dead, someone who needs her and who will thus distract her from the terrors of selfhood. Her telling Holstius, a mentor whom she imagines into existence near the end, that she may have seen him in a train station or a hotel, gathering places for the itinerant, points up her homelessness. This leggy, bony forty-five-year-old has no intimates. Though she accepts freedom with all its dangers, her bravery is forced upon her by events beyond her control.

Her moral pilgrimage doesn't start when she leaves Australia. Rather than enabling her to drop out of workaday society, where she never had a place to begin with, Julia Goodman's death lets her probe more deeply the fire-and-ice region of her inner self. If this plunge is dangerous, it also offers rewards not available in social relationships. Most of White's characters vibrate most keenly when alone; as Veronica Brady reminds us, "For White, solitude, not society, is the true human milieu, and passivity, not action, the proper mode of being."[4] *The Aunt's Story* shows what happens when a plain, middle-aged spinster confronts freedom for the first time. Early on, Theodora wins us to her side by twice outfacing her conventional, domineering sister—when her closing their mother's coffin robs Fanny of the chance to mouth middle-class pieties about last glimpses and when Theodora, who had cared for their mother since Fanny's marriage, claims all of Julia Goodman's small estate for herself.

Her ensuing pilgrimage looks modest. Theodora wants to be a part of reality, not to control it. She dresses quietly and sits in shadowy corners because, neither arrogant nor shy, neither ideologue nor artist, she has no vision to sell. She envies no one and, having renounced the trophies of her pragmatic consumer society, manages well without the approval of others. Rather than imposing herself, she seeks strength in tables, chairs, and rocks. Her ability to exist on a level with simple objects deflates grandiosity with the same dispatch shown in her rejection of middle-class consumerism. Asked if she believes in God and the saints, she voices her faith in a table and a pail of milk. She constantly feels herself in the presence of living, countersupporting things. But people resist her, offended by her indifference to the prizes they seek. Because they can't understand her, they can't control her. What is more, they feel embarrassed, even intimidated by her because she has the courage and self-possession to live according to her own lights. This serenity can make them envy, fear, and sometimes hate her; her convention-bound mother would like to destroy her. Outside the home, the malice directed against her works more slowly and subtly. Not knowing what to say to her, the guests at the Parrotts' ball feel uneasy in her presence. Because her looks clash with accepted norms of femininity, the young men at the ball avoid asking her to dance. Frank Parrott, who does dance with her, probably because he is drunk, perpetrates a blacker insult, to himself as much as to Theodora. After being swept into a euphoria by the dance, Frank leaves her, denying the lyrical communion he has shared with her, and within days asks Fanny to marry him.

Frank turns so quickly from Theodora because he feels embarrassed, largely because of her appearance. He doesn't want others to connect him with her. Had he the patience and the wit to look beneath the surface, he might not have rejected her and, along with her, the poetry in himself. It must be said on his behalf that Theodora's appearance does indeed pose a challenge his middle-class ethos hasn't taught him to cope with. Called "some bloke in skirts" (p. 60) and "the long dark slommacky thing in the striped dress" (p. 67), she looks like nobody's dream girl. Her oft-mentioned mustache, together with her age and her bony angularity, turn into a badge of exclusion and deprivation. The same negation attaches to her skill with a rifle. A sign of her acuity, her sharpshooting discourages Frank Parrott and the rich lawyer who wants to marry her, Huntly Clarkson, because it also goes against accepted social norms; debutantes don't usually go to the rifle range. She refuses to let these rejections daunt her. For her first forty-five years, others have discouraged Theodora from growing in her own way. But she is an "Adam woman" as John Fowles defines it several times in *The Aristos* (1964), fusing female gentleness and male reason. The suddenness with which she can move within this range of human potential shows in the symbolism connected with her. Already mentioned has been the phallic rifle, whose destructiveness not even she can flee, as is proved by the reactions of Frank, Huntly, and herself after the shooting of her alter ego, the red-eyed hawk. A less explosive yet similar image that comes to symbolize her is the hawthorn tree blossoming outside her room at Miss Spofforth's academy. The hawthorn flowers quickly, resembling the swift brightness of Theodora's vision. That this brightness can blind, and even burn, White reminds us through dramatic event. The major epiphany of Theodora's life comes on her twelfth birthday, when a spear of lightning splits the ground some three hundred yards from where she is standing and slams her to the earth. As Hurtle Duffield and Elizabeth Hunter will learn, God's "stroking," no gentle caress, carries a heavy charge of terror. Because of our awful separation from God, any divine emanation, bridging great distances, must wring and wrack.

Emanations can come in pairs, with God aiming his lightning bolts at least as accurately as Theodora does her bullets. Proving that divine lightning can strike twice in the same place, the Man who was Given his Dinner walks onto the Goodman property within hours of Theodora's escape from death. These apparently unrelated events form twin halves of the same event—Theodora's discovery of her uniqueness. The hungry nondescript has come because, having once panned for gold with George Goodman, he believes he is justified in asking his ex-mate for food. His sense of justice meets opposition, and he nearly leaves Meroë hungry. Though he does get his meal, he is forbidden by Julia Goodman to eat it in the family dining room. Theodora's later leave-taking from the man on a bridge inaugurates her passage into maturity. She knows she will never see him again. But she also knows that, because he has won a place in her heart, she needn't spend any more time with him. Spiritual kinship does not rest on physical proximity, as Laura Trevelyan and Voss will discover. Theodora's survival of the lightning blast and the stranger's rejection at the hands of his ex-mate both sharpen her awareness of freedom. An untamed flair for adventure in the stranger makes her want to travel with him, even though she knows she can't. She isn't saddened. Although she must wait more than thirty years, till her mother dies, before she can indulge her wanderlust, her identity as a wayfarer comes into being on her twelfth birthday. Other byproducts of her maturity surface quickly: she reaps the benefits of the civilized art of compromise, for instance. By suggesting that the prospector eat in the enclosed veranda after her mother denies him access to the dining room, she not only ensures him a meal in a sheltered place where she can keep him company; she also avoids offending the carping, superior Julia.

White continues to vary both the steps and the components of Theodora's development. In contrast to the impact made by the single visit of the Man who was Given his Dinner, the influence of music on Theodora comes piecemeal. It is first spelled out as part of a running contrast between Theodora and her sugary, predictable sister, Fanny. The chief difference between the Goodman girls inheres in Theodora's having both the honesty and the self-detachment to perceive moral ambiguity: "Fanny understood most things. The emotions were either black or white. For Theodora, who was less certain, the white of love was sometimes smudged by hate" (p. 4). Fanny, trading on her good looks, hews to society's formula for success and happiness, marrying a local property owner and rearing a family with him in a well-to-do suburb. A similar contrast held good in the girls' childhood, again favoring Fanny at first glance. Fanny's skill at the piano makes her an ideal display piece for her mother. Although Theodora can't match the technical virtuosity of this pink cloud of loveliness, she allows music to move her much more deeply. As Miss Spofforth, her headmistress, predicts, she is "torn by all the agonies of music" (p. 56). But she is torn to be remade and more finely tuned.

The dance with Frank Parrott discloses hidden dimensions in both partners: "They were pressed into a dependency on each other that was important" (p. 68). Theodora undergoes a similar ecstasy when she hears Moraïtis play his cello. Because she is older by then, her communion with Moraïtis is more spiritual than physical, and it makes a subtler, more memorable impression. Says White of the audience assembled to hear the cellist play, "At the concert, as at all concerts, everyone was rounded and well fed" (p. 103). While others view the concert as a social event, Theodora has come to hear the music, and she expects to be stirred. Despite her discreet appearance, the strong, sensuous music strikes depths in her beyond joy and grief; she is transported. But her ecstasy, like any other, passes quickly, and she returns to the drab prose of everyday with the same wooden flatness she experienced after dancing with Frank. In neither encounter does the return to prosaic reality quiet the echoes caused by her transport. She leaves the Parrotts' drawing room alone to recover her wits. Later she leaves the concert hall without applauding because she has attained sufficiency; her spirit already aquiver, she has no room for further stimulation.

Much of Moraïtis's power comes from his being Greek. White always describes Greece as gray and primitive, windswept and rugged, a land of essences whose elemental bleakness stands light years from the gentility of a suburban society like Australia. The last paragraph of "The Woman Who Wasn't Allowed to Keep Cats" (*Australian Letters*, 1962) contains an image that expresses the primitivism of the Greek temper: "The columns of the Parthenon glittered with openly revealed veins." Living among such images of anguish has taught generations of Greeks to accept pain and privation. Moraïtis has also pared his life down to basics rather than seeking comfort. Just as a Greek shipping mogul in *The Vivisector* asks for bread and water at a lavish dinner party, so does Moraïtis reflect a peasant heritage of earth, sky, water, and rock in *his* choices. He can't practice his cello in a furnished room. Music, for him, embodies the same brutal simplicity that has fed and then honed the classical temper for generations. To make it, he needs an empty room. He explains his passion for bareness to Theodora in their only two conversations. No further words are needed. Theodora takes his meaning so well that she needn't attend any of his scheduled concerts; she only hears him play because he agrees to perform one more time. He has also read *her* accurately, calling her his compatriot in the land of bare bones. This tribute makes her exchange with him strike as deeply as the one with the Man who was Given his Dinner. Each man has touched her heart; each has strengthened her for her coming ordeal and trauma.

II

Part Two of *The Aunt's Story* tries to capture the subterranean flow of Theodora's mind. The unit also features the same contemporary materials that fascinated the surrealists of the late 1930s: economic stagnation, dictatorship, civil violence, and the coming war. The people at the Hôtel du Midi, in the south of France where the action takes place, span some fifty years in age and include a Cockney woman, a man from the English midlands, a set of Jewish twins, and others from France, Germany, the United States, Russia, Greece, Italy, and (with Theodora) Australia. This array of backgrounds conveys the Western temper at large. Appropriately, the guests grumble about the leading issues of the day, Hitler and communism. Their words often sound as if they have been filtered through a maze of echoes. Technique accounts for much of the effectiveness of White's cultural collage. Shot through with obsession, the contrivancess of Part Two have hallucinogenic force. The surface of "Jardin Exotique" is sharp and clear, but under it lie layers of fantasy and mystery that provoke large questions. What does the action mean? Is it taking place or being dreamed? Like much of Salvador Dali, the White of "Jardin Exotique" uses realistic techniques to create surreal effects. His practice of grounding the outlandish in the believable depicts, with disarming force, the fundamental wrongness of things in 1930s Europe.

European decadence makes itself felt in many ways. Walls yawn, arms ask for pity, a drinking glass glitters, trembles, and melts in the same sentence. Characters will tap in on each others' thoughts. Their compulsive babble can take the form of riddle, paradox, or *non sequitur*: "General, you are on fire," calls out a character. "Come, and we shall put you out with crushed strawberries" (p. 220). The foibles and addictions displayed in the Hôtel du Midi mirror the madness gripping Europe. Only a rotten-ripe mentality sacrifices all to style. The lodgers at the hotel have moved too far from the mainstream of life. Their verbal polish can no longer hide their desperation. They can complete each others' thoughts because their decadence has made them interchangeable. This hopelessness permeates the garden adjoining the hotel. Fittingly, much of the last chapter of Part Two takes place in the garden, which provides the section's title and from which many of the guests watch the hotel burn. "The garden was completely static, rigid, the equation of a garden" (p. 134), says White, ascribing some of its deadness to its "sceptical, dry, chemical air" (p. 135). The plant dominating the dessicated garden is the cactus, thorniest of flora; other blossoms die quickly, owing to swarms of attacking flies. The formalized artificiality of the fly-haunted garden scorns life. The fruits have all been plucked and gathered. The garden is empty now, a ransacked, dusty place no more deserving of its fame as a tourist attraction than is Madame Rapallo's nautilus of the energies of its claimants.

The hotel's most long-standing guests, both of whom enjoy the garden and visit it often, are an American and a Russian. General Alyosha Sokolnikov and Madame Elsie Rapallo have converged on Europe from opposite directions, each of them enthralled by Europe's wealth, beauty, and high level of civilization. Each, too, craves acceptance within this time-honored splendor. Though as artificial as their favorite haunt and as hollow and empty as the nautilus, the prizes they seek nonetheless draw great waves of energy from the two expatriates. Predictably, most of this wasted energy goes unnoticed by the other guests, each pretender working furiously to distract nonexistent attention from his own thin credentials. The efforts of these two natural enemies constitute fine satire, much of the fun inhering in the way the figures face the world. The General's tragic sense of life is trapped inside a cocoon of rhetoric. Garrulous and self-dramatizing, Sokolnikov conceives of life as a nineteenth-century Russian novel, his nonstop talk incorporating the long sentences, anecdotal melancholy, and pseudo-philosophy of tsarist fiction. Tallying with his inflated talk is his balloonlike appearance. This bellowing gasbag is as empty as the trophies he craves. His military rank never rose above that of major. Like any other praiser of his own past, he needs an audience; his self-serving talk alienates people, however, nearly everyone finding him offensive. So poorly equipped is he to live in the present that anything on which he sets his great rubbery hand, like the nautilus, will smash.

Clinging more stubbornly to a faded past is his foil, Madame Rapallo. Her fraudulence and her mindless worship of Europe represent a frayed edge of James's international theme. With her lace-and-bone fan and her alleged descent from old Dutch settlers in New York, she reeks *haute monde* imperiousness. But this self-declared New World aristocrat speaks ungrammatically. A little prodding reveals that she wears a wig and false teeth, and that she possesses neither a husband nor a daughter married to an Italian prince. The row caused by her nautilus is absurd, because the beauty that she and Sokolnikov see in the shell cannot be captured. Yet her ability to live her dreams generates pathos, unlike Sokolnikov's pneumatic clowning. So fierce is this barren woman's need for a daughter that she sends herself letters allegedly written by the Principessa and, more touchingly, uses a pet monkey as a substitute child. Her refusal to leave the blazing hotel discloses a failure to adapt to social change; indeed, she has been out of step with reality for years. But it also shows her following any number of Jamesian heroines brave enough to see their commitments through, regardless of the consequences. Madame Rapallo burns for her beliefs.

Theodora is the person who interacts most vitally with both Elsie Rapallo and Alyosha Sokolnikov. Coming from a non-European country without much history, she, too, covets the shell and then watches its destruction. Though the two impostors confess to her, she remains patient with them, entering their fantasies without bringing judgment. Her ability to imagine herself into their lives constitutes a creative act: "I am Ludmilla Sokolnikov, and I keep house for my brother in St. Petersburg," she says, reciting her impromptu litany to perfection. "We have a house which is almost empty, because we have sold most of what is in it. Sometimes we go on short visits to richer relatives who have estates in the country" (p. 201), she adds, adopting both the vocabulary and syntax of Russia's pre-Bolshevik squirearchy. Her impersonation expands and enriches her psyche. Rather than posing between mirrors, she has renounced herself, her intellect, and her hold on things. This ego attrition goes beyond acting, giving her the insight and control needed to participate imaginatively in other people's lives. The withholding of judgment has helped her help others. Only she can make Sokolnikov happy, not merely by playing the roles of both his sister and his lover but also by hopping intuitively from one role to another. She has intuited the bogus General's psyche so well that she can reconstruct his fantasies more quickly than he can. Other benefits follow. Besides invoking an image of tsarist St. Petersburg, which he values as his spiritual home, she even addresses different incarnations of herself imposed by him.

Theodora plays pseudo-sister and aunt so well because she lacks encumbrances; she has no family of her own, and, as an Australian, she needn't worry about cultural burdens. This freedom serves the selflessness and invisibility she must assume to merge her life activity with that of another person. Because she has no hardened identity, not even a socially approved female identity, the others thrust identities upon her. She can be many things to many people. White's attitude toward her fluidity is characteristically mixed. Though uniqueness is to be cherished, it can also be enhanced or overcome; loss of self leads to the discovery of hidden aspects of self. Conversely, clinging to one's identity blocks the drive to self-transcendence. The parallel with Sartrean existentialism is exact: any person encumbered by possessions, relationships, or a self-image will tend to preserve selfhood as the cost of seeking new limits. Theodora doesn't perpetrate such bad faith. Her stay at the Hôtel du Midi represents a midpoint for her (as the hotel's name implies), not a terminus. The blaze that consumes the hotel leaves her unscathed, as did the bolt of lightning that struck Meroë on her twelfth birthday.

But does she bear inner scars? White's unified world disallows both accidents and loose ends. Theodora is implicated in the fire, having extended and reinforced the madness she found at the hotel. Even though the action of Part Two describes her attempts to merge herself with other selves, its division and breakdown impress us more than do its patterns of unity. What emerges from Part Two is a vision not of wholeness but of a divided self in an exploding world. The hotel fire claims Madame Rapallo; in addition, the Henry Miller epigraph to "Jardin Exotique" includes words such as "split," "splitting," "dividedness," "fragments" (twice), and "fragmentation." The rapid scene shifting, the speed with which Theodora moves between roles, and the blurring of actuality and fantasy make the very act of reading Part Two a plunge into the bizarre. Amid such havoc it is difficult to feel solid.

Aesthetically, the extravanganza is consistent. White depicts disorder without lapsing into dementia. In his review of the 1958 Eyre and Spottiswoode reprint of *The Aunt's Story*, Peter Hastings found some "excessively irritating faults," namely White's "resort to mysticism in describing human experience and relations and his preoccupation with a subjective approach to characters."[5] This disclaimer rests on misreading and oversight. The mysticism that offends Hastings comes from Theodora, from whose point of view the action is perceived and told. Had White shifted to another perspective, he would have forfeited the control of a fixed reference. Had he resorted to the more naturalistic descriptive mode of Part One, his portrayal of Theodora's weird clarity as an ongoing process would have become blurred, along with the psychological lines of force leading to Part Three.

"Jardin Exotique" flags occasionally, as White's tendency to flip through his card file or to reach into his bag of literary tricks dulls the comedy. Because of this showing off, the brilliance of Part Two sidetracks the story as often as it advances it. All is swept indiscriminately into the final blaze without any explanation for that blaze's emergence. The hotel might have burned at any time after the shattering of the nautilus, and the nautilus could have smashed at any time at all. On the positive side, White both controls the events of "Jardin Exotique" and ensures a unified portrayal of Theodora by alluding to elements from Parts One and Three. Often, too, he uses comic understatement to undercut melodrama or to stop the action from peaking too early. The banal detail, "She [Theodora] would have to ask Monsieur Durand to recommend a cordonnier who was both reliable and cheap" (p. 155), ends chapter 7, a mélange of wild fantasies. The attempted theft of the nautilus in chapter 9 (which may have been modeled on the dramatic climax of James's *Aspern Papers*) also keeps a comic focus, thanks to timing and selection. The presence of dust everywhere in the room, the bilingual nonsense that the bald Madame Rapallo mutters in her sleep, and, finally, the pet monkey's holding onto Theodora's neck during the caper rule out suspense while promoting the grotesque; its ironic symbolism simultaneously spoofs and heightens the drama of the nautilus.

Theodora has seen herself reflected in the unlikeliest people, such as Jack Frost. The similarities reach into Part Two with appropriate variations. Herring has observed that the "destructive impulses"[6] of the German lodger Lieselotte reflect Theodora's. The tie-in is important; each guest at the hotel represents an aspect of Theodora, dredges up an episode from her childhood, or summons up an unfulfilled, perhaps even unconscious wish. Without identifying with either Elsie Rapallo or Sokolnikov, she merges sufficiently with both characters to gain access into their obsessions. Other imaginative likenesses are more oblique. Miss Grigg, the Cockney governess (Theodora calls herself a governess [p. 137]), enjoys picnics, as did Gertie Stepper, the Goodman family servant in Meroë. The poet Wetherby's face reminds Theodora of that source of beauty and strength, Moraïtis's cello. The reminder strikes home. Like Theodora, Wetherby is a visionary expatriate. He comes from Birmingham, England, but Birmingham is also a place in Alabama. Theodora comes from Australia and ends her days physically in America and spiritually in Abyssinia; all searches end where they began. Other elements in the book induce a bipolar tension whose impulses range over a wide field. The Hôtel du Midi stands in a volcanic region, recalling the earthquake-destroyed city of Meroë in ancient Abyssinia, after which Theodora's childhood home, itself surrounded by volcanic ash, is named.

Except for Theodora, the people, setting, and narrative voice of Part Two all differ from those of Part One. Yet repetitions and correspondences linking the units restore, amid the chaos of the hotel, some of the wholeness of Theodora's childhood. Because exact parallels would belie life's mystery, events overlap, touch briefly, or cross at different angles; the recurrence of zinc—a dull, opaque metal—in all three sections reminds us that life is unknowable. During a conversation on France's southern coast Theodora notes, "Far away a mouth of glass bit the darkness" (p. 239). For some unrevealed reason, she has invoked the image of a man she had seen years before in a Sydney pub "with a talent for eating glass" (p. 120). She also connects other far-flung events. Violet Adams wrote a poem in quatrains while attending school with her; years later, Theodora reads a four-lined stanza (unrhymed) by Katina Pavlou, written in purple (violet) ink. Katina's age when she writes the poems, sixteen, probably parallels that of both the schoolgirl Violet and Theodora's niece Lou in suburban Sydney. This second parallel deserves mention because it calls forth yet another: just as Part One ended with a conversation between Theodora and Lou, so does the finale of Part Two show Theodora and Katina, her surrogate niece, talking together.

The dovetailings and convergences carry into Part Three, "Holstius." A motif binding the book's three sections is that of waiting; lacking a fixed routine of her own, an aunt awaits the pleasure of others. Part One opened with Theodora waiting for her sister Fanny to come to their dead mother's house; the outset of Part Two shows Theodora waiting for the desk clerk of the Hôtel du Midi to book her into her room; the novel ends with her waiting to be admitted into an asylum. Her waiting signals faith—anyone with a goal in view converts her waiting into a waiting-for. The events of Part Three add to this affirmation, but only just. The atmosphere exudes promise. In contrast to the sterility of the cactus garden, the American heartland where Part Three opens teems with fertility and abundance. The compassion of the people Theodora meets and her own quiet resolve also exude a calmness we find soothing after the gleaming macabre farce of "Jardin Exotique." But Theodora's retreat into the shadowy recesses of her mind restores ambiguity. "Holstius" is full of imponderables. When her insight is keenest, Theodora seems most adrift and deranged. She even silences White, who either finds her bewildering or respects her too much to intrude on her innermost thoughts. The mysteries that scramble the surface of her mind he only records, without pretending to fathom them. Like us, he can only wait for the asylum's door to close behind her.

As Theodora wanders farther from civilization, she burrows deeper into her new, free self. Yet the commonsense, workaday world pulls her back from the deserted shack that she finds and then appropriates. This traveler, hotel dweller, and nursemaid-governess had turned the shack into the only home she could have ever called her own. No matter that it stood near some crumbling hills and only contained sticks of worn old furniture; she scrubbed it, built a cozy fire in it, and believed it to be her own. At the end, she becomes a passenger again, walking toward the car that will take her to the mental hospital.

III

Given its irrevocable finale, how should her global journey be judged? Theodora has never fit comfortably into her surroundings. She manages no better when those surroundings are shaped by her own hands. On her twelfth birthday she decided against a settled existence, but she delayed her pilgrimage for more than thirty years, and it lasted only a year or two. Thereafter she is more hemmed in by her surroundings than she had been in Sydney, where she served as her mother's domestic drudge. The woman who vowed to know everything ends up unable to take care of herself. She has hardened, blistered, and become black, the color of rot, frost, and volcanic rock in the novel, because she has raised questions that ignite the consuming flames of God. Either she has failed to make good the affirmations conferred on her by both Moraïtis and the Man who was Given his Dinner, or else she has fulfilled them all too well. In either case, she feels uneasy enough about herself to summon up Holstius to rebuke her for defining reality too rigidly. It is difficult to find grounds for this rebuke. Theodora has already confessed to being self-destructive; she killed the red-eyed hawk in chapter 4 rather than letting Frank Parrott try to do it because she wanted to know her feelings, even the self-destructive ones. Called "that imaginary composite of the men from whom she [Theodora] has learned wisdom" by Herring and "a . . . half father-figure, half *alter-ego*" by Hadgraft,[7] Holstius accuses her of misunderstanding permanence. According to him, she views it as a fixed state and not as a merging and a flowing.

On what grounds does he base his charge? Surely she deserves no blame for wanting her own place, the dusty, ill-furnished shack in the hills. She needs rest from her travels, and her ability to transform the shack into a home reflects creativity as well as a recognition of her need for roots. She has found what she wants and has the wit to claim it. What is more, she backs her claim with hard manual labor, scrubbing the floor without soap. Like that avatar of vision, the infant in Wordsworth's "Intimations" ode, the power of her vision exists inversely with her ability to state it.

Theodora has become the originator and arbiter of acts whose import she can never share. The epigraph to Part One of the novel, from Olive Schreiner, sets forth opacity as the culmination of vision: "She thought of the narrowness of the limits within which a human soul may speak and be understood by its nearest of mental kin, of how soon it reaches that solitary land of the individual experience, in which no footfall is ever heard." The passage refers to the whole novel. Though Theodora's deeds touch others, their effects bounce back to her, where they get reabsorbed. She remains a private person, unknown and perhaps unknowable throughout. In Part One she lives alone, prior to setting forth on her worldwide trip; in Part Two she lives in a hotel, a way station for the homeless; in Part Three, where she is in transit, she spends as little time as possible with others. So isolated has she become that she may even be cut off from herself. Ironically, at the end the wayfarer gives in to the reason and social conformity she has been resisting since age twelve. The black rose bobbing on her hat may keep a life of its own, symbolizing the inviolability of her spirit. But this fragile, trembling freedom threatens to starve for want of outlets. Not that it ever prospered: Elsie Rapallo's cloak also led a life of its own. When brought to the test, Theodora rarely rises above tables, chairs, and rocks.

Did White write a brilliant, complex novel only to contrast the physical enslavement of its heroine with her unfulfilled creativity? If such was his intention, he merits censure for vagueness and indeterminacy. The novel needs a stronger closing statement in any case. Every opposition doesn't form a dialectic or a bipolar tension, as Theodora's actions prove. After having been at odds with her environment throughout her life, she finally tries, in vain, to merge with it by transforming the abandoned shack into a home. Certainly, White distinguishes between her and the baroque Elsie Rapallo; otherwise, he wouldn't have built the novel around her. But to describe her freedom at the end as a quivering rose of black gauze is to symbolize the death throes of her mind—like winter earth giving a last shudder before it hardens, or once-raging lava trembling in protest before it settles into basalt. Only by a farfetched reading could one infer that the restrictions imposed upon Theodora in the hospital will foster a new self-awakening. Most of the evidence foretells a steady decline for her, not a creative bipolarity between her and her surroundings. Either she lacks the energy and purpose to resonate against her environment, or else she has drifted past the point where any breakthrough she might muster can be recognized as such.

Symbolism both extends and deepens Theodora's plight (and White's). Two colors associated with her throughout are black and yellow. She is last seen as a yellow-faced apparition wearing a black hat. Now yellow expresses, besides her drabness, the stone facade of Meroë and a dress which Julia Goodman finds unflattering to Theodora. Yet White also associates the color with vitality: a calf is born amid buttercups at the Parrotts' property in Audley, the teeming cornfields through which Theodora's train passes at the start of "Holstius" pulsate with yellow, and her happiest childhood memories are bound up with warming sunshine. Others beside her both feel and transmit the vibrancy of yellow. Although dancing with her turns Frank into "a blaze of fiery gold" (p. 68), this strange tumult frightens him, and his conventionality douses the elemental fire. His fear is understandable, for the fire is blind and amoral, a creative force that can destroy if it is not controlled. Theodora has already proved that energy can devastate as well as strengthen, and the color symbolism supports the idea. Lou draws a picture of a yellow thunderstorm, and the lightning bolt that felled Theodora has a yellow tint. (Danger always accompanies illumination in White.) The yellow and the black come together both in Theodora's appearance and in the place that influences her most, Meroë. Fittingly, both she and her childhood home fuse elements of transcendence and breakdown: the forces of creation and destruction run through, rather than around, all. Unpredictable mixtures of good and evil, we are all potential Jack Frosts. Thus Theodora and Meroë call forth ambiguities that resist pat answers. Theodora's complexion is yellow, along with her school desk, the estate of her suitor Huntly Clarkson, and a bar of soap she uses in America. Blackness recurs just as often, usually in a deathly context, black being the ashen residue of that which once had a yellow flame and glow. Aside from a dead crow seen in church, there are the flies who feed on decay at Meroë, the decay itself, a black frost forecast by George Goodman, and the *Monstera deliciosa* growing in the winter garden of the Hôtel du Midi. Sokolnikov's mention that the fruit of the *Monstera* gives most nourishment when black with putrescence invites a parallel with Europe, in whose soil the plant grows and which comes before us in its death throes. Theodora, by extension, having been strengthened by her brush with decadent Europe, acquires zest as *she* rots or lapses from sanity. Only a heightened sensibility like hers can be part of everything it touches; only a heart as open as hers is so vulnerable.

Meroë, with its yellow grass, yellow house, and black basalt hills, reflects the same ambiguity. Theodora draws an imaginative parallel between the black outcroppings she sees from her window and the fiery innards of the Ethiopian volcano that razed the ancient city of Meroë. This fusion of the legendary and the immediate gives the Australian Meroë an inclusiveness that makes Theodora think of it as eternal. But even stone crumbles. George Goodman's death forces the sale of the family property and sends Theodora and her mother to Sydney. the fixity Theodora ascribes to Meroë is an illusion; no single meaning can encompass the place. "There is another Meroë . . . a dead place, in the black country of Ethiopia" (p. 15), said George Goodman in a poetic moment; a local man calls the Goodman property "Rack-an'-Ruin Hollow" (p. 17); Theodora cherishes the permanence she ascribes to it. Although the permanence comforts, it also comes to grief, the devastation that consumed its legendary counterpart returning to send Pearl Brawne away, to split the earth with a lance of lightning, and, finally, to displace the Goodmans. Ironically, the displacement strengthens the tie between the Meroës and thus raises the mundane to the level of myth. The processes may differ, but the effects are similar enough to sustain the parallel between modern Australia and ancient Abyssinia and, therefore, to drench the everyday with the grandeur of antiquity.

Bespeaking Meroë as eloquently as its yellow grass and black bedrock are the many roses that grow on the property. Roses recur throughout White's work, for several reasons. Earth and flesh are not barriers to be overcome before the goal of illumination is attained; on the contrary, all value takes root in the material world. White's rose symbolism endorses this rootedness. Although the rose may evoke Paradise as God's loveliest creation, it also grows out of the soil of the fallen world. That it may grow best in the stench and filth of a manure pile shows waste as an appropriate seedbed for transcendence. Broadly speaking, the rose in White symbolizes the comfort and security of the family. Part of its joy, like that of family living, comes from its transience. The soft, dewy fragrance given out by its delicate flesh can't last; accordingly, George Goodman's death leads to the sale of rose-thronged Meroë. Its proudest bloom, Fanny, then plants a metaphorical rose garden of her own by marrying Frank. Yet careful nurturing can prolong the life of roses, just as judgment and patience can protect one from their sharp thorns. Beatson's insight, "Roses evoke the sensuous happiness of childhood,"[8] applies vividly to Theodora and to the warm sense of belonging she feels at Meroë. The red, white, and golden roses that blossom there have "a power and an influence" (p. 13) that makes her stable, loving childhood "an epoch of roselight" (p. 14).

White will vary to the point of overturning his basic identification of roses with the coziness of family life. As *Eye of the Storm* shows, family members can savage as well as console. What is more, roses needn't relate only to childhood. In "Dead Roses," a story that describes the breakup of two families, a man brings a woman "the largest bunch of crimson roses." He soon proposes amid the fragrance of rose perfume. Pearl Brawne, the discharged servant in *Aunt's Story* described as "a big white rose" (p. 20), becomes pregnant in a bed of nettles. Roses and thorns come together again in *Voss*, where another servant, whose name is Rose, gets caught in a rosebush, "roselight . . . flooding her face" (p. 154), soon after being impregnated. Both servant girls have violated a precept of middle-class family morality—thus their association with thorns and nettles. The family, both image and nucleus of Western society, can be cruel as well as nurturing. Roses sometimes gash and rip: "I've seen roses tear a roof off" (*Four Plays*, p. 203), says a man in *Cheery Soul*. In perpetuating the family, the two servants, Rose and Pearl, have also dishonored it; though not sinners, they have committed a social crime. They must feel the thorn. One of them drifts into prostitution and the other dies, neither of them rearing her illegitimate baby. Cut roses can die other deaths in White, the influence of family spreading widely from the domestic hearth. Dorothy and Basil Hunter leave Australia, land of their fathers, and wilt. Europe also depletes Eddie Twyborn. Eddie lives as a woman in France, and, twenty-five years later, in England. Only in Australia, where he was born and reared, does he mesh with his manhood.

Like the Hunter children of *Eye*, Eddie flees roseflesh and attar because they can lull the senses. The thorn on the rosebush they all fear is social conformity; the individual must sacrifice freedom to belong to any social unit. Much of the warmth of family living comes from obeying received values and hewing to fixed norms. An emblem of middle-class propriety, the rose threatens uniqueness. Fear of being punished moved Eddie out of the roselight. To become intoxicated by roses dulls the instinct and undermines personal freedom. Roses confer status, which can confine while comforting. Julia Goodman forbids Theodora to touch the roses growing at Meroë not to preserve their beauty, but to maintain her own reputation as a homemaker in the neighborhood. This scold, associated throughout with jagged, scraping objects, proves that roses can crystallize into garnets (her favorite gem) if not approached with a tender heart. Another perversion of roses enters the novel with Fanny, described as a child as "pink and white as roses" (p. 19). While White doesn't begrudge Fanny her respectable husband, suburban home, or three children, he does regret her having become socialized at the cost of her individuality. The creativity that enabled her to play the piano has dwindled to proprietorship, leaving her a stout, grasping matron: "Her life was a life full of cupboards. She kept them locked. She made inventories of her possessions" (p. 9). The profit motive governs all, her basilisk look having turned the soft fragrance of roses to brambles. So calculating is she that she uses the visit to the city and her dead mother as an occasion to buy clothing for her children.

Neither Parrott was pushed into conformity by a stroke of authorial will. White's people all exhibit inclinations and tendencies which may entrench themselves after years of unconscious trial and error. Often a value, and thus a social stance, asserts itself through conflict with another. Frank wasn't always a thick-waisted, henpecked clubman happy only when talking shop to his cronies. At least twice Theodora stirred the heart of this once-athletic horseman. Nor would Theodora necessarily have turned down a proposal from Frank. White's characters don't represent moral or temperamental extremes. Fluid and many-sided, they are capable of anything. If Theodora can imagine herself committing Jack Frost's murders, she might have also enjoyed marriage to Frank: "Fanny is a rose, felt Theodora, but I am a lesser rose on the same stem" (p. 18). She finds comfort in the family, even though she has never had her own except from a dubious distance. Her quickly adopting Katina Pavlou and Zack Johnson as surrogate niece and nephew proves that, temperamentally, she wheels in the cycle of the family. Though White never claims that Theodora would be happier as a suburban homemaker than as a spinster, he supplies enough evidence to convince us that the duties of wife and mother wouldn't have crushed her.

But her homemaking skills are never tested. No roses blossom for her after Meroë, nor will anything else blossom for her, so far as we can tell. Shrubb's 1968 statement on White's technique of persuasion and revelation applies as strictly to Theodora as to any other figure in the canon: "In the most ordinary and everyday of us there are resources of understanding that we do not normally call upon. . . . We are able to utter truths that we cannot defend in argument."[9] The image of Theodora's face beneath a black gauze rose describes her privilege, her punishment, and her mystery. It also defines our participation in her tragedy. Though none of us would want to trade places with her, most of us would agree that the world needs heroines like her to test the existing order. Theodora and her kind keep social institutions like the family from going flat and stale because, though outsiders, they have also participated enough in these institutions to view them from the inside. The novel's crowning irony, which White has the bravery to face head on, shows Theodora, denied a home since childhood, going to the only home where her needs can be met. She has come to the United States, a land of rugged individualists, to write the closing chapters of an odyssey marked by Yankee self-reliance. Now she must rely on others. The woman who suppressed her own needs to merge with others has finally lost the thread of selfhood. *The Aunt's Story* succeeds because its main figure puzzles, frightens, but, above all, enriches us.

5. Strange Truths along Well-Trod Byways

A WORK DEALING with family life and the shaping of the wilderness, *The Tree of Man* forgoes the cosmopolitan touches of its two consciously modern predecessors, *The Aunt's Story* and *The Living and the Dead*. Nor does the work feature characters who are either projections of or symbolic stand-ins for the author, like Elyot Standish, the effete, self-disparaging intellectual, or Theodora Goodman, the mustachioed spinster whose madness deepens the longer she stays away from Australia. The White of *Tree* leans less on personal experience than on an Australian heritage that goes back four generations. Its ancestral roots give his 1955 novel a ripeness and a resonance heretofore lacking in the canon. The forerunner that most resembles it, *Happy Valley*, which also takes place in rural New South Wales, has little of its heft and scope. *Tree* pairs the founding of a settlement with its main characters' groping efforts at self-discovery; as the Parkers tame the land, add livestock, and improve their standard of living, they create themselves. By contrast, the remote, inconvenient settlement in *Happy Valley* is already formed, having enjoyed its heyday before the time of the novel, and most of its inhabitants live there reluctantly. *Happy Valley* also lacks the descriptive verve and the concentration of character found in its more mature successor. The vision put forth in *Tree* is one of bare statement, not thesis. So assured is the work that neither argument nor verbal brilliance accounts for its grip so much as does White's commitment to his materials. *Tree* has a heartbeat. Perhaps the least intellectual of White's books, it is busy, warm, and old fashioned in its ability to draw us into the lives of its people and make us experience the action along with them. Speaking of the work's rootedness and its continuity between people and setting, Vincent Buckley said in 1958, "It has a real relationship with the earth. It does not ponder, does not consciously accept or reject its bonds with the earth. It simply has, *is* those bonds."[1]

The book's portrayal of a bygone age simpler than ours shows what we have come out of and what we have come through. *Tree* gains legendary grandeur from its common background. The struggles it depicts with flood, fire, and drought could take place almost anywhere. The unconscious solidarity that the locals display in these crises evokes, along with the artifacts and tokens of a shared rural heritage, the infancy of our urban culture. Set in a timeless, suspended world, *Tree* celebrates the archetypal homesteading experience of clearing and fencing, tilling and sowing. White's omission of all dates, all public events except for the Great War, and all mention of Australia till Part III of his four-part novel also directs the primitive bigness of the novel to the common ancestry of man. The action opens in a featureless scrub, a rough, unpeopled place not connected with the rest of the world. The huge sky and silent earth could eat Stan Parker whole. The place has no past, and the only certainty about its future is the toil necessary to make it livable. Stan must cut his farm and home out of solid bushland. Cut he does, and White admires him for it. As the first sentence of Part II shows, the district where the Parkers homestead has acquired a reality from the antlike efforts of its dwellers: "About a mile from Parkers', where the road forks, a store had been built, and a post office was added in time, so that Durilgai did exist physically, these two buildings proved it" (p. 101).

Those buildings stand on Australian soil. Though rarely mentioned, Australia infiltrates the action. Haunted by both its convict heritage and its cruelty to Aboriginals, turn-of-the-century Australia felt demeaned in the eyes of the world. It stood far from cultural centers, and it had nothing like the New England Puritanism that set a tone, laid down laws, and created the sense of mission that still permeates American public and private life. What is more, Stan and Amy Parker are children without parents. Because they must create themselves without psychological aids in a land that offers no guidelines for behavior, they grope in the darkness, sometimes colliding painfully, for a few grains of light. Like all people who live together, they baffle and bore, injure and comfort each other. Decent kind people often caught in a net of events beyond their understanding or control, they portray the tensions of close, spontaneous living. The trials posed in *Tree* aren't restricted to heat, storms, and hunger. White also wanted to describe the contradictory impulses of estrangement and suffocation generated by family life. These impulses form a pattern whose meaning both puzzles and strengthens. His 1958 description of his imaginative intent in *Tree* reveals his preoccupation with the mysterious, life-giving interchange between the ordinary and the eternal. The tree of man is both rooted and soaring; wonder can blossom as radiantly in

Australia's hardscrabble soil as in the gardens and lawns of the northern hemisphere: "I wanted to suggest in this book every possible aspect of life, through the lives of an ordinary man and woman. But at the same time I wanted to discover the extraordinary behind the ordinary, the mystery and the poetry which alone could make bearable the lives of such people, and, incidentally, my own life since my return."[2]

I

The poetry and mystery surface so quickly that the Parkers gasp. As a wedding present, the parson's wife who had introduced Stan and Amy gives the couple the same silver nutmeg grater that she herself had received as a wedding present but never knew what to do with. The useless, worrisome object conveys life's wonder because the Parkers believe that their first visitor, a nameless Bible salesman, stole it before slipping unannounced from their home. The ingredients of transcendence are at hand. Divine emanations flow out from both the parsonage where the nutmeg grater lay for some years and from the Bibles of the itinerant salesman. The Parkers' makeshift home provides the mundane actuality in which vision takes root. The salesman gives the marriage its first jolt and helps turn the shack into a home. The acts of serving him a meal and then giving him a bed for the night establish Stan and Amy as a family in their own minds. This confidence needs to survive the test of shock before acquiring legitimacy. The strange disapparance of their guest, following his gripping words about Africa's mysterious Gold Coast, gives their marriage a dark intimacy which strengthens and soothes.

Later, too, the transcendent flares out of the actual. "The mystical is not hidden beyond appearances, but hidden in them,"[3] says W.D. Ashcroft of White's faith in material reality. Because the real contains the ideal, it must be dealt with directly. White's so-called excremental vision, which insists that illumination can even break through filth and corruption, will reach its zenith (or nadir) in *Vivisector* and *Eye of the Storm*. Elizabeth Hunter has her crowning, final vision while seated on the toilet (called several times, appropriately, a "throne"). Hurtle Duffield, after having contemplated God while himself at stool, dies when his vision of the heavenly blue (the indigodd) coincides with brute reality; matching, and thus providing an earthy context for, his revelation is the fart that constitutes his last living act. The Bible peddler in *Tree* helps the Parkers because he explains to them the same truth that will come to Hurtle during his first stroke and to Mrs. Hunter when she is pounded and wrung by a cyclone on Brumby Island, viz., that God reveals Himself in travail: "The Almighty 'asnt shown 'Is 'and," mutters the peddler through his rum; "You 'ave not been 'it over the 'ead, kicked downstairs, spat at in the eye"

(p. 36). White supports the idea quickly. The Almighty does show His hand in the next chapter exactly as the drunken salesman had predicted. Soon after the man's disappearance a cyclone frightens Amy and Stan, making them reach out instinctively to each other. The humanizing effects of the storm carry God's signature. By showing them their mutual need, the cyclone brings the Parkers together. They have learned from it that they can face life's storms better in each other's arms than alone. The chance for self-transcendence comes to all, since all partake of the same indwelling life-spirit. But the sacrifice and danger that self-overcoming entails make us shrink. Our faintheartedness creates the need for storms and other crises. Both of Stan Parker's major epiphanies stem from catastrophes, his inner turmoil in each case answering and tallying with a disaster that pelts his body. Both epiphanies leave him elevated and diminished; his sharpening vision puts him in mind of man's smallness and transience. Other important truths follow. That the storms occur in the first and the last part of the book shows, along with other patterns of recurrence, Stan's life wheeling in a cycle as well as moving straight ahead. But experience never repeats itself in exactly the same way. In chapter 20 he catches a chill and a fever from being rained on. The ailment that races through and overtakes his system provokes one of several revelations. Unconsciously he will build on the experience. Attainment comes to him piecemeal (in the war, in his visits to Sydney, and in storms) rather than all at once, as with Mrs. Hunter.

Chapter 20, which describes his fight with pleurisy, ends positively. Though flattened, Stan has also been renewed, as is indicated by his learning of carpentry, a new skill, late in life. His newly won intensity shows, too, in his reactions to a production of *Hamlet*, which he had read as a boy. Seeing *Hamlet* performed in Sydney raises ghosts for both Parkers, in fact, confronting them with some of their darkest insecurities. Stan's lost hopes for self-knowledge push to the fore, together with a premonition of his death; Shakespeare shows him that he may die before exploring his heart. But he doesn't share his stabbing revelation with Amy any more than she shares hers with him. Because her secret thoughts turn on guilt, her silence is understandable: she is more shaken than she can show. Even though Stan's boyhood reading and great emotional range both make him an up-country Hamlet, he may be less deeply stirred by watching the play than is Amy, who sees in it various reflections of her incestual craving for her son, Ray. The difference in the playgoers' hearts is spelled out by their reactions to Madeleine, a beautiful socialite who visited Durilgai some thirty-five years before and whom Stan rescued from a burning house. Of the different memories that watching *Hamlet* revives in the Parkers, none surpasses in force the dredging up of Madeleine. Stan recalls her as someone with whom danger once created a strong, wordless bond. Amy, who even believes she sees Madeleine in the audience, remembers her as a cool, poised rider of horses, identification with whom will ease her own sexual guilt. But her guilty longings make her identify instead with both Gertrude, Denmark's semi-incestuous queen, and the Player Queen, who poisoned her husband so that she could marry his brother. "I want Ray, I want Stan, said the queen" (p. 419), murmurs a disoriented Amy to herself, amid memories of Leo, the commercial traveler with whom she committed adultery, and Glastonbury, an imaginative stand-in for Elsinore, where Madeleine nearly burned and where Amy last saw Ray. Amy's reaction to *Hamlet,* "This play is a lot of nonsense" (p. 420), is as defensive and dishonest as Gertrude's insistence that the Player Queen doth protest too much in her declarations of innocence. In this play all women tinged with sexual guilt see themselves mirrored, and the recognition hurts. Amy will never regain Ray, and she has only frustration and guilt to show for her sinful attempts to make good the loss.

Now art unleashes the same revelations that unfold much more slowly in daily living; Stan and Amy react so strongly to Shakespeare because they resemble him. A play like *Hamlet* or a violin conceto like the one Thelma hears at the moment of her father's death resembles the lightning bolt that illuminated Theodora Goodman while knocking her down; artistic creation has some of the urgency seen in the natural disasters which are wisely termed "acts of God." But if God didn't reveal Himself in everyday reality, too, Stan, Amy, or Thelma wouldn't respond to His more spectacular self-disclosures. The difference between the ordinary person and the artist is one of degree, like the difference between a drizzle and a downpour. The poetry and the mystery in all of us perceive gleams of the divine. Other tenets of White's metaphysic fall into place, downfall and disintegration accompanying growth and expansion at all levels. Although working outdoors builds sinew and perhaps moral fiber, it also coarsens and wears down the body. The smell of death clings to life's greenest offshoots. An old couple who soon die are among Durilgai's first settlers, the Quigley family. A dead horse at the side of the road marks the way to the O'Dowds, whom Amy visits on an important mission in chapter 6. The closing chapters of *Tree* show this reversible rhythm pressing outward: as urban sprawl ensnares Durilgai within Sydney's web, the home of its first pioneers, the Parkers, gets reabsorbed into the bush. Attuned to the same rhythm, nature itself gives and takes away. One of spring's cleansing, refreshing rains lasts too long and pelts down too hard, damaging property, drowning livestock, and splitting families. Summer is mellow, golden, and bountiful, yet its heat also causes droughts and raging brushfires. It culminates in a fire in Part Two that destroys the area's richest house, Glastonbury, and burns all the hair off the head of its proudest beauty, Madeleine. This counterpoint then begets an antiphonal phrase of its own.

Stan is rewarded by the Armstrongs, owners of Glastonbury, for rescuing Madeleine, whose baldness destroys Amy's bogus-romantic image of her. Amy's inner world goes flat and gray when her illusions about Madeleine collapse. Whereas she admires Stan for the courage he displayed in the rescue, she also resents him for ending her novelette.

Feelings usually run in channels with hidden currents. Beyond the destructive range of both misplaced love and hate is life's underlying mystery. Amy tries in vain to appropriate the foundling who materializes near the butcher's shop, but the boy is no hunk of meat to be sliced or sold. He takes his meaning from another setting connected with him, the drowned church that supplies the fragment of glass whose red curves render the world a crimson miracle. Part One of *Tree* ends not with the flood, but with the disappearance of the foundling. The invasion of loss and mystery into the Parkers' home strengthens the couple, as it did earlier, when their only other overnight guest also left unannounced. That Stan and Amy make love within minutes of discovering the boy's absence affirms their marriage and puts them in phase with a mirroring universe. As they did after discovering the disappearance of the Bible salesman, they take the world on its own irrational terms and, wisely, they take it together. Some roads in Durilgai bypass the butcher's shop.

Hardship encourages the Parkers' neighbors to join ranks and, by stages, welds them into a community. One family will help lighten another's burden, as when the O'Dowds loan Amy a goat to nurse a calf whose mother has contracted milk fever. Many families take part in the novel's next instance of social bonding. Responding to the damage caused by the Willunya floods, local men form volunteer rescue teams while the women dispense bread and soup. The "iron rain" (p. 67) fosters valor, generosity, and a community spirit the area has never before known. With the mayor and the governor applauding their efforts, the men and women of Durilgai have affirmed the value of their scrap of sodden turf by risking their health and their lives. The emergency has also razed class barriers. Like the war of Part Two and the fire of Part Three, the flood, besides promoting local pride, also marks a big step in the growth of democratic feeling.

Through it all Stan and Amy keep adapting to the needs of the moment, belonging, at different times, to both the one and the many. *Tree* records not the triumphs of colonizing the frontier but the grim daily realities which are more psychological and moral than social or political. People count more in *Tree* than does milieu. The adventure of pioneering means constant toil. Amy and Stan start out as newlyweds, barely acquainted with each other and with the tough, remote area where they settle. They leave us, and each other, some fifty years later, just as puzzled with the key realities of their marriage. "The novel relies for much of its strength on

White's feeling for the awkwardness and fumblings of human relationships,"[4] said Wilkes about the work's grasp of psychological complexity. Controlled by an incommunicable mystery, Stan and Amy experience sharp and sudden changes of feeling as they look both inward and outward. Golden moments of intimacy pass before they are savored or understood. On the other hand, pain and darkness persist. *A Life Sentence on Earth*,[5] White's original title for *Tree*, conveys the stress felt by finite hearts yearning for the infinite; the rare glimpses of transcendent reality vouchsafed them, usually after a crisis, leave the Parkers confused and shaken, heightening the severity of their sentence.

Stan toils in the thickets of ambiguity. He takes his pick, axe, and shovel into the wilderness, where he builds a house, grows crops, and raises livestock. As he acquires ballast and social standing, he makes the land fruitful and orderly. He is a real homesteader; rather than digging in the earth, extracting minerals, and moving on, this stoic, earnest son of the soil fosters a healthy, life-giving interchange with his environment. He immerses himself in the productiveness of daily routine. Whereas clearing and fencing, planting and animal raising, enrich the area, they also make him feel whole. But even though he equates moral principle with work routine, he lives much of his life outside the equation. This part of him seems blocked. Neither his marriage nor his soul thrives as his farm does. His productiveness and his good name walk together with a growing sense of isolation, puzzlement, and sorrow. Buckley has complained of him, "Stan is either a clod or an enigma; that is the trouble. . . . We are given no adequate clue to his stoicism, and so we cannot see just what it is that the tree of man is rooted in."[6]

Stan would share Buckley's chagrin, having searched in vain for a clue to his inner life. As his strong boyhood response to the Old Testament and *Hamlet* shows, his soul contains poetry, but he lacks the key to release it. A practical man, he acts out his feelings, channeling them into activities like sinking fenceposts and doctoring sick animals. The feelings that bypass this routine he doesn't deny so much as fail to share or analyze. For one thing, he lacks language. He can neither explore nor express his deepest impulses; any self-inventory he might prepare would end in a litter of fleeting impressions, smudged memories, and inchoate ideas. Another inhibiting force is his early training. His inability to touch his children reflects both a British fear of displaying feeling and a frontiersman's disregard of tenderness. No Theodora Goodman, Stan also recoils from the impulses that arise from his dark self. More of a Henry IV, or Boling-broke, than a Hamlet, he never undertakes his long-deferred pilgrimage. A long, steady look into his heart would have forced him to face truths that both his instincts and his training have taught him to suppress. Impulsiveness rattles him.

The moral complexity that middle life brings nearly finishes him. Endurance, toughness, and other outdoorsman's virtues won't see him through his ordeals. His wife and children move out of his reach and understanding. The hurts pile on in old age. As he grows older, he sees that insecurity is the norm in life; nothing and nobody can be taken for granted. His first great setback comes with the news that a race track scandal has driven his son from Sydney. The news, hard enough on its own, has a sting in its tail: not only did Ray probably dope the favorite in a big race, but the favorite was also trained by an old family friend in whose house Thelma was living at the time. Stan goes immediately to Sydney, but not in search of primitive justice. Rather, he wants to comfort Ray. Though he could never communicate with his son, he cares enough about him to go to Sydney after the turf scandal and, again, after Ray is shot to death. To call him unfeeling is both inaccurate and unfair. Love draws him out of his hiding place. To say that he needs the legitimacy imposed by family or work before he can show his heart argues only self-distrust. He overrates his failings. Much of the trauma caused by his discovery of Amy's adultery comes from the suspicion that he doesn't deserve a faithful wife. Were his heart calcified, it wouldn't have responded so dramatically to Amy or to Ray. Stan's torment bespeaks a sensitive soul. White's saying that "he just failed to shoot himself" (p. 422), when a dizzy spell causes him to fire his gun a page after the *Hamlet* outing, discloses the suicidal streak often found in morbid, not stolid, natures. The word "failed" infers intent. Also, White had shifted to the present tense in the previous paragraph to alert us to the significance of the drama at hand.

Leonie Kramer overlooked this dramatic moment when she faulted Stan's dying revelation, several chapters later, for being stage managed: "I would argue that White's assertion at this point [the intrusion, "One, and no other figure, is the answer to all sums" (p. 497)] shows up a weakness in the handling of Stan's dying revelation. The only way in which White can make the point about wholeness and oneness is by stating it himself; he cannot, though, validate it in terms of Stan's actual experience."[7] Kramer's argument carries force in its claim that White is putting thoughts into Stan's head, but all fiction writers determine what their characters say and when they say it. The only issue that matters is that of plausibility. Is Stan's perception dramatically motivated? What must be established first is the need for some psychological or, better, metaphysical breakthrough by Stan. Stan does not understand himself well enough to know either other people or why things happen. Suddenly he sees that One is the answer to all sums. What has provoked his revelation? Why should we buy it?

An important clue lies in White's dovetailing of psychology and narrative structure. With one exception, the spot-on recognition of Amy's lover's car parked outside his house, Stan always discovers the truth piecemeal. In Sydney the old man meets Ray's widow and son. Ray's son by an earlier (and perhaps only) marriage has been visiting him often in Durilgai, where they enjoy an unstated, productive love grounded in handicrafts. Stan sees that his two grandsons have fulfilled his longing for permanence. He has perpetuated himself through the blood, even though his hopes languished for most of Ray's misspent life. He can now accept the deaths of Ray, Madeleine, Mrs. O'Dowd, and Bub Quigley. He even welcomes his own death. White builds a religious frame for it by stressing Stan's readiness, by showing Stan at the end with a dog, an image of God in *A Cheery Soul*, and by intruding on Stan, in his last hour, a young evangelist who tries to convert him. Although Stan dismisses the evangelist's pieties, he fastens onto the mystery nourishing them. Soon Amy comes breathlessly to him to display a different facet of the mystery, the silver nutmeg grater which had been out of sight for the past fifty-odd years. The mystery has been confirmed: things from the past assure continuity, just as do progeny. Stan's dying words, "It's all right" (p. 497), show that he has achieved peace and clarity, if only briefly, before his death. Amy's last response in our presence, "Stan is dead. My husband. In the boundless garden" (p. 499), glimpses the purity into which Stan has been gathered. Amy knows that he has found his true home. What she doesn't know is that his revelation just moments before allowed him to go peacefully.

During their long years together Stan makes Amy feel glad, puzzled, and resentful. Like him, she craves permanence but finds herself pinned to ambiguity and change. Also like her husband, who becomes seamed and gaunt with the years while she thickens, she views her marriage as an anomaly of intimacy and estrangement. Manfred Mackenzie calls her "a profound study in neurotic self-destruction,"[8] noting, as evidence for his claim, her incestuous feelings toward Ray and her adulteries with Leo, the traveling salesman with the blue car. But her behavior with Leo and Ray doesn't diminish Stan. She, not he, feels deprived and unfulfilled. No Hedda Gabler (as Mackenzie believes), the comforting, maternal Amy harbors needs that her brooding, incommunicative husband can't meet. Her maiden name, Fibbens, suggests a penchant for deceit and doubleness that comes no nearer to her animating core than the pastoral uprightness of Stan's surname comes to his; no person can be explained by a single idea or formula. Amy is a sensualist, unlike Ibsen's Hedda. She eats greedily, and she also feels tempted to eat her husband, son, and grandson. Leo she kisses with bruising passion, yet she wouldn't have turned to him if either Stan or Ray had paid attention to her. Leo, furthermore, is less a surrogate husband to her than a surrogate son. He has Ray's build and coloring; he travels a great deal, like Ray; he follows Ray's practice of showing up in Durilgai unannounced; he might even be closer to Ray's age than to Stan's. No wonder Ray and Leo fuse in her mind as she watches *Hamlet*. The fusion persists. When Ray comes home for the last time, Amy sends him away to spare Stan from seeing how far his son has fallen from youthful grace. But she is also protecting herself; to walk into the house with Ray would be to parade her adultery before her deceived husband.

Because no such parade occurs, the guilt that it symbolizes festers within Amy, transferring itself subtly to her children. Both of them waste their lives; their futility is spelled out in kind, sexually. The mincing, finicky Thelma seems asexual, and the bullet that kills Ray lodges in his groin, suggesting sexual revenge. Born in the summer, Ray at first warms his parents' hearts like a beam of sunshine, but then this cheerful, glowing baby gravitates toward darkness. As a child he stones hens, kills puppies, bullies his sister, cheats and lies to the local simpleton, Bub Quigley, and throws the rock that splits the lip of the old German who for years helps the Parkers before anti-German sentiment during the Great War drives him away. As an adult, Ray becomes a cheap crook. The paltry £20 he pries from his sister as a bribe to stay away from her respectable home reflects his meanness. So corrupt and rundown is he that even his common-law wife shuns him in public. The rumor surrounding his death—that he informed on a mate—fits a personal history which includes a couple of jail terms, the fret of near-constant movement, and a shameful homecoming which involves summoning his mother to a local ruin under cover of night. "I would like Ray to be something in the government, or a famous surgeon. . . . We would read about him in the newspaper" (p. 125), says Amy about her small son. She and Stan do read about him, but, rather than learning of his triumphs, they discover that he has been murdered in a Sydney dive. They read this news report separately, not together. Not only has Ray put a blot on the family; he has also helped to divide it.

Thelma goes wrong because, unlike her anti-social brother, she becomes completely socialized. One reason that Australia's hardy pioneer stock weakens in the new generation is the new generation's denial of its frontier past. Ray's underworld dealings weaken his tie with his decent parents. The coiffed, manicured Thelma tries harder to shed her rural background, and, ironically, she succeeds less well. To sidestep embarrassment, she avoided inviting Stan and Amy to her wedding to a smart Sydney lawyer. This "thin woman of taste" (p. 385) feels ashamed of her parents, whom she pronounces dowdy and unaware at a time when, curiously, their rebelliousness and intuition have just begun to flower. In denying her parents, she denies herself. Furthermore, she underrates the tenacity of her roots. Just as her husband, a city man, gains strength from the tangy, bracing air of the Durilgai countryside, so does she surprise herself by visiting her parents much more often than she had expected to. Her stylish city routine of concerts and charity committees, of diamonds and expensive furs, answers fewer of her needs than she knows.

On one of her visits Thelma brings an "old friend" whom she has known for two months. Her mother's response, "Here we know people for a lifetime" (p. 443), infers that Sydney's hurry and fret blocks the formation of close personal ties. Sydney, city of Australia's dreadful night, is where Ray thickens, coarsens, and dies and also where the nervous, anemic Thelma negates herself. Her becoming Christine to her new friends completes her self-inflicted butchery: "Thelma's nonentity was complete" (p. 491), are White's last words about her. Unlike her, her parents avoid the baleful city. Amy visits Sydney only once, as an old woman, when the experience of watching *Hamlet* upsets her. Perhaps Stan finds the Shakespearean production less shattering because he has learned to expect trouble in Sydney. The jar and jostle of the city had already undermined him. He felt weak, lost, and helpless wandering Sydney's mazelike streets in search of Ray. Chaos had overtaken all. During this nightmare visit, he sees a car crash; a man vomits in a street littered with rotting vegetables and used contraceptives. Nobody will help him reach Ray. He gets drunk. The world looks so flat, rank, and godless to his anguished eyes that he contemplates suicide. Thelma has to visit the countryside to boost her spirits after living amid Sydney's trash, noise, and moral depravity. *Riders in the Chariot* also describes a degraded Sydney strewn with garbage, neon-lit bars, and sleazy restaurants. The Aboriginal artist Alf Dubbo dies in Sydney, his lungs weakened by the city's bad air and his faith in humanity mangled by his association with drunks, prostitutes, and transvestites. Not until *The Vivisector* will the country-reared White brighten Sydney's moral darkness with some gleams of hope and cheer.

II

White keeps the passage of time in *Tree* vague for the same reason that he describes physical settings with such sharp particularity: Parkers exist relative both to their immediate locale and to the forces of nature. *Tree* mentions no date or, except for the start of World War I, no public event by which a date can be inferred. The Depression and World War II pass unnoticed, and Stan's military service with the ANZAC forces is glossed over in a subordinate clause: "When the years of mud and metal were over, Stan Parker would seldom talk about them" (p. 203). This sentence, the first of chapter 14 and Part III, reflects an important verbal tactic. To give the reader his bearings in a nearly timeless world, White will often indicate the passage of time in the first sentence of a new section or chapter. Thus chapter 4 begins, "Life continued in that clearing in which the Parkers had begun to live" (p. 26); chapter 7 opens with the summary, "Several times in those years Amy Parker attempted to have their child, but evidently this was not intended to happen" (p. 63). Relating the effects of time to a broader curve, chapter 18 starts, "When Stan Parker had reached this age of life he did sometimes wonder what was expected of him" (p. 302). Changes indicating time's passage can take other forms. Not only does Amy thicken while Stan grows gaunt; the arrival of Fritz in chapter 7 also turns Stan from a hireling to an employer of an odd-jobs man. Other changes have already touched the Parkers. They entertain their first visitor in chapter 4, and in chapter 5 Amy meets their first neighbors. Even though the O'Dowds live two miles away, their presence in the district robs Stan of Amy's total attention. Later external changes touch the Parkers differently. Animals are born and die. New inventions, like the radio and the telegraph, come into vogue. As the district becomes settled, it adds a general store and a post office. Social gradations form; someone who has visited England comes to Durilgai, and the Armstrongs build Glastonbury, where they entertain guests from Sydney. But time's forward flow is sometimes diverted, or even checked. Each of the book's four parts corresponds to a season, creating a cyclical pattern which rivals the straightforward chronology. Smaller touches support White's presentation of time as multi-dimensional. Though Stan replaces his horse-drawn wagon with a motorcar, Amy prefers to ride around town in a trap given her by Thelma. Ray's death also smudges the linear chronology, reminding us that family members needn't die in their order of birth.

Ray's dying before his parents also describes life as a network of breakdown, persistence, and recurrence. "The tree of man was never quiet" (p. 389), says the A.E. Housman poem which supplies the book's title. Included in this activity is time's sly trick of reversing its effects. Mrs. Gage, an early settler and the village's first postmistress, visits Durilgai after having moved away years before. A trick of time also brings back Ray, who reminds Amy of Leo, whose lover she became to begin with because of his resemblance to Ray. Time destroys but also resurrects in other instances. Figures from Amy's past return in her old age. Madeleine, her girlhood idol, returns with Thelma, who had met her in Sydney, for tea and scones. The foundling Amy wanted to adopt after the Willunya floods comes back as her grandson, who finds and cherishes the curving of red glass that the foundling had left behind. His discovery shows Amy that her first two visitors had added to her home, rather than subtracting from it. The Bible seller told the unheeding Parkers exactly how God manifests Himself. An embodiment of resurrection, the foundling both exists miraculously and, in the glass fragment that inspires his foil's poem, bequeaths a legacy that only begins paying dividends fifty years later.

Glastonbury, the Armstrongs' brick mansion, reveals another facet of time. That its English namesake presumably holds the Holy Grail relates its potential for transcendence both to the Bible salesman's wares and to the foundling's bit of glass, which came from a church window. But

Glastonbury comes to ruin and grief because of its owners' pride in it, its pretentious English name, its false security, brickwork, expensive trappings, and many servants—and, perhaps, too because of the leveling mood of the times. A clue to the breakdown comes from White's personal life. The real-life Glastonbury is located in Gloucestershire, near Cheltenham, where Connie Tiarks of *Living and Dead* and Ellen Roxburgh of *Fringe of Leaves* both droop and where White suffered as a college student. Nothing connected with Gloucestershire can serve wholeness or joy in White's work. Within Glastonbury's brick shell festers corruption that can ignite spontaneously. Although White may savage the building's occupants unjustly—burning Madeleine's beautiful hair, blowing off her fiancé's face in combat, and shocking young Tom's father so deeply that he becomes a shriveled, grieving wreck—Glastonbury's solid, elegant appearance still clashes with its sordid reality. Whatever promise the place offers is doomed. Another example of its futility is the marble nude adorning Glastonbury's grounds. The expensive statue traces the same decline as (and thus comments ironically upon) the mansion itself. At first it awes the locals; Armstrong is so rich that his show of female nudity, expressing his aristocratic scorn of prudery, neither offends nor titillates his rude neighbors. After the fire burns away much of the statue's glamor (as it did Madeleine's), a villager makes jokes and dances lewdly in front of it. The statue now symbolizes both the vulnerability and the crushed vanity of the Armstrongs; now that Glastonbury has burned, neither its owners nor any of their effects provoke awe. The next time the statue is seen, one of its hands is missing. This brilliant effect symbolizes the furtive exchange that will soon take place between Amy and Ray, the criminal-outcast who can't face his mother in daylight or in public. Curt, coarse, and evasive, Ray only wants food and money. What does Amy want? The isolated, moonlit setting for the tryst whets her erotic passion for her son. Her first question in the disused ruin, "Is that you, darling?" (p. 360) includes a term of endearment she has never used with Stan. Ray's response both to her words and to the lamp she lights, "Cut it out. . . . You'd blind a man" (p. 360), besides rejecting her Oedipal overture in kind, also establishes dark, deserted Glastonbury as the proper milieu for someone with nothing but a police record to show for his years away from home.

Ray's reentry into the action at the end of Part Three helps show how Durilgai becomes a community and how the Parkers cohere as a family. The two processes moved ahead in phase at the book's outset. Chapter 1 begins with wilderness and ends with the establishment of a family, its last paragraph showing the newlywed Parkers approaching their crude homestead. The public ordeals in the novel's first three sections reflect tense private drama. The great spring flood at the end of Part One culminates in Amy's rejection by the foundling boy. The summer heat of Part Two climaxes in the fire at Glastonbury. The pressure created by the midsummer madness does not decrease, as a local menace gives way to one in Europe, 12,000 miles away. Even though no bullets fly in Durilgai, the war separates the Parkers and causes the wringing of Fritz, in one of the book's most moving, because most simply recounted, episodes.

The drowsy, late afternoon autumnal settings of Part Three relax the tensions only briefly. Just as Part Two described the early years and growth of the Parker children, so Part Three, following it in time, shows Ray and Thelma leaving their parents' home. The action swings away from Durilgai for the first time since chapter 2, following Thelma to Sydney, where she has enrolled in a business college. Even Stan's overseas duty was enacted from the standpoint of the family, who stayed home and to whom Stan wrote letters, mostly dealing with the management of the farm. White's treatment of Thelma's early days in Sydney reveals careful selection: he avoids describing her courtship with her future husband, and he recounts the news of Ray's part in the racing scandal in a letter whose contents are read in Durilgai, where they make their greatest impact. Ray's disgrace constitutes but one element of the contrast in Part Three between the slow golden mellowness of fall and the turmoil gripping the Parkers. This wildness declares itself with the arrival of the young Greek immigrant, Con. The first English word Con learns at the Parkers', "apple," prefigures the sexual magnetism he will exert. Amy, who teaches him the word, invests him with the storybook glamor that had melted away when she saw Madeleine bald. Con fills another big need for Amy because she can redirect her sexual longing for Ray to him, a much more acceptable target. But she must share the field. Her children are just as obsessed with Con as she is, searching his past, finding ways to be with him, and craving physical contact. Thelma fills her diary with words of love for Con. Rocked by feelings he can't understand, Ray destroys Con's most cherished object, his mother's picture, to punish him for leaving Durilgai without returning his, Ray's, tormented love.

Amy expresses love more subtly and postively than Ray, as is brought out in chapter 18, which turns inward to take psychological stock of her marriage. This concentration refocuses the action. Con left at the end of chapter 15, and most of the next two chapters took place in Sydney. Accompanying the restoration of the Parkers' acreage as the novel's chief reference point is a drought which scatters dust in cupboards and drawers. The drought has extended its effects beyond the corn rows and the paddocks. It also brings along Leo, the salesman of women's dress materials who arrives on a still, dry day claiming to be as "dry as a snake" (p. 309). The thirst in Amy's soul, aggravated by Con's departure and by Ray's disgrace, comes forth immediately; Amy contradicts herself within minutes, claiming to have everything she wants and then voicing a wish for a spring. Leo catches her drift, mouthing, mauling, and clawing at her moments after he enters the house under the pretext of wanting a glass of water. Her rut with Leo, her first instance of adultery, doesn't refresh her; rather, the dryness she felt when she wished for a spring has increased. Leo (named after the astrological sign which represents the coldest time of year in Australia) has chilled her heart while leaving it parched. Her flinging a tomcat, the second of its kind to enter her bedroom that afternoon, against her dressing table indicates her frustration. No penitent, she receives Leo in her home two more times. But this man who is likened to a snake, a tomcat, and an invading rat only feeds her self-contempt and compounds the tensions in her marriage. Part Three ends with a break in domestic ritual: Amy takes her evening tea alone after Stan spurns her invitation to join her.

Part Four takes up the ominous mood created both by this rift and by the reappearance of Ray after a ten-year absence. Winter sets in quickly. Stan becomes dizzy and faints after helping a neighbor move a rock early in chapter 20. Because cold weather brings people together, community spirit reasserts itself as a value in chapter 21, which contains several visits by Thelma to her parents, the theater outing in Sydney, and a church service. This show of communality is the book's last; winter soon freezes the lifelines joining people. Amy and Stan don't commiserate with each other when they learn, separately, of Ray's death; their joint sorrow and loss haven't united the stricken couple. A grieving, dilapidated Stan goes alone to Sydney on one more errand of sadness before he dies. Thelma is alone at the concert hall when she later intuits his death. In addition to Stan and Ray, Madeleine, Mrs. O'Dowd, and Bub Quigley also die in Part Four. Then there is the moral death of Doll Quigley. Throughout the action Doll has represented constancy amid change, but the ageless, enduring Doll kills her idiot brother because she fears that he won't be able to look after himself after she dies. The mercy killing recoils on her: "Doll Quigley was in hell" (p. 484), notes Amy on a visit to her old friend at a local asylum. Attempting to resurrect the brother she killed out of love, Doll impersonates Bub. The impersonation touches our hearts. Having lived in Durilgai nearly as long as Stan and Amy, the Quigleys have a chapter to themselves at the end, albeit a short one. White shows great humanity by accounting for this decent, simple brother and sister. They deserve his tribute. Their role in the action, though small, has been steady. They have helped shape Durilgai's personality and legend.

III

Another truth emerging from Amy's visit to Doll is our impenetrable isolation. In Doll's last, straitened moments of sanity, Amy has no comfort or wisdom to offer her, even though the two women have been friends all of their adult lives. This opacity would support Mackenzie's argument that *Tree* is a pessimistic book: "In Part IV, the disintegration of the tree of man continues piecemeal until complete. Stan and Amy Parker live on together out of mere habit; Ray, now a petty criminal in Sydney, is murdered; Thelma loses all identity, even to the point of becoming 'Christine' to friends; Sydney, an impersonal and labyrinthine city of the plain, practically envelopes the original Parker property."[9] This negation, though powerful and pervasive, doesn't overcome. As is seen in the novel's many cyclical and dialectical patterns, life will continue. Trees are mentioned in both the first and last paragraphs. The novel's last sentence, "So that in the end, there was no end" (p. 499), defines life as process, not as message, fact, or idea. The seed of love can grow in the poorest soil. White's metaphysical tree may not yield sweet, healthy fruit all the time, nor will its blooms be always beautiful. A bent Ray and a spindly Thelma are normal offshoots of the pioneer stock. The tree's role as life-giver goes on. The sapling has taken root in the tract of scrubland Stan cleared for it. Its leaves branch out in ever widening arcs, and its roots sink ever deeper in the nourishing earth. Its portrayal of life as action makes *Tree* a massive celebration of the commonplace. While describing the world in operation, the novel also assigns meanings. It is unique in the White canon: only *Tree* portrays a tragic sense of life, the feeling that each day brings us closer to death and that we reveal something timeless, yet irrecoverable, in our daily acts. The book gives courage and joy, showing, through Amy and Stan, that people matter. Even its transitional passages release poetic force. The following quotation describes a little drama enacted by peripheral figures, yet its vitality, expressed for the sake of the unity it describes in a single sentence, discloses the heartbeat of a family: "Once the father struck out at him, and the boy screamed, he pretended to cry, it was a great game, and the father also liked it" (p. 376).

As that passage implies, everything that happens in *Tree* matters. The scenes moving the action are made up of tender exchanges and personal struggles that reduce distances between characters and their deeds; the characters nearly fuse with their passions. The style of the book sustains this emotional pressure. Straining the bounds of naturalism, White captures both the solidness and the imaginative properties of landscape. Homesteading is no dry intellectual exercise. The inscrutability of distance and silence can overwhelm; rocks groan, cold air slices through trees, and darkness crushes sunlight. The big fire in Part Two demonstrates the book's stylistic range and control. It may materialize from the inside of Glastonbury. Sometimes it is experienced from the point of view of one of the firefighters; the firefighting crews may be seen at a distance, black specks moving like hectic ants under clouds or plumes of smoke. It may also be felt as a hot gust or heard as a chewing, roaring engine of destruction. The burnt-out farms, scorched, leafless trees, and stricken animals tally its destructive effects. For variety, some of the destruction is summarized by an eyewitness after the fact. A local man's description of the devastation shows White's remarkable instinct for a tag line. The concluding image both summarizes the torment and provides an unexpected moral context for it. The vividness of the effect and the disturbing notion on which it leans—that humans resemble snakes—generate a primitive force that makes us wince: "The animals were burning . . . the wild ones, and snakes, they were lashing on the hot earth, as their flesh burned they lost shape, and knotted, and shrivelled. He had seen a snake bite on itself before it died, to hold someone responsible" (p. 167).

White doesn't need violence to inspire a stylistic felicity. His reference to girls "writing scenty letters to friends" (p. 13) provides a perspective beyond the evocative range of the more conventional adjective. "Scenty" is perhaps a word callow girls would use to sound stylish; it also refers to the cheaply sweet odor of the perfume used to douse their sentimental letters. White finds new uses for adjectives elsewhere in the work. In his reference to the "bronzy sheen" (p. 132) of Madeleine's hair, the playful adjective remains separate from the noun it describes, pertaining more strictly to the person from whose standpoint the hair is seen. Other stylistic effects lack this evoctive range. *Tree* uncovers in White a new penchant for alliteration. "Already it was cold, a curdle of cold cloud" (p. 3), we read in the book's second paragraph, and we are obviously expected to feel an icy wave from the succession of voiceless velar stops. A more serious stylistic failing is White's wordiness. His tendency to overwrite begins in *Tree*. Curiously, much of the verbal padding comes at the ends of sentences. The first sentence in the quoted passage below would gain swiftness with the removal of its last five words, as would the third sentence if its last ten words were cut: "She kept it for those friends . . . lest they should break the relationship for some reason or other. So she offered them 'Christine' as an earnest of closer intimacies. Besides, she loathed "Thelma" more than anything else that had been inflicted on her" (p. 445). "The iron . . . flung across the yard and slapped a pig's arse fairly hard" (p. 469) shows worse stylistic judgment; its last two words pad the jolt created by the seven straight monosyllables, three out of the last four of which are stressed. Had White wanted to soften the whack of the flying iron shard on the pig's bottom, he might have picked a weaker verb than "slapped."

Such errors, though worth noting, constitute but minor snags in a grand tapestry. *Tree* matches richness of execution to nobility of idea. The life that happens to Amy and Stan comes in big chunks, yet it consists of small things like milking cows and baking scones. The mystery and the poetry make their lives greater than the sum of the parts. The interplay of simplicity and complexity, of the trivial and the majestic, both sustains and puzzles the Parkers. Though ignorant of the secret places in their hearts, they sometimes intuit the grandeur in all things. *Tree* describes the prose and dailiness of prosaic daily living. Mostly, there is nobody to love and nobody to hate. All passions subside. This rhythm of stasis and flux can't be described in terms of beginning, middle, and end. In place of a linear plot, White substitutes an intimate knowledge of his people and an absorption in the matter of their lives. He isn't the first writer to describe his characters as mysteries surrounded by a mystery, yet few other writers have put us so close to their people's hopes and setbacks. He deserves special praise in *The Tree of Man* for the vigor, amplitude, and humanity of his vision.

6. The Immensity That Enfolds

LIKE *A Fringe of Leaves,* White's other novel set in the nineteenth century, *Voss* (1957) stands more firmly as a period piece than as a historical novel. Stressing mood over documentation, it captures the Australian spirit at a time of burgeoning nationalism. The distinction between suburban gardens and the vast, mysterious outback, the importance of emancipists, those former prisoners who stayed in the colony after serving their time, and the growing popularity of the word "country" over the earlier "colony" all describe Australia trying both to define herself and to discover a sense of common purpose. The book's narrative technique gives the rich period flavor a dark, dissociated vitality. Though *Voss* celebrates individual heroism, it is neither an action story nor a pre-Freudian saga of frontier adventure. White shuns smooth plotting, straightforward pace, and swift declarative prose to work in a modernist tradition reaching from Conrad to John le Carré. Crammed with ideas and impressions, *Voss* bombards the reader with data rather than filtering those data through a mediating intelligence. Whatever form is imposed on the welter of materials comprising the novel comes largely through dreams, telepathy, or poetic foreshadowing rather than through direct statement. How is the reader affected? The novel that copies reality rather than ordering it rationally often suffers from a tortured density. The tightly-packed *Voss* fits the usual pattern. Though intense and varied, the book lacks pliancy of mood, its specificity often taking on the same hallucinating glare that muddles Voss and his colleagues as they trudge across the outback.

The reader relates to the drama viscerally, not intellectually. The sharp particularity, twisted grammar, and heavy cadencing of *Voss* combine well. In 1971 Brian Kiernan called *Voss* "the most imaginatively daring and impressive of all White's novels to date."[1] His praise is easily supported. The following description of the murder of a white explorer by two Aboriginals, for instance, makes us feel we are witnessing a real-life event:

> Then one black man warded off the white mysteries with terrible dignity. He flung his spear. It stuck in the white man's side, and hung down, quivering. All movements now became awkward. The awkward white man stood with his toes turned in. A second black, of rather prominent muscles, and emotional behavior, rushed forward with a short spear, or knife, it could have been, and thrust it between the white man's ribs. It was accomplished so easily.
>
> "Ahhhhh," Palfreyman was laughing, because still he did not know what to do.
>
> With his toes turned in.
>
> But clutching the pieces of his life.
>
> The circles were whirling already, the white circles in the blue, quicker and quicker. [p. 337]

White has translated the violence into a series of physical impressions, rather than moralizing or noting the responses of the onlookers. The vagueness of the phrase "it could have been" sustains, instead of lowering, the excitement. In the heat of the moment, nobody can ascertain what weapon is used by the second murderer. Nobody has the presence of mind. The lesser physical movement, the short blade thrust, has all but vanished inside the larger impression created by Tom Palfreyman's awkward, reeling attempts to remain standing. Moments later, White describes the angry reprisal against Palfreyman's murder. But again, rather than saying that Albert Judd shot the muscular second murderer in the stomach, he transforms the shooting into an immediate physical sensation: "Judd had discharged his gun, with none too accurate aim, but the muscular black was fumbling with his guts, tumbling" (pp. 337–38). In its quieter passages, too, *Voss* gives textures and masses a pulsating immediacy that precludes analysis; only after a physical sensation wanes can it be reasoned about. Above all, the book's slow-tracking, gnarled prose conveys the toil of the expedition, with some of White's sentences reproducing the strain of crossing dry, rocky terrain under a baking sun rather than merely giving information. The tensions and the pressures exerted by this physicality also help organize the mighty distances traversed. White wants to make this space palpable because *Voss* is a book about distances—the physical distance dividing lovers, the gulf separating both ambition from achievement and dream from actuality, the difference between pride and humility, and the split view of Australia as a fusion of suburban gardens and desert wilderness.

Finally, the book's tough, twisted rhetoric befits Voss, whom Geoffrey Dutton calls "an impatient eccentric who tears all that is ordinary up by the roots."[2] Perhaps White's most restless, inquiring hero, Johann Ulrich Voss is much more complex than either Stan or Amy Parker, and he comes to us in greater detail than Theodora Goodman. White needed to find a voice and a vocabulary that captured both his intensity and the grinding physical pressure of his desert march. Did he succeed too well? Reviewing *Voss* for the *Sydney Morning Herald,* Kylie Tennant quipped, "When the book strikes off into the deserts of mysticism, I would sooner slink off home." Following suit, Alan Nicholls, writing for the [Melbourne] *Age,* found "muddy affectation" together with "bad prose and philosophic posturing."[3]

The span of years since the book's publication has quieted this hostility, and readers today agree for the most part that a smoother, more affable style would have dimmed the novel's brilliance. Though plodding and solemn, *Voss* generates tragic force. Nor can it be indicted for looking with contempt at human purpose. If life can suddenly turn monstrous, that monstrousness can also inspire our best energies; nearly every character in the book grows both morally and spiritually. As is usual in White, the growth occurs when the characters disdain reason, respectability, and social acceptance in favor of a mystical-intuitive approach. Finally, there is the question of stylistic originality. Twelve years before the publication of Fowles's *French Lieutenant's Woman* (1969), *Voss* made the breakthrough of matching a Victorian setting to a Victorian idiom. White has not received enough credit for his pioneering rhetoric. In fact, the granite ambitiousness of the novel has prompted much misreading and wrongheadedness. The same critics who ask that a literary work be fresh, impromptu, and firsthand become flustered when faced by these virtues. Standing much closer to the life it describes, much of which is interior, than does any earlier White novel, *Voss* challenges some of our oldest assumptions about the longstanding but ill-defined reader-writer partnership.

I

Another ill-defined connection involves Voss and the German explorer Ludwig Leichhardt, a botanist who made two long treks across Australia in the 1840s. In *Cooper's Creek,* Alan Moorehead discusses the march which took Leichhardt to the Gulf of Carpenteria in Northern Queensland and then on to Port Essington, near Darwin, in the Northern Territory. (Voss, a botanist himself, explored the northern reaches of Australia before the time of White's book.) Moorehead also mentions Augustus Charles Gregory, surveyor-general for Queensland, who went on two different expeditions looking for Leichhardt.[4] The line of descent joining Gregory to White's Colonel Hugo Hebden, who also spent time in Queensland and goes searching twice for Voss, is much clearer than the one between Voss and Liechhardt. In 1958 H.J. Oliver noted the parallels between the two explorers. Ten years later Marcel Aurosseau said that Voss and Leichhardt were dissimilar, that White's Laura Trevelyan and the Sydney woman with whom Leichhardt fell in love had nothing in common, and that Voss's western journey followed a different route from that of Leichhardt.[5] Perhaps White can solve the problem of Voss's ancestry himself. In 1962 he claimed, "It was only long after I had started writing *Voss* that I realized that there was a parallel between my explorer and Leichhardt. I certainly did not conceive the book in these terms."[6] Conception differs from execution, however. White obviously hadn't yet written so much of *Voss* that he couldn't add a few comparisons between the two perished German botanist-explorers after he discovered the parallel. Nor would the late entry of Colonel Hebden, the A.C. Gregory figure, wrench the book's technique. White's moving of the expedition from 1848 (when Leichhardt went out) to 1845 looks like a calculated maneuver to keep Voss out of the way of his counterpart. By all appearances, we can believe White's statement that he had written a good deal of *Voss* before stumbling on any parallel between his title figure and Leichhardt. On the other hand, White was too much the artist to bypass opportunities created by the parallel once he discovered it.

In the same 1962 interview where he denies having published *Voss* with Leichhardt in mind, White claims that the main push behind the novel came from "the idea of a megalomaniac explorer."[7] This definition of Voss, which tallies with White's 1973 view of his man as "a monomaniac, rather than a hero, and like all human beings flawed and fallible,"[8] fits the underlying metaphor of the trek. In a waggish half-truth, the reviewer of *Voss* in the [Sydney] *Observer* located the book's heart in the idea "that life can be considered a series of mad expeditions."[9] The nineteenth century was an age of expeditions, both fictional and realistic, in which the individual pitted himself against the forces of nature. H.M.S. *Beagle,* with Charles Darwin aboard, roved the southern hemisphere; Captain Ahab piloted the *Pequod* in search of the white whale; Stan Parker of *Tree* was named after Stanley, the English explorer of Africa. The wild urge that drove Dr. Livingstone, The Swiss Family Robinson, and Conrad's Mr. Kurtz to seek new limits also spurs Voss. White's explorer snubs the consolations of love, family, and friendship to look for some mysterious deeper fulfillment. From the outset, though, the purity of his mission is smirched. Preferring to cross the desert alone and barefoot, he accepts money, provisions, and companions, even though they mar his heroic ideal. His resentment expresses itself vividly in his treatment of his patron,

Edmund Bonner, the rich draper of Sydney and suburban Potts Point. Reasonably enough, Bonner feels entitled to have a say about the trip he is financing. Voss registers his contempt for this interference by accepting Bonner's cash, rejecting his friendship, and, wildest arrogance of all, asking to marry his niece. Such high-handedness typifies him. Little moves him at first besides imposing and expanding his ego. Though a botanist, he displays little interest in flowers. When Laura shows him one of her uncle's camellias in chapter 4, he replies lamely, "Interesting" (p. 83). The same terse boredom marks his response in chapter 8 to a lily shown him by a colleague. Not only can't he identify the variety of lily; when he is told that the rest of the trip may not disclose another lily so fresh, he also says, with a yawn, that the lily looks commonplace. He responds no more keenly to fauna than to flora: he beats mules, shoots a dog, and orders a horse killed.

Voss's world is a poor show. He reacts no more imaginatively to people than to animals or plants. Socially awkward and easily flustered, he can neither grant nor receive hospitality. He offers his visitors no food or drink in his Sydney room, and he lacks the social grace to accept a dinner invitation, even after a walk of four kilometers has hungered him. He looks so starved after leaving the Bonners, having claimed that his belly is full, that he is offered a scrap of bread by a stranger. Characteristically, he turns down the offer, preferring to indulge his dreams of loneliness. This demonic scarecrow can't pay for a scrap of bread with some polite conversation, let alone sit down with others to dinner. The backs of his trouser bottoms are frayed, as if his bloated self-esteem has tilted his head toward the clouds and set him walking on his heels. The Bonners' servant, Rose Portion, refers to him as a man rather than a gentleman when he turns up unannounced in chapter 1, and her opinion of him doesn't improve. He inspires so little trust in her that she balks at having him wait in the study, lest he steal something. After the Bonners arrive home, he continues to go against etiquette, speaking out of turn and looking hungry when trying to convey good will. His blunders go beyond offending social graces. He mistakenly believes that Laura "would wear her faith cut to the usual feminine pattern" (p. 44). The error speaks poorly of him. Laura's absence from church during his unannounced Sunday morning visit to her uncle would have hinted to anyone less self-absorbed than he that her piety was not conventional at all.

His obtuseness hampers the overland trip. Voss doesn't champion justice, reason, or the rule of love. He harbors no dream of founding a new and better society. Besides seeing some beauty in a German poem, which he refuses to share with others, he shows little interest in art, extending an icy look both to Laura's piano music and to some Aboriginal cave paintings he finds in his travels. He will even negate the uplift of aesthetic response: to punish himself for enjoying the scenic beauty of Rhine Towers, he rejects an offer of a roof for the night in favor of camping outdoors. Only a fainting spell by one of his men persuades Voss to accept his hosts' hospitality. His tendency to vex people needlessly casts strong doubt on his ability to lead. Kiernan's reference to "Voss's absurd incompetence as a leader"[10] can be amply supported. Voss lacks common sense, to begin with. He wears thick, dark clothes in the summer; he sets out on the desert trek shortly before Christmas, i.e., both in the blazing heat and at a time when some of his colleagues would prefer to be with their families; he can't build a fire to cook the food he hasn't thought about rationing; he commits the costly error of not studying the terrain. After resting on Christmas Day, he orders the march be resumed in the cool of the evening. Unfortunately, the darkness more than offsets the advantages brought about by mild breezes and lower temperatures. The horses stumble in potholes, losing their balance, upsetting their mounts, and risking broken bones. At a heavy cost in time and morale, the march must halt within minutes. One shudders to think of the damage that might have occurred had it continued. The appearance of a snake in the men's path and the theft of some cattle on Christmas Eve, making the going-out an inverted night journey, show the fatuity of Voss's marching order. Such blunders come often. In the early going, when the sheep delay the march with their slowness, Voss refrains from killing them—only to do so later, when their reduced numbers and the refreshing rains have made them less of a liability.

"He would . . . experience fits of humiliating helplessness in the face of practical obstacles" (p. 28), says White of this visionary who can't cope with the mundane. In Chapter 1, a scant two weeks before setting out, he has yet to study a map of the land he wants to cross. "The map . . .? I will first make it" (p. 19), he says in a grandiose evasion, displaying no knowledge of map-reading, let alone map-making, in the coming action. Out on the western trail, he finds excuses to impose his will. He can neither humble himself nor accept the humble offerings of others, so anxious is he to live up to his own idea of leadership. When Judd offers him the ritual morsel of honor, the liver from the Christmas lamb he has cooked, Voss insists that the heat has taken away his appetite. Such behavior limns a parallel between him and his mules, who, suitably, both read and forecast his moods. A mule also shows him the folly of his mulishness by kicking him in the stomach. The richly deserved kick gives him a bruise which delays the trip for two days.

Others come to appreciate the appropriateness of the kick. "You no stop when ready" (p. 209), says an old Aboriginal of Voss's stubbornness. He is right to defect. A stranger to moderation, the self-tormented Voss makes such unfair demands on himself and his cohorts that only a mule, his mirror-image, can restrain him. Excess keeps haunting him. Anyone who denies his own feelings will likewise deny the feelings of others with impunity. In a leader, this suppression kills morale; all can't be sacrificed to expediency in a joint venture. Claiming that Gyp the sheep dog no longer serves a purpose after the sheep which start out with the expedition are all dead, he shoots the dog despite the men's protests. His purpose, to sacrifice a creature he himself loves for the sake of utility, backfires quickly. Gyp may no longer serve a practical use, but she helps morale, distracting the men from their worries and giving them a chance to be kind. Even the most grasping, whining expeditioner, the mutinous Turner, agrees to share his food with her if she can't find enough on her own. As with the ancient mariner's killing of the albatross, this denial of love by Voss brings on disaster. Much of the political wisdom of *Voss* stems from White's knowledge that, though all followers profit from their leader's wisdom, they all pay for his mistakes, as well. Gyp's death reminds the weary, gritty wayfarers that they, too, are dogs and could die as quickly and as arbitrarily as their former mascot. This inner malaise extends outward. Within hours of Gyp's death the men are battered from without as well as from within. "Rain like bullets" (p. 262) pelts them, making them chilled and feverish and corrupting them with self-pity as they trudge through hostile, spearlike grass.

Although he never admits his guilt, Voss links these adversities with his willful, pointless killing of Gyp. His asking Palfreyman if he will follow Judd when Judd decides to defect both fosters factionalism and calls his own leadership into question. He continues to incite mutiny, telling Judd, without provocation, that the presence of only one compass in the party's store of supplies will create awkwardness if the party divides. Nor are these references to mutiny his first expressions of guilt. In chapter 8 he gave Jackie, the young Aboriginal guide, the clasp knife with which Jackie will behead him in chapter 13. White handles the exchange discreetly, letting it convey its own meaning. The bleak, isolated Voss is choosing neither his murderer nor his murder weapon; on the other hand, he knows his present life isn't worth prolonging, and he doubts that he can improve it. Beatson says shrewdly of him, "He is a sick man rather than a sinner . . . terrified of love and suffering. He wants to mortify and destroy his body. . . . He is almost monastic by temperament, but his monasticism is perverse and deluded."[11] The trek exaggerates his delusions and perversions. The sterner the demands, the better, he reasons, glad for the chance to tend the anguished bowels of Frank Le Mesurier. Yet his assistance is calculated and hence corrupt. Rather than extending compassion, he nurses Frank in order to feel virtuous. Whatever humor he musters makes Frank feel worse, not better. He reminds Frank several times of his indebtedness, and he assures him, while he is cavebound, that dying in a cave is preferable to dying in the open. The remark gives scant comfort. Frank is more his victim than his patient. To discredit Judd, his rival for dominance within the group, Voss defies his better judgment, feeding Frank some goat's milk that Judd had brought and thereby causing the expected onslaught of diarrhea.

His men's welfare leaves Voss indifferent throughout. In the same episode in which heavy rains have pushed the men into a cave, Palfreyman plants some greens intended to help cure Turner's scurvy. As a botanist and former medical student, Voss, having happened upon the greens, should have connected their healing properties with Turner's complaint. As a leader, he should have rated the needs of his subordinates over his own. Instead, this selfish fanatic, who will later sponge up dew from rocks and plants for his private use, eats the cress and mustard sprouts, "stuffing the green stuff into his mouth, like an animal" (p. 283). A last perversion of leadership in the cave episode involves the violation of privacy. While Frank sleeps, Voss goes through his gear and takes out the notebooks containing the prose poems that the invalid has been writing but has refused to show any of his colleagues.

Surely there must be more to this monomaniac than pride, ignorance of morale, and selfishness. Otherwise the shrewd businessman Edmund Bonner wouldn't have offered to finance his expedition; Frank Le Mesurier wouldn't have called him "sir" in Sydney weeks before deciding to follow him into the outback; an independent, intelligent woman like Laura Trevelyan wouldn't have fallen in love with him. What these people admire in Voss is his fearlessness and his disdain of money. Even if his motives for crossing Australia's dry heart outpace those of money and fame in their arrogance, how many of us would dare to dream on such a grand scale, let alone live our dream? Voss needs no one's approval; he acts to impress no one; he asks for no rewards other than those he can wring from self-mortification. The trek is its own object. In an oft-quoted passage he defends his belief in God on the basis of his own preening vanity. The divinity he intuits within himself impels his belief in an all-powerful God: "Atheists are atheists usually for mean reasons. . . . The meanest of these is that they themselves are so lacking in magnificence they cannot conceive the idea of a Divine Power" (p. 84). The vastness of the desert he deems an apt challenge to his capacity for heroism. He needs no reason to cross Australia, only a purpose which, coming from within, needs no external justification. Goaded by mystery, he can encounter his demon, a mirror image of the dryness and blankness he sees in the desert.

But he has misjudged. Faced directly, the desert is more than a huge, monotonous waste. The buzzing insects, the swirling air currents of sand, and the rising shimmers of heat make Voss and his men dizzy. The heavy rains that fall during the wet season flood the dry creekbeds and leave the rest of the sandy terrain impassable, immobilizing him and his party. Meanwhile, hostile blacks have been stealing whatever provisions the insects and the humidity haven't already spoiled. The wilderness is not the abstraction Voss thought it was. One reason why Judd effortlessly surpasses him as a leader inheres in his having suffered physically; he knows what to expect from the wilderness. An emancipist, he has a first-hand grasp of the brutishness of reality, whereas Voss's is all derived and self-willed. Several forces ripen Voss. Judd does physically and morally what the desert achieves topographically and what Laura accomplishes romantically: he shows Voss that he is not the God he had thought he was. Voss sets out to conquer distance; instead he conquers himself. Only in defeat does he attain vision. Defeat gives him cause to rejoice. Crossing the desert successfully would only have hardened the pride that blocked his path to the divine. The desert trek—and White knows that many of the world's great prophets have come from the desert—causes several inversions. Voss's most significant journeys become spiritual, rather than geographical. Ironically, no compass will help him reach his goal, for his inward journey counts more than the one he takes across terrain. In a Nietzschean transvaluation of values, he reaches the point where depths lead upward. Suffering teaches him humility, which he had previously despised as an inferior emotion. He both extends compassion to other sufferers and learns to accept help, even from strangers. Seeing that ordeals take on new meanings when they are shared by others joins him to the human community. In weakness lies strength; that is a truth that defies both reason and vanity. Suitably, this reversal of values comes to him in a dream, where his practical, striving self can't refute it. In his heart Voss wants to be led. The process, though not sectarian, fuses Christian epistemology and teleology; paradoxically, he must shed his godlike airs before becoming godlike. We must be shown our dreadful apartness from God before we can piece out the identity. The fate of the man-god on earth is to be broken physically and then reborn in spirit. Man only confirms his divine origins indirectly. Laura, who plays the archetypal role of intervening woman for her man, describes the steps by which spirit descends into matter, merges with it, and then rises from it to blend with the world spirit: "How important it is to understand the three stages. Of God into man. Man. And man returning to God" (p. 380).

Diminution is necessary to Voss. Relaxing his grip on his pride and seeing half his expedition party break away from him help him pierce the closed circuit of self. Although he fails to win his predetermined prize, he gains a more important one whose very existence he had been unaware of. Learning to value humility gives vent to the woman lurking inside his man's heart. Other benefits follow his attaining a full, balanced growth. Once he establishes the flow of feeling, he frees himself from the corrosive action of the will. Revelation replaces struggle as life's actuating principle. "The paradox of man in Christ, and Christ in man" (p. 336) replaces rational formulations and the quest for tangible proofs. Wholeness replaces division, profane or human love showing itself to be a category of divine love. Just as Voss's tie with Laura strengthens in direct ratio to the miles that separate him from her, so the recognition that he is not divine show him ways to develop his divine potential.

II

His recognition comes slowly. At first, the expedition is led by a Captain Ahab figure who tries to subordinate all to his own purpose. Like the crew of the *Pequod,* the membership of the expedition—a German, a Frenchman, two Aboriginals, and three Britons—is a microcosm of humanity. This carefully selected lot of wayfarers breaks down from different perspectives to include a scientist and poet, a landowner and an emancipist, a stoic and a grouch, and a youth and an adult. White obviously wants to lend his insights universality. The men's steady, grinding contact with each other as they slog across the desolate, unfeatured desert directs this breadth to thematic ends. New standards of judgment and new alignments take hold as the march presses on. The ornithologist Tom Palfreyman and the gentleman Ralph Angus both profit from their association with Turner, a whining gutter rat they'd never have bothered to know if the march hadn't brought them together. The solicitude with which Turner is cared for by Angus and Palfreyman when scurvy takes him exposes the self-seeking behind Voss's attentions to Frank Le Mesurier, as well. We have already seen Voss worsening Frank's suffering in order to score against Judd. His surreptitious reading of Frank's books sharpens his fears of inadequacy. Both he and Frank are searching for a transfigured, ennobled self, and the prose poems show that his follower is much further along in the quest than he, the leader. G.A. Wilkes has said of the poems: "They are the work of a man who has exposed himself to the reality of the material world that Voss's egoism has rejected, and who has been able to shed his sense of individuality in that exposure: a state in which he finds himself nearest to humility and love. Le Mesurier looks to the complete disintegration of the self in death, with his spirit then distributed everywhere, as the ultimate fulfillment."[12] Before reading the poems, Voss had based his program of self-fulfillment on the qualities he had brought to the expedition. Frank's wish to realize himself through destruction shows Voss that negation precedes rebirth; one incarnation of the self must die before another can come into being. The process has already started, the leader learning from his follower just as the healer gains strength from ministering, however selfishly, to his patient. Voss sees that Frank has broken through the structures of a corrupt world. Having transcended both causality and selfhood, he follows Job and Milton's Samson by accepting divine inscrutability. He has allowed God to be God rather than a projection of his own ideas about divine order, justice, and love. Yet his suicide shows that he lacks the physical endurance and moral courage to do justice to his vision. Having learned from his example, a less self-enclosed Voss carries on his metaphysical work.

A more threatening rival-partner to Voss is the adaptable, all-purpose Judd. Bonner recounts Judd's virtues accurately when he explains why he added the emancipist to the team of explorers: "a man of physical strength and moral integrity. An improviser, besides, which is of the greatest importance in a country where necessities are not always to hand" (p. 18). Judd lives up to this advance billing. Always busy, he builds a raft, keeps and reads the instruments of navigation, mends both a bridle and a torn shirt. Having suffered, he has both the skill and the insight to relieve suffering in others. He helps strengthen the convalescing Palfreyman before the action begins by spooning out rum to him; in the early part of the trek, he binds Voss's head wound with his own clean handkerchief. These acts of mercy show him to have attuned himself to the spirit as well as to physical reality. He understands morale, for instance, much better than does his leader. Judd recommends that the march be halted to celebrate Christmas; Judd roasts the Christmas lamb. His mastery, all the more impressive for not calling attention to itself, cheers all. Even though Voss resents and feels menaced by it, he, too, is impressed. Thanks partly to Judd, he comes to view compassion and humility as strengths, rather than as faults. Womanly grace and gentleness can temper the male virtues of hardiness, endurance, and physical courage in the toughest old bull. Whenever Voss opens himself to this soft, healing glow, his soul expands, though his tense, angry pride often rebels. With Judd, as with Laura, who teaches him the same humanizing lesson, he must be force-fed wisdom, and he balks even at the unconscious level. Two conflicting motives led a sleepwalking Voss to put in Judd's saddlebag a compass that is later declared missing. Whereas his competitive, insecure self wants to discredit Judd, making him look like a thief and a usurper, his honesty and sense of fair play prod him to hand over the instruments of navigation as a tribute to Judd's superiority.

The sleepwalking, though enacted with a divided heart, adds to the unity that builds through the expedition. Blurring the margin between dream and walking, it joins with the woman-in-man and Christ-in-man motifs. Other narrative materials have already been worked to serve wholeness. Expressing the book's belief in its characters as people rather than as symbols, Laura both misreads and resists the tie joining her to Voss. Although she admires him for his fearless, unmaterialistic outlook, her admiration expresses itself more sexually than she credits. She is both repelled and fascinated by the hairs sprouting from his wrists and fingers, such hairs always symbolizing male sexuality in White. Only after she intuits his death does she realize that her attraction to him was physical, and even then she admits nothing. The lovers' moments of mystical communion rise from dreams and attacks of delirium, and the couple deals guardedly with sex. Other implications follow. In chapter 10 it is Frank Le Mesurier, not Voss, who repeats Laura's experience of feeling mystically refreshed and engulfed by a rainstorm. One meaning of this exact parallel may be that Frank would have suited Laura better than Voss under normal conditions.

The distance dividing Voss from the tenderness he needs to become human shows in both the rhetoric and the content of his letter of proposal. But the stiff, withdrawn style of the letter counts less than his reason for writing it. Giving his effort the credit it deserves, John B. Beston notes that "Voss has . . . opted for the path toward humanization by writing the letter."[13] The explorer has moved as close as he can to another person, yet he hasn't moved far. Sounding more defensive than vulnerable, his words lack the abandon of an anxious lover's. Feelings scarcely enter his plea. Instead of mentioning his heart, he refers to "the plan of life that fate has prepared for each of us" (p. 148). If he and Laura are fated to marry, why fog the issue with emotion? Need and passion continue to get short shrift. In the middle of his letter, in its shortest paragraph, he tells Laura that he'd like to marry her—but he never explains why. In fact, he never returns to the topic of marriage at all. The pleasures and excitements of love have never influenced his thinking, he would have Laura believe. He ends not by voicing soft words, but by looking forward to the opportunity to describe for her benefit various details of the flora and fauna he expects to find in his coming travels.

Beston sees more anger than affection in Laura's reply. "In this letter she writes of their mutual hatefulness and common arrogance,"[14] he argues, noting that Laura has taken her cue from Voss's self-protective aloofness. Some of Beston's argument flows well. He understands the problems facing Laura in writing her letter of acceptance, and he explains how she copes with them. The problems demand discretion. Whereas she wants to marry Voss, she understands that she couldn't bear living with him on his bleak, bloodless terms. Thus she must stop him from setting the style for the marriage without discouraging him from wanting to marry her. She will attack his balance and his pride. If he is consistent, she will appear to waver and reverse field; to break down his detachment, she will introduce religious (but not sexual) fervor. Her letter begins sarcastically and ends devoutly, starting on a note of divisiveness and doubt and closing with the promise of unity. It replaces judgment with faith. Laura challenges Voss's assumptions, his stance, and what she believes to be his view of her. She has been duelling skillfully. If Voss accepts her acceptance, she stands a good chance of controlling the marriage. The success of the letter will also show her how to maintain control. Much of her carefully mapped strategy consists of anticipating his responses. Her self-demeaning start contains a hidden lure. Because she esteems Voss, she must credit his contempt for her. This attitude he had never voiced or held; otherwise he'd not have proposed to her. On the other hand, his vaulting ego could trick him into adopting it, were it to originate with her. Then she says that, despite her confusion (hoping that her logic is confusing *him*), she sees him as her mirror image; his pride runs as deep as her humility. Next comes her proviso: she will marry him providing they pray together, he to beat back his arrogance and she to quell those self-doubts that make her so unworthy of him. But she doesn't feel unworthy, and she never did. The condition she poses is absolute; he can come to her only on her terms. This absoluteness clashes with her self-demeaning words. She has fabricated inferiority in order to bring Voss to a level where she can understand and control him.

The self-sufficiency Laura demonstrates in her letter also marks her behavior elsewhere. She receives Voss in her aunt and uncle's house in the opening scene because her skepticism kept her from joining the family at church. Then she defends Voss to the family, who find him stiff, shabby, and remote. Her greatest show of compassion also hinges on her ability to resist the majority. In the teeth of her relatives' objections, she looks after the servant, Rose Portion, when Rose is discovered to be pregnant. Installed in the best bedroom during the last stages of her confinement, Rose dominates and sets the tone for her employers' household, thanks to Laura's recognition of her need. Although a servant's unwanted pregnancy could easily become a subject of comedy in a work dealing with a nouveau riche household like that of the Bonners, White treats it from the Jamesian standpoint of moral perception and growth. Existence itself is at stake, as only Laura has the clarity to see. Preferring to love rather than to judge or analyze, she takes her stand in favor of life, its sacredness, mystery, and right to be protected. This love is untainted. If Mercy becomes her adoptive daughter after Rose's death, she didn't pique Laura's acquisitiveness before it. Laura knows the hurdles facing Rose's unborn baby because she is an orphan herself. That her tie with Voss arouses her maternal instinct certifies the love as a productive, reversible process. Just as the strength Voss gains from her allows him to push forward on his desert march, so does the love he sends back build and refine her feelings. She comes alive in places she never knew existed.

Barry Argyle has summarized the effect of Laura's growth on both Voss and the action: "She fulfills the demands of the novel, which requires her to be Eve, the Virgin Mary, Gretchen, and a young woman of Australia in 1848."[15] Perhaps an aesthetic miscue helps her meet some of these requirements. Laura's honesty and independence smack of self-congratulation. When she spurns the idea of using her uncle's store to entice eligible bachelors, she exposes the half-baked values of suburban Sydney's upper crust as neatly as the country squire, White, could wish. He rewards her by making her beautiful, by arranging that she be born in England, as was he, and by giving her the resoundingly English surname of Trevelyan. But his critics have objected less to his endorsement of Laura than to the telepathic communion linking her and Voss during the tormented last stages of the explorer's life. Concentrating their wills, Voss and Laura send their spirits out to each other, their mutual love overcoming great tracts of space. So keenly attuned is she to the fiancé whom she knows she will never see again, let alone marry, that she comes down with brain fever during his death throes. This flow of instinctive or telepathic understanding between lovers or soulmates has precedents in English-language fiction; Jane Eyre and Edward Rochester and, later, Leopold Bloom and Gerty McDowell in the "Nausicaä" (the name Nausicaä riveted George Goodman in *Aunt's Story* [pp. 59–60]) section of *Ulysses* communicate wordlessly.

"Telepathic communication does exist," said White in 1973, "I'm continually receiving evidence of it myself. I'm convinced that life is built on coincidence and strange happenings."[16] Many others have believed in acausal connections, so telepathy can't be dismissed as a cheap mystical indulgence. Nor can White be faulted for invoking it indiscriminately. Laura and Voss commune telepathically at a time when hallucination and delirium have razed barriers imposed by reason. What is more, the communion, besides bridging the gulf between lovers, connects the human to the divine; much of the novel's metaphysical bite comes from its depiction of faith, mercy, and humility as forces more powerful than those set up by pragmatism and motives of material gain. The issue isn't whether telepathy belongs in a closely observed narrative like *Voss* or whether White uses it to sidestep the rigors of plot building. A more legitimate grumble stems from its inappropriateness to White's view of sexuality. Does White's portrait of Voss and Laura's all-transcending love match Voss's elitist scorn for the everyday? Voss and Laura have attained the poetry of spiritual intimacy without having first dealt with the prose of each other's foibles. After a life of close sharing, Stan and Amy Parker still don't know each other. How has the superfine mutual comprehension of Voss and Laura, who spend much less time together, bypassed the tensions of human dynamics? In yoking Voss and Laura as soulmates, White is deriding the same palpable, contingent world that he puts forth elsewhere as the seat of all value. The lovers don't know each other well enough to scale heights attained briefly by the Parkers perhaps two or three times in a marriage spanning fifty years. White has made them soar without first proving that they can walk hand in hand. Furthermore, his couples rarely walk together, their sexual tie causing much more grief than joy. The mystical union of Voss and Laura doesn't fit with the numerous bad marriages and broken love affairs described elsewhere by White. It takes place largely because the action calls for it. Lacking human content, it fails to erase the sad realities that love flows more smoothly from a distance and that embracing a spirit is less taxing than embracing a person.

Another mystical connection works better than the one joining Laura to Voss. It involves the coincidence of Voss's arrival in the Aboriginal camp where he later dies and the appearance, in the heavens, of a spectacular comet. The comet symbolizes the patriarch in the Aboriginal pantheon, "the Great Snake, the grandfather of all men, that had come down from the north in anger" (p. 373). Because Voss's arrival in their camp coincides with the sighting of the comet, the Aboriginals equate the two phenomena. Voss expands into a God while his body shrinks and dries. Like a comet, he strews his residue across the Australian outback. His hosts believe in his divinity all too well, killing him and then eating his flesh in order to win strength from his supernatural powers. In Sydney his name is also written large. People speak of him as God or the devil; "He was more than a man" (p. 437), Judd says of him twenty years after the expedition, at the unveiling of a statue in his honor. But his sufferings have not merely passed into the officialdom of bronze statuary and "garlands of rarest newspaper prose" (p. 434). Anxious to unearth the meaning of the expedition, Colonel Hebden goes looking for Voss in the outback two years after the explorer is declared lost. Hebden's coming within earshot of the mute remains of Angus and Turner and his just missing Dugald and Jackie, the two Aboriginal guides, before their deaths look like stage-managed events. But White isn't so much gloating or mocking as delaying the discovery of information about Voss's pilgrimage. The greater the energy, the more explosive its release. By falling short of his goal, Voss has created goals for others. Colonel Hebden is the first of these others; he has been inspired to test his energies in fresh ways. By such steps individual development channels into the growth of a national self-awareness. In the book's last chapter Hebden resolves to search for Voss again, some eighteen years after his first try. But the Australian future that Voss has helped shape isn't exclusively white or European. Like his murder victim, to whom he is eternally linked, Jackie becomes a legend and a prophet, moving constantly and voicing truths that vex the souls of his hearers. White invites the possibility that one of these dark-skinned hearers will feel vexed enough to discover Voss's place in the Aboriginal consciousness. His hint is well advised. By the end of the book, Voss's impact on the land in which he dreamed, toiled, and suffered has not yet been assessed. Many options and approaches remain open. For White to gauge Voss's impact would be for him to impose a limit on the powers both of Voss's spirit and of spiritual activity itself.

III

The desert, where Voss suffered most, is the arena in which his legendary role will work itself out. The different views of him taken by Aboriginals and whites rest on differences which the grindstone of Australia's dry interior sharpens. *Voss* describes what happens when one culture tries to impose itself on another. Like Twain and Conrad before him, White shows that touching the wilderness spoils it; the trek brings out the worst in the simple Aboriginals and the complex Europeans comprising the team of explorers. The European mind lacks both the training and the patience to make sense of the outback, a bleak, nondescript vastness but also an imaginative landscape full of subtlety and awe. Western man's passion for control can't upset its natural balance, which proves pervasive and unconquerable. The menace conveyed by its stark, stony emptiness takes different shapes. Its sandhills, rocky, treeless slopes, and featureless flatlands broken only by tufts of saltbush provide no shade or shelter; its insects and heat spoil food; its hammering rains puddle swirling, blinding dust into mud. Such hardships encourage motives of endurance, not conquest, showing Voss his limitations and moving him to new depths of concentration. Dorothy Green judges well when she calls the expedition "a metaphysical success."[17] It is the majestic desert, with its blazing days, cold nights, and hostile blacks that purifies the hearts of the pilgrims and forces the metaphysical confrontations.

But the hot, dry stretch of land that the travelers cross isn't the book's only desert. Suburban Sydney is another wilderness. White loathes snobbery most of all when it parades as generosity. In the passages just before Voss's overthrow, White's comparisons between Potts Point and the desert go beyond satire. Chapter 13 alternates between the desert and the Bonners' home, where Laura is reeling from brain fever. It is while she is believed to be dying that she sees most clearly into Voss's pain. Her spirit also goes out to the others on the vast overland trek. Her turning green during her attack of brain fever relates her to Frank Le Mesurier, Harry Robarts, and Turner, all of whose skin goes green at or near the time of death. These resemblances don't exclude Voss; the savagery and horror of chapter 13 promote unity rather than division. Again, symbolism helps build wholeness. Voss's death isn't the finale of the throbbing chapter, let alone of the book. His spirit reawakens in Laura, who breaks her fever within moments of his death. Her recovery is carefully prefigured. The middle act of the seventh, or middle, subchapter of chapter 13 had shown Voss declaring his faith in God. His trusting God rather than relying on his own energies both fulfills the condition set forth in Laura's acceptance letter and confirms his spiritual tie with the child Mercy.

Then the thematic focus either swerves from Voss or expands. His beheading makes him more a precursor than a savior. Other scriptural

parallels invite themselves. Jackie, who was badgered into killing his
master, profits as little from his treachery as did Judas. No one will hear his
confession with enough compassion to absolve him; children run from his
wild looks; each tribe he visits sends him away. After hearing that "the
black . . . gives up the gold" (p. 356) in the act of burning, Voss sees
Jackie's body as "black-gold" (p. 356). The process of burning away
impurities resembles that described by Abyssinia's volcanic eruption in
The Aunt's Story. Jackie's spiritual translation may be more fascinating
than Voss's because, having sinned more darkly, Jackie must dig more
deeply into himself to win contrition, repentance, and expiation. But
White, forced to be selective, can only hint at this rich spiritual drama.
Narrative consistency rules out its development.

Unity also inheres in White's artful foreshadowing of Frank's death.
The first words we hear of Frank, before meeting him, come from Voss:
"Frank has great qualities, if he does not cut his throat" (p. 17). In chapter
2, during a talk in Sydney, Frank tells Voss that he hasn't yet decided to
join the expedition because "I am not sure that I want to cut my throat just
yet" (p. 31). The headlessness created by his throat-slitting installs Frank
in the role of John the Baptist *vis-à-vis* Voss's Christ without negating
Voss's role as headless precursor to Australia's unidentified, perhaps even
unborn, redeemer. This overlapping or extension of roles enriches the
novel. It also cooperates with other narrative elements to organize the
reader's responses; the suggestion that Frank is a precursor implies the
interpenetrability of spirit. Often attacked for willful obscurity, the Patrick
White of *Voss* will use various structural or poetic devices to help the
reader. As a surprise he introduces, in the last chapter, a survivor of Voss's
expedition twenty years before. But he makes us read halfway through the
chapter before identifying the survivor. His deliberation in revealing the
impact of Voss's letter of proposal on Laura and Laura's written response
also keeps us turning pages anxiously while acquiring information which
may color her thinking.

White gains a major benefit by withholding the contents of the reply:
he can telescope the world of the trek with that of Potts Point. If Laura and
Voss are to defeat distance and absence with their love, they need a
common foothold. Chapters 6–12 don't provide this steadiness because
they alternate between the two settings. Yet the alternation contains
echoes and leaves residues. White uses repetition and foreshadowing to
spell out the interdependence between the stationary female-dominated
world of suburban Sydney and the moving male one of the expedition. In
chapter 7 Laura has some peaches on her dessert plate which look "almost
bloody" (p. 158); the sky to the west of Jildra, where the travelers arrive
early in chapter 8, is "of a blood red" (p. 162). Such references prefigure
the literal bloodshed that will haunt the lovers, as Laura relives Voss's

hardships both physically and spiritually during her sickness. In addition, some of the same topographical conditions prevail in the book's two main settings. Rose Portion's coffin is carried up "a crumbly slope" (p. 229) to Sand Hills; shortly before her burial, Voss's party crosses some "spent and crumbly" (p. 205) ground while trudging through a particularly hot and barren stretch of wilderness; finally, "the desert the house [in Potts Point] had become" (p. 352) to Mrs. Bonner during Laura's sickness shows heat and dryness turning a fashionable suburb into a wasteland.

The garden-and-desert interplay begins subtly in the first scene. In fact, the book's short opening sentences, evoking vastness and a sense of immensity with the tracts of white space to their right, launch a narrative in which distance and blankness predominate. The three characters intro-duced straightaway also figure most prominently in organizing the blank-ness and distance. None of the three was born in Australia; two, Voss and Laura, will adopt spiritually the daughter of the third, the emancipist Rose Portion, but only after great suffering. The suffering is hinted at by the embarrassment Voss's unannounced visit has caused. The German has arrived at a bad moment; his first recorded instance of poor planning and bad timing comes about because his prospective host is at church. Voss should have known better than to visit Bonner unannounced on a Sunday morning, but, a chronic victim of tunnel vision, he repeats his mistake shortly. In chapter 3, another of his impromptu visits causes embarrass-ment. He arrives at the Bonners' just as the family is setting out for a picnic. A plan of action must be adopted quickly. Although the picnic can't be delayed, neither can Voss be turned away after having walked from Sydney. He is invited to join in, even though his puritanical disdain of fun might spoil the outing for the others. The worries of these others are justified quickly, as he bangs his head climbing into a carriage full of women. Stiff, sweaty, and unkempt among the well-dressed female pic-nickers, he continues to exude discomfort. Laura picks up many of his vibrations. She is more deeply stirred during the picnic than she lets on, just as her body language and word choice showed her to be fencing hard for position with Voss in chapter 1. The consistency of her responses is revealing. The shabby, bearded Voss's ill-advised Sunday morning visit got the book off to a strong start. The explorer entered Laura's life soon after she renounced her belief in God. Without either of them understanding the process, Voss soon replaces God in her imagination. She says to him, a week after their first meeting, "I am fascinated by you. . . . *You* are my desert" (p. 84).

Laura's rising interest in Voss contrasts admirably with the sinking spirits of the explorers. Alternating rhythms of hope and gloom within the expedition further counterpoint the crescendo achieved by Laura's com-bined romantic and spiritual affirmations. The trip starts badly. Chapter 5, most of which takes place at Sydney's Circular Wharf, is full of hesitations, stops, and false starts owing to the lack of wind; Voss's ship can't sail out of the harbor. A spot of comedy does produce a gust, but not of the needed kind. The send-off speech given by the governor's deputy, one Colonel Fetherstonhaugh (the pronunciation of whose name, Fanshawe, sounds like a breeze) bulges with bombast. A 125-word sentence (pp. 109–10) describing the nervous movements of the captive dockside listeners conveys the colonel's windy pomposity. As a proper finale to the speech, a neighing horse drops its dung. One discharge of gas and waste has replaced another, the onlookers' recognition of the similarity between the two restoring life to its normal ambiguities.

Elsewhere moods shift without the help of comedy. Chapter 12, for instance, begins positively; the end of the rainy season has allowed the party to move ahead after a delay of two or three months. Suddenly negation sets in. The loss or theft of a compass disorients and soon brings the expedition to grief. In an act of Coleridgean portent, the second of its kind, Turner shoots a bird. Death continues to have its way. At Voss's command, Judd kills a sick horse; Palfreyman is slain by Aboriginals; Judd, Turner, and Angus defect from their leader and turn back, with only Judd surviving the long pull home.

But the efforts of the three mutineers finally serve the same ends as do those of Voss and his loyal retainers. The music put forth by *Voss* does indeed disturb us with its stubborn sonorities.[18] The work's pattern of rises and falls sets up an emotional rhythm that pulsates in the blank, unexplored reaches of the heart. Its dark emotional power makes *Voss* perhaps White's most intense, frightening book. In addition, the characters, most of whom start out prizing the abstract and the mechanical over the human, are an unsympathetic lot. Yet their energies serve richly human purposes; nearly every one of them grows both emotionally and spiritually. *Voss* refutes the critics who have scathed White for using literature to indulge his bitterness and revulsion over mankind's follies. Rather than positing an elitism of suffering, the book puts the goal of self-transcendence within reach of all. The grit and the glare, the thirst and the screaming monotony of the desert form White's metaphor of the pilgrimage some of us must undertake. The ordeal can hearten as well as distress; security and stability can be plucked from the remorseless flow of time.

No one is denied access to heaven, either. Though strewn with torments half-buried under sandy wastes, *Voss* points the various paths to attainment. Some are rockier and steeper than others; some call forth heretofore untapped energies. None rules out the validity of any other. The suburban matron Belle Bonner Radclyffe, the secular pragmatist Albert Judd, and the visionary poet Frank Le Mesurier all carve out permanence. Conceived as a study of a monomaniac, the mystical, inquiring *Voss* extends White's democratic principles into the orbit of metaphysics. Voss's worries about dominance get swept into God's politics; sexual love becomes a category of divine love; the spirits of its black and white sufferers give Australia an intensity of self-awareness that encroaches upon religion. *The Aunt's Story* lacks *Voss*'s range of well-drawn characters; the more secular *Tree of Man* cannot match its thematic richness. Perhaps White's breakthrough novel, *Voss* sounds greater metaphysical depths and extends greater compassion over a landscape more insistently abrasive than any other work by his hand.

7. The Sowing
of the Seed

Riders in the Chariot (1961) treats time the way *Voss* treated space—conveying its mystery, displaying its effects, and, with a metaphysical fillip, downgrading its import. Life obeys a strict economy in White; effects follow causes, and what happens is inevitable, even if its meaning bypasses most. The shabby figure of Israel, the Dyer of Holunderthal, in northern Germany, reveals the pervasiveness of home truths. The grubby, mousy dyer, indelibly stained with the colors of his craft, remains a force long after leaving the action. He indirectly introduces Himmelfarb to his future wife; he attends the wedding, the only member of the older generation to represent the parentless bridegroom; after not seeing the dyer for decades, the once-nervous groom, now a widower of sixty, mistakenly thinks he spots him in a shed into which he and other Jews have been herded by the Gestapo. To convey the impact of early influences like that of the dyer, the novel alternates past and present episodes, teasing out parallels between them. This strategy frees the novel from the shrillness of the present while providing the unity that comes from a single setting. The two benefits interlock. Whereas the fixed reference of an Easter season shortly after the end of World War II sharpens White's investigation of redemption and resurrection, the echoes created by going back to early twentieth-century Germany and England give the investigation added force.

Like materialist-conformist Australia after World War II, the past seethes with conflict. War is mentioned twice in the book's opening pages. In chapter 3 Mary Hare tells how she lost a parent in each world war. Himmelfarb fought with the German infantry in the First War and came to Australia because of the Second; during the time of the novel, he lives on a street called Montibello (after Latin *bellum,* meaning war) Road. The turmoil seizing the soul of the artist Alf Dubbo has made him a battlefield of conflicting drives. Nor is he alone in his self-division. All the characters in the novel struggle against an internal enemy. Because none can reach an armistice, their wars are as deadly as any fought with bullets or bombs; as usual, White's people tend to hurt themselves more than their enemies hurt them. David Bradley has shown how each of the novel's four apostles carries a long-standing burden of failure and guilt: Mary Hare suspects that she could have saved her father from drowning; Ruth Godbold watched her brother die after falling from a hay cart; Himmelfarb fled Germany rather than searching for his wife after her capture by the Gestapo; Dubbo deserted the cleric who raised him.[1] The four apostles, or illuminati, don't suffer alone. Bradley's roster of the guilt-laden can be extended by adding Harry Rosetree, or Haim Rosenbaum, whose denial of his Jewish heritage becomes self-denial, and those two harpies, Mrs. Jolley and Mrs. Flack, who live together in enmity after forfeiting the love of their families. As these three sufferers learn, adherence to reason and social convention redeems nothing. The novel's four immaculati all transcend the self by negating it and denying the will; like the four living beings in the prophet Ezekiel's vision of God, they attain a wisdom and a freedom beyond the reaches of common sense. None of these paragons of inwardness perceives reality piecemeal; none attains vision by walking in socially approved paths. Rather, each grasps truth as a whole, perceiving on the inner planes of consciousness and making connections while forgoing analysis. Purveyors of special insights painfully wrested from life, they also recognize and accept each other. Like White's visionaries in *Aunt's Story*, *Tree of Man*, and *Solid Mandala*, they are not ordinary and forgettable but ugly, despised by others, and antisocial. However, their refusal to regulate their lives by reason has instilled in them a humility, an intimation of life's terror, and a faith in their power to direct this terror toward higher ends.

The same religious outlook that permeated *Voss* pulsates through *Riders*. White said in 1973 that the later book's four main figures "lead religious lives, Himmelfarb and Mrs. Godbold consciously; Alf Dubbo's attempts at painting are worshipful acts [as is Mary Hare's 'crawling on all fours through shrubbery']."[2] Patricia Morley has indicated how White varies the backgrounds of his four riders in order to universalize the book's religious vision: "A brief look at the four protagonists—Jew, mad spinster, half-caste artist, and washerwoman—reveals the true universality of White's vision. The Riders include two women and two men; two formal adherents of recognized religions, and two who seek the deity independently, in nature and in the truth of art. Their geographical origins and varieties of racial type (Jew and Gentile, Anglo-Saxon, European and aboriginal Australian) . . . suggest all men and all countries of the world. The social spectrum represented by their backgrounds is equally inclusive."[3] In 1979 Edgar L. Chapman expanded Morley's categories to identify each rider with one of the elements, with a lifestyle, and with both a sensory and an unconscious mode of perception.[4] The rich variety coloring the meeting of Mary Hare and Mordecai Himmelfarb at the end of Part One of *Riders* bears out the insights of Chapman and Morley. The meeting of the European city dweller and the Australian property owner invites contrasts of male intellectual and female primitive, of widower and virgin, and of Jew and pantheist. Mary Hare and Himmelfarb have attained their higher states of life both differently and similarly. The similarity stems from the chariot of the novel's title; the riders' response to the chariot provides the difference. Though each rider is fascinated by the chariot, none has a firm hold or full picture of it. One mumbles about it in a dream or trance; another is moved by a painting of it; a third learns of it from some Kabbalistic lore; it comes to the fourth as a hymn. None sees it clearly, none discovers its purpose. Those who discuss it speak guardedly and try to dispose of it quickly. Argyle's reading, besides explaining the chariot's universality, justifies the humility and doubt of the riders: "In using a symbol so universal, with its associations of Plato, Apollo, Ezekiel and Blake, White is able to tie up the three strands of European (and therefore Australian) culture: namely, Hebrew, Greek, and Roman Christian."[5] This manysidedness suits the novel. The Kabbala, perhaps the novel's chief source of ideas, endorses plurality. No single interpretation or opinion, it asserts, can explain the Torah. The meaning of this treasure of Jewish religious writing will take centuries to emerge, and that emergence will occur unpredictably. Some eras build on the findings of their predecessors, while others reject them. Some beliefs die; others resurface after lying quiescent; still others remain in force for a century. Himmelfarb's belief that history reflects spirit reworks the Hegelian idea that the essence of a people will emerge slowly.

But slowness makes us fret. We want truth in our lifetimes—the sooner the better. Expressing this natural urge to impetuosity, the chariot stands as one of the two main bodies of mystical interpretation in Jewish lore, the other being the creation. Jewish mystics have used the flight of the fiery chariot, from Ezekiel 1, as a means of describing heaven, which isn't seen in the Bible. In a deathbed dream Himmelfarb becomes Kadmon, transitional figure between God and Adam to the Kabbalists. He is about to wed the Shekinah, the feminine aspect of God. The marriage signifies greatly. Having exiled herself with the Jews (and thus identifying with Jerusalem and Israel), the Shekinah left God's side. Himmelfarb is also separated from his wife, or female self. His constant brooding over Reha's probable murder by the Nazis explains his dream of supernatural union as wish projection. He can't live his dream.

Himmelfarb's failure to merge the real and the ideal refers to another chariot—the one from Plato's *Phaedrus*. Plato describes the soul as a charioteer drawn by two horses. While one horse aspires to the heavens, the other pulls earthward. The metaphorical task of the charioteer is to stop the darker, vicious horse from running the chariot aground. His task applies to Himmelfarb because the Jew followed a wild youth with an ascetic, self-denying maturity. The dialectic engendered by the opposition of denial and indulgence begets no synthesis during his lifetime (that his dead wife's name is the same as that of the wife of Kronos the titan puts her beyond his reach). His three fellow riders share his plight. Fallible mortals all, they either fall short of blessedness or fail to credit themselves for achieving it. When Himmelfarb learns that atonement rests upon failure he says, "In that case many of us are saved who never expected it" (p. 171). To gauge the value of our achievements calls for the self-detachment of a mystic. But because the mystic scorns all goals other than that of gaining oneness with God, he would also recoil from all self-inventories based on worldly standards of success and failure. Only rarely will a divine intimation flash before him; still more rarely will he glean its meaning, as the novel's last paragraph insists. *Riders* follows the other work of White's maturity both in its close look at the interplay of the finite and the infinite and in its attempt to disclose the meaning of that cosmic interplay.

I

Morley judges well to call Mary Hare, the first apostle in *Riders,* a "nature mystic."[6] A shaman of sorts, Mary leaves her body to enter spiritually into the thoughts and feelings of animals. She seems poorly attuned to her physical self. One of her first acts in chapter 1 consists of upsetting a post office inkwell; when she was a child her father complained about her breaking valuable objects. But the stumpy, grubby Mary is only clumsy indoors and around manmade things; outdoors she thrives. She loves her home, the ruined Xanadu, all the more for the tree that has caved in one of its walls, for the insects that breed in its carpets, and for the moss and mildew patterns on its curtains. Her belief that life is drenched with goodness keeps her from distinguishing between indoors and out—and between the seen and the unseen: "I believe in what I see, and what I cannot see," she says in chapter 3; "I believe in a thunderstorm, and wet grass, and patches of light, and stillness. There is such a variety of good. On earth. And everywhere" (p. 57). She demonstrates her belief by crawling and burrowing through the underbrush around Xanadu and by putting herself on a level with whatever life she encounters. Literally in touch with nature, she will free a chick from its shell, warm it inside her blouse, or feed it from her mouth.

Her tunneling wisdom has revealed wonder in places where others wouldn't deign to look. Not only does she entangle herself in brambles and vines, befriending life without making exclusions; she also becomes spiritually absorbed by tables and chairs, and she observes, mimics, and interprets the behavior of animals. Unlike her housekeeper-companion, Mrs. Jolley, who has set ideas about right and wrong, Mary has escaped the prison of self. She has accepted the reality of the nonhuman world to the point where, instead of judging or coveting it, she wants to fuse her being with it. It provides the standard for her to live and judge by. Elsewhere she describes the steps by which the lowly can rise: "I was the servant of the servants. I was a very ugly little girl" (p. 82), she says of her lonely childhood. Embarrassed by her ugliness, her parents neither trained her socially nor encouraged her to make friends with other children. She had to seek out animals for company. Covered with dirt and scratches and wearing her wicker hat, she still finds joy in simple, humble things. Her return to Xanadu after visiting the local post office shows her going home with the same excitement that most people (like her father) only muster for foreign travel. The homecoming provides one of the book's great moments, as Mary's sense of awe makes Xanadu both a vision and the fulfillment of a dream. To the humble, oft-repeated acts can bring gladness and wonder. Mary's modest ambition to exist on a par with her surroundings endows Xanadu with such grandeur that seeing it, after being away for only an hour or so, nearly overwhelms her.

Though inferring moral genius, this outstanding freshness of response exacts a high cost. Mary has mingled her energies so intimately with her physical milieu that she has nearly dissolved into it. Acts like feeding a snake and rearing a nestling induce a subhuman mentality. (In an interview, White called Mary "slightly subnormal.")[7] Like burrowing through thickets and shrubs, these solitary acts also foster contempt for people. "She found it impossible to like human beings" (p. 15), Mary admits. First seen from the rear, walking away from Sarsaparilla's post office, where two women are talking, she underrates the human. She even answers idly and keeps walking away when her fellow apostle, Ruth Godbold, offers words of help. Although she admires Mrs. Godbold, she can't treat her with courtesy. The only person for whom she troubles herself, Himmelfarb, appeals to her chiefly as a fellow victim or extension of herself. What is more, his outstanding ugliness and his Jewishness might make him seem more animal than human to her.

Besides her relationship with Himmelfarb, the ties that mean the most to her are the ones with her pet goat and with her father, a gourmet, collector, and dillettante. The deaths of these two, like that of Himmelfarb later, define her as a dangerous intimate. Death had already touched her family before her birth. The death of his rich wine-merchant father allows Norbert Hare to defy the Australian ethic of practicality by building the pleasure dome of Xanadu, but the expensive marble, crystal, and gold he has imported from Europe do not spare him the ugliness of his munching, red-faced daughter. Feeling cheated and angry over having daily to face an ugliness he himself created, he empties his shotgun into his glittering drawing room chandelier. The cold musical fire of the chandelier, a symbol of privilege, turns out to be empty and meaningless, "an excruciating crystal rain" (p. 32) that stimulates no growth. Unable to go on living with his blotchy daughter, he drowns himself. White doesn't excuse the repulsion Mary rouses in her father; his substitution of affectation for a loving heart has weakened Norbert's hold on life. Nor did he ever try to understand, let alone love, Mary, avoiding her and speaking curtly to her as a matter of policy. On the other hand, his despair shows the strain of living with a girl who seems to bring out the worst traits of those close to her.

Mary's own faults are also an issue. Like Theodora Goodman, she knows herself to be capable of doing evil. One of her darkest regrets inheres in having burned her pet goat to death. Narrative selection shows White condemning the burning as wasteful and wanton. Having supported himself by breeding goats in Castle Hill,[8] Sarsaparilla's real-life counterpart, White speaks of goats with unusual fondness. In *Voss* he refers to them as "rational creatures" (p. 271); Mary calls them "the animals which see the truth most clearly" (*Riders*, p. 314); Elizabeth Hunter, perhaps White's most astute and dazzling person, claims an affinity with goats: "I never kept a goat, but know from looking at one or two that we might have understood each other" (*Eye*, p. 87); the wisest character in the play *Night on Bald Mountain*, a goatherd, presumably acquired her wisdom by spending so much time with her charges. Goats encompass enough to teach wisdom. Writing about White's 1964 play, Robert F. Whitman calls the goat "the very incarnation of animality and sexuality."[9] The goat has also been identified with betrayal, that which is most rank but perhaps most fundamental in human nature. This ill-favored, ill-used animal sometimes forages in nettle patches for food. The contents of his digestive tract and his identification with both betrayal and sexual lust reveal that he can't escape nastiness. Yet he can rise above it. That he eats nettles and plays Judas to sheep led to slaughter can't disguise the truth that, despite his notoriety, the goat is one of the most docile, good-humored farm animals. To kill one of these kindly creatures, not to mention torturing one to death with flames, is to destroy what may be best in creation. Mary chides herself justly for killing her pet goat.

Himmelfarb is another self-blamer whose isolation White studies minutely from the inside. Along with Joyce's Leopold Bloom (whose father, like Himmelfarb's, became a Christian a year before his death), Malamud's fixer, Wallant's pawnbroker, and Robert Shaw's man in the glass booth, Himmelfarb has helped make the self-condemning Jew a familiar figure in contemporary literature. Himmelfarb doubts his very right to live. In choosing to work as a low-paid menial in Australia, which he imagines as perhaps the most bitter place on earth, this distinguished academic frustrates nearly all his civilized needs. His decline in living standard can be traced historically. Although a proud, sensual youth burgeoned into a maturity rich in honors and achievements, a chance encounter with Jewish mystical writing soured him on intellectual activity and its rewards. Judaica taught him to supplant reason with faith. No secular Jew, he comes to believe in the dynamism of faith, praying to the Supreme Infinite and prizing spirit as the most intimate, sacred part of life. Because pain comes from God, like all other things, he won't resist or relieve it. The prospect of living in a termite-infested, cold-water weatherboard shack appeals to this "elderly, refined Jew" (p. 211) as much as do washing dishes and cleaning public lavatories. (Like his apostate father, he renounces a key reality of his life in his maturity.) Following what he believes is the Lord's will refines his soul as it ages and wastes his body. His physical ugliness betokens spiritual honor.

After he leaves Germany, most of the major events of Himmelfarb's life happen by chance, by impulse, or through the will of others. Passivity ennobles him. He doesn't fear the roughnecks and rowdies who crucify him, nor does he pass on the malice that brings about his crucifixion. His calmness on the rude cross makes his persecutors feel cheated. Rising above their proletarian male tribalism, he leaves the crucifixion site with dignity, whereas Blue, his chief tormentor, vomits. Blue is deeply moved, perhaps even redeemed, by his victim's passivity. That he quits his job at Brighta Bicycle Lamps, where he had worked with the Jew, and flees to another state suggests that the crucifixion prompted a spiritual self-examination. Named for the color designating both hope and the Virgin Mary, he plays an essential role in the drama of the crucifixion. His matey brutality serves transcendence. Without it Himmelfarb wouldn't have bled. And without the Jew's pain to prod them several other characters wouldn't have risen to saintliness. It is because of Blue that Himmelfarb's agony creates outlets for spiritual love in these others. Blue's centricity in the miracle can't be suppressed any more than the miracle itself.

Yet Himmelfarb (who follows his fellow German, Voss, in dying in the thirteenth chapter of a novel which opens in suburban Sydney, where he is a misfit) feels no uplift from the miracle. He would permit himself no such luxury. For one thing, knowing the extent of his spiritual achievement might make him smug and vain and thus destroy the humility nourishing his piety. His blessedness, ironically, depends on his ignorance and suffering. Pointing the dependence is his identification with fire. The flames that burn his hometown, the Polish prison camp where he is taken, and his shack in Sarsaparilla occur in the Bible both as the miraculous pillar of fire which leads the Jews out of the desert and, later, as the symbolic presence of God. But if his holiness feeds on loss, pain, and destruction, does his ruthless self-denial bring him closer to God by deepening the negation? White discourages reasonable answers because, like the three other riders, Himmelfarb acts as if he exists to absorb sorrow and punishment. So much goes awry with him and his counterparts that they appear destined to suffer. Ruth Godbold accepts her husband's worst abuse. Her refusal to question, discourage, or avenge her husband's cruelty gets her far fewer knocks, though, than his compliance does Himmelfarb. He was wounded in battle in World War I; after losing his professorship, he sees his home-town burn and finds that the Gestapo have taken his wife. In Australia he is turned away by a fellow Jew on Passover night, the time when Jewish hospitality is traditionally affirmed. The next day he is crucified when he reports to work after being told to stay home. He complains about none of this, his Jewish legacy of pain heightening his guilt over surviving. If he must live after his German friends and family have all died, his life will be mean and sordid.

His blaming himself for whatever goes wrong makes Himmelfarb a creature of caricature or fable. Instead of feeling lucky, he experiences only uprootedness and shame. It is as if in leaving Hitler's Germany he did wrong, and to compensate he must work at a dull job in degrading surroundings and live in a shanty. He even balks at enjoying the consola-tions of water and sunlight. Unable to shed the past, he reels through the present, punishing his body, numbing his mind, and insulting his soul. (Boring is boring, runs White's unstated joke about the Jew's job drilling holes in steel disks.) A problem with the book arises from the certainty, which emerges early, that Himmelfarb will end badly. The events which later chasten him look more convenient to the book's overall plan than causal in terms of his character. What happens to him turns *Riders* into an essay-novel written to degrade happiness and achievement and to hint at the spiritual profit that may be gleaned from suffering. Himmelfarb couldn't dodge trouble if he wanted to.

The pages recounting his youth, education, marriage, and professional career surpass by far the ones describing him in Israel and Australia. In Germany he is a person; when he leaves his homeland, he flattens into a symbol. Idea sometimes goes it alone in *Riders,* razing all in its path. The belief that salvation lies in sacrifice and self-denial hinders White, whose close supervision cuts off Himmelfarb's supply of oxygen. The symbolism heaped upon the Jew limits his freedom, rather than lending him dignity. It can be all too easily inventoried. When Himmelfarb flees the burning Polish prison camp, the barbs from the wire fence through which he crawls pierce his brow; he is taken to an enclosure that smells of pigs and straw where he is reborn; three days later he has his first German-language conversation since his escape. The parallels with Christ continue to mount in Australia, after his temptation by worldly prizes in Jerusalem and Haifa. He cuts his hand with his drill at Brighta; Ruth Godbold provides him with a roof, and Mary Hare warms his feet after the crucifixion (the two Marys appear in Pietà paintings by Raphael and Caravaggio); he dies on Good Friday. This symbolic paraphernalia, White's clumsy cue that we should side with his victim, shows poor judgment as well as heavyhanded technique. If Himmelfarb hasn't already won our hearts by the time of his arrest in Germany, the novel has failed to make its point.

The introduction of Alf Dubbo, the half-caste Aboriginal painter who sweeps the floors at Brighta, enlivens the action. He is the book's most compelling figure, with his sick, battered body and visionary mind. He also inspired White to base *The Vivisector,* his longest and most ambitious novel, on insights about the artistic process and the artist's psyche set forth in *Riders.* Dubbo is a perfect outsider to both Australian and non-Australian readers. He makes no attempt to be white as he drinks, wanders, and takes low-paid, menial jobs. His white blood and the refinements he learned from the white family that raised him have excluded him from the black world, as well. He chooses to stand apart. Even when not painting his wildly inventive pictures, he spends most of his spare time alone. Perhaps his weak constitution has convinced him that he can ill afford to waste time with others. He rarely speaks, and what he says is usually too deliberately trite to prompt an answer. "Alf, you got something shut up inside of you, and you bloody well won't give another person a look" (p. 378), says a Sydney landlady. She is right. He can't afford to share anything vital; friendship threatens to distract him from his vocation, as money does. Perhaps he squanders his cash in drink in order to drive out both threats.

Like the other three immaculati, Alf Dubbo takes turns being despised and feared. Further proof that he is one of the blessed comes in his many hardships. He has been infected with syphilis, denied a home and family, robbed by his landlady, and kicked from one slum dwelling to another. He rarely comes before us without coughing up blood or displaying multicolored facial bruises. But White does not use his aches to invent a new separatism. Rather, Dubbo helps him fight past both social and religious barriers toward a new harmony, one born of great conflict. Both Dubbo and Hurtle Duffield reveal the artist as a battlefield of warring impulses. Recalling Adrian Leverkühn, the musician in Mann's *Dr. Faustus,* White speaks of "the two poles, the negative and positive of his [Dubbo's] being: the furtive destroying sickness, and the almost as furtive, but regenerating, creative act" (p. 366). Art comes from the bipolar tug between Dubbo's physical weakness and the soaring inspiration he gains from reading the biblical prophets. The process both renews and destroys him, as is seen in his dying from the effort of painting his most inventive picture. The practice of art also immobilizes him, denying him the consolations of moral action as well as those of friendship. His quest for proper aesthetic distance demands that he keep aloof. Though outraged, he can't save or protect Himmelfarb on the Friday afternoon of the Jew's crucifixion. The four immaculati never appear together for the same reason that Dubbo can paint the crucifixion but can't stop it. He stands outside Ruth Godbold's shed during the Jew's last overthrow, looking in but, again, not participating directly. Getting caught up in the emotional or moral issues of an action would distract him from that action's spiritual truth. Dubbo denies himself in order to enrich his art.

II

Some of the local people who can't understand Dubbo and his fellow riders malign them and would like to destroy them. The two outstanding foes are Ada Flack, Blue's putative aunt, and Mrs. Jolley, a Melbourne woman who has come to Xanadu as Mary Hare's companion-housekeeper. The contrast between these opinionated, self-righteous widows and the riders is sharply drawn. Whereas Dubbo will talk sparingly, preferring shadows to spotlight, the widows drone, chatter, and bawl at great length. The voiceless fricatives ending one of their exchanges, while invoking the hissing of snakes (Mrs. Flack is later called a pythoness [p. 239]), also show them leaning on the safe and the officially sanctioned, whereas the four apostles all stand alone and look within: " 'See you at church!' hissed Mrs. Jolley. 'See you at church!' repeated Mrs. Flack" (p. 229). As the exchange implies, the women presume that the church and the family, those bulwarks of the middle-class consumer state, stand behind them. Their policy of rating the collective and the official over the personal and the spontaneous has robbed life of its mystery, tragedy, and glory. Mrs. Flack's home, where Mrs. Jolley settles after leaving Xanadu, reflects White's ongoing practice of associating his people with their houses. Located on Mildred Street, the setting for White's 1962 play, *The Season at Sarsaparilla*, the modish texture brick home embodies its owner's preference for what is pink, plastic, and prefabricated. But its name, Karma, also suggests literalness and retribution. It soon becomes clear that Mesdames Flack and Jolley live together less from choice than from necessity. Their domestic arrangement obeys the same iron morality they exact when judging others. "People must always pay" (p. 239), Mrs. Jolley says one afternoon, and her sentiment is repeated straightaway by Mrs. Flack. Their living together gives them just what they deserve—each other, and the knowledge that hatred binds them. Their mutual karma decrees that a bond forged in hatred (for Mary Hare and Himmelfarb) will not run its natural course until its principals also hate each other. The two women are well matched. Each helped cause her husband's death; their baiting, carping ways have exiled each from her family; each knows that the other is both her mirror image and her punishment (or karma): no one else would take either woman in. Having initially closed ranks through hatred and fear, the two then turn their malice on each other, discovering each other's secret sorrow and then twisting the knife.

White portrays Mrs. Flack and Mrs. Jolley with stunning intimacy. His photographic accuracy, unerring ear for speech, and historical sense disclose evil permeating the banal. The two women are always predictable, yet always frightening. As obvious as they are, no one can afford to lower his or her guard around them. White's ability to mold danger out of such common clay shows real inventiveness. On the other hand, the danger doesn't tempt us. One of the writer's hardest jobs is to depict a character who will both attract and repel the reader, and the wickedness of these two is never engaging. Using the women as moral opposites to his four riders, White never lets either one of them do anything right or good. His nasal, preachy condemnation trivializes the conflict between the two camps.

Mrs. Flack sometimes claims to disown her friend's loveless brand of moral judgment and punishment. Denying that people should account for their actions, she says things like, "Who will ever decide who killed who?" (p. 240) and "Only a person can know the truth and then not always" (p. 429). Such statements pervert moral relativism. Mrs. Flack doesn't struggle internally, as do Mary Hare, Himmelfarb, and Dubbo. She believes that morality is subjective because such a stance frees her from blame. Blue can be talked into damaging Himmelfarb because aggressiveness "lets out the bad" (p. 427). Perhaps she worries justifiably whether Blue's evil will fester and infect him unless he vents it, for the ease with which he crucifies Himmelfarb suggests that he may have killed another older man—his father. To suppose that Will Flack, a tiler, fell accidentally to his death from a roof defies belief. A more likely explanation for his fatal fall stems from his widow's refusal to admit that Blue is her son and not her nephew. If Blue didn't murder his father, then perhaps Ada Flack pushed Will from the roof where he was working when she found herself pregnant by another man. But then her lover, frightened by her crime, fled instead of marrying her. In any case, Ernie Theobalds, Brighta's foreman and a longtime resident of the district, both insists that Blue is Mrs. Flack's son and believes that Will Flack's death was planned. (Our not knowing the date of Flack's death prevents us from naming a murderer or ascertaining motives.) His convictions fit her practice of invoking moral relativism to hide her guilt. She lacks the loving heart, the religious faith, or the artistic vocation which might allow her to release her secret sin. That Mrs. Jolley, whom she must face each day, knows of the sin makes it unbearable.

Pressure also builds within Harry Rosetree, or Haim Rosenbaum. Although he would like to deny his Jewish ancestry in order to play the cheerful, extroverted Australian, he is too sensitive and self-questioning. He has all the outward signs of the assimilated Australian—a texture brick home in a good suburb (shrewdly named Paradise East), a Ford Customline, membership in a local church, and a wife who wears a fur coat. White also gives him an inward sign—an aliveness to pain. He is more compassionate than his ruthlessly conformist wife and the two Mildred Street widows, and he suffers more than these women do. His suffering also breaks him. His dying suggests the facile argument that death is better than a comfortable, painless life; we are meant to admire Rosetree for choosing a literal death over the living one that he has been enacting as a prosperous suburbanite. But the process by which he replaces his shiny, stereotyped image with his stricken individuality generates the drive of tragedy. The denouement comes at Passover. Having decided to play the guest rather than the host for Seder, Himmelfarb goes to the Rosetrees', but he is snubbed so that they can move ahead with their Easter preparations. The rejection of any visitor on Seder night is a denial of Jewish tradition; when the visitor is another Jew, the denial becomes a defilement—of hospitality, heritage, and self. The consequences of his behavior drive Rosetree to suicide; he can't suppress his Jewishness any more than the Dyer of Holunderthal can wash away the stains of his labor. The sickness that overtakes him, his decision to forgo his Easter holiday, and his wish to hold a *minyan* for Himmelfarb all reflect more spiritual growth than Rosetree's socialized self can accommodate. Rosetree commits suicide because his mistreatment of Himmelfarb has flooded him with guilt. Rosetree lacks the fiber to challenge his wife and her suburban ethic of normality with his revelation. Faced with social, marital, and spiritual pressures, he hangs himself.

As the suicide implies, Himmelfarb attracts a great deal of attention in the days surrounding his death. It is as if an unseen hand is leading his survivors to follow their truest impulses. Not only does Rosetree die; Mary Hare also disappears into the bush, and Blue quits his job and moves to another state. Finally, Dubbo recreates the Jew's death in paint and dies of the effort; whereas the businessman Rosetree kills himself, Dubbo's art can rechannel the pain caused by Himmelfarb's death. This pattern reinforces another that holds good throughout the work. Most of the present action takes place in Xanadu, in Himmelfarb's poor shack, or in the temporary shed in which the laundress Ruth Godbold has settled permanently. Once again, the shadowy but pervasive figure of the dyer explains the apparent anomaly. Accident doesn't bring the rich, the worldly, and the comfortable to these rundown places. (In chapter 15 Rosetree goes to the Godbolds' rude shed; he discovers that an act he had been planning to do out of duty, burying Himmelfarb, has already been performed out of love by the widowed laundress.) Although they may claim superiority over the inhabitants of these places, they also sense that the latter have found something they themselves lack—self-sufficiency and inner peace. "It was an old and rather poor church . . . but such churches are the best for praying in," reads one of the epigraphs, from Dostoevski, to *The Solid Mandala*, White's next novel after *Riders*. The prospect of harmony both beckons and reproaches. Whether in search of victims or atonement, the less insightful, more ego-bound figures can't stay away from broken-down dwellings and their twilit owners. They also know that they lack the moral courage to confront their needs. Mrs. Flack and Mrs. Jolley embarrass each other by meeting accidentally at the razed and rebuilt site where Xanadu once stood.

The squalor, ugliness, and filth dominating *Riders* neither shocks nor offends. Several important characters besides Mrs. Flack and Mrs. Jolley return in chapter 17 to the torn, dusty ground where Xanadu once stood. Himmelfarb's bus ride home through greater Sydney, after he is spurned by the Rosetrees, discloses vomit, urine, and used contraceptives under a neon glare. After his conversion to Christianity years before, the Jew's father married a woman with hair "as heavy and yellow in its snood as horse's dung" (p. 126). Toilets figure conspicuously: Himmelfarb and Dubbo hold their only conversation (about the Old Testament prophets) in a factory bathroom; Mrs. Jolley resigns as Mary Hare's companion-housekeeper while she is in a bathroom; Harry Rosetree, whose vision of the Savior in chapter 15 includes the smell of urine, hangs himself in a bathroom. Much of the demolition and waste permeating *Riders* serves higher ends; whereas the plastic and the prepackaged promote empty values, the natural processes of decay and corruption can enlighten and enliven hearts, revealing breakdown as an agent of rebirth. In hearts already illuminated, the process can forge strong bonds. Pain and blood-shed bring Himmelfarb and Dubbo together within a context of biblical prophecy when the Jew goes to Brighta's men's room to wash his wounded hand; the injury brings the Jew and Ruth Godbold together the same afternoon; at the end, the ravages caused by Himmelfarb's crucifixion send Mrs. Godbold and Mary Hare to his side. Collapse stimulates vitality in other ways as well. A highly subjective work, *Riders* portrays life as spiritual understanding rather than as having and doing. Simple, ordinary existence is miraculous: "It is the same" (p. 482), blubbers Rosetree about the universal parity of existence just before his death. The legacy of heart knowledge that Else Godbold inherits from her mother allows Else both to love and to accept love from Bob Tanner; the son created by their marriage expresses their healthy, life-giving interchange. The interchange reverber-ates elsewhere. Though neither Mary Hare nor Himmelfarb presided over the relationship, both of these apostles knew the couple, asked for their help, and benefited from their good will. The moral contrast with Mesdames Flack and Jolley, who appear for the last time immediately after Else and Bob, gains dramatic heightening through narrative structure. It deserves this special treatment. Whereas malice turns on itself, the kinetic drive of love reaches into and enriches the future. One of the reasons why chapter 17 leaps ahead several years is to show that Bob and Else have married and become parents.

This transit into the future strengthens the impression that dowdy, slow-moving Ruth Godbold is the book's moral avatar and leading figure. Associated with the bread she often bakes for her six daughters and the clean laundry often seen billowing and freshening on her clothesline, she represents compassion and mercy. Ruth measures her life in loving acts. First we learn that she kept Mary Hare clean, warm, and fed when Mary was sick. No definitions can explain her, nor need any be invoked. The tragic hero sees and confronts the existential chaos; the religious hero looks beyond it to its cause; the artistic hero interprets and reshapes it. Mrs. Godbold's loving heart excludes her from these categories. That she is the only rider both to survive and to have children expresses White's admiration of her. "Of the four central characters, only Mrs. Godbold lives out the action of the book," says Colin Roderick, adding, "Religious fervor and artistic creation pass away; love only is left."[10] Her brand of love hinges on the simple belief that God ennobles and sanctifies our commonest acts. From this simplicity comes strength. Mrs. Godbold's escape from the shackles of self has driven out fear. Appearances and the threat of nasty gossip can't shake her sense of conviction. Perhaps the quietest character in the book after Dubbo, she nonetheless acts decisively. Needing no fanfares, she emboldens herself several times—coming to Australia from England's cozy fen country, doing Himmelfarb's laundry and dressing his wounded hand without being asked, and going to the bawdy house where her husband is a paying customer.

Her goodness baffles the bawd just as it overpowers and negates the evil both of her drunken bully of a husband and of her onetime employer, Jinny Chalmers-Robinson. As a tribute to Ruth Godbold's goodness, Mrs. Chalmers-Robinson invokes her spirit, some twenty-five years after Ruth worked for her, while lunching in a smart Sydney hotel. The invocation is well judged, for Mrs. Godbold reconciles and elevates all discord. The finale of Part Four, during which her husband dies, shows this pasty-faced saint transcending her grief to bestow compassion on all humanity. Her epiphany crowns the book's middle section.

She serves unity to the end. The leg of Easter lamb she brings to Himmelfarb matches the shankbone he puts out for Seder. The gift mirrors her faith in the nonsectarian uplift of the holidays; Easter and Passover can support and ennoble each other if celebrated, however informally, by a loving soul. Mrs. Godbold again rises above sectarianism in giving a Jew a Christian burial: "It is the same," she tells Rosetree, who feels bilked of his chance to conduct a Jewish service for Himmelfarb: "Men are the same before they are born. . . . They think they will change their coat. But remain the same, in themselves" (p. 480). The idea of our basic oneness so moves Rosetree that it constitutes his helplessly repeated last words. His struggles to suppress his Judaism have all been pointless. White conveys his own admiration for Ruth Godbold and her values structurally. Chapter 9, the middle of this seventeen-chapter novel, belongs to Mrs. Godbold, describing her English past, her early years in Australia, and her marriage. Her unqualified love is the centerpiece of the work. White reaffirms his faith in her by matching chapter 9 with Part Four (which also comes midway into the seven-part book); Part Four *is* chapter 9, just as Australia's national boundaries match her continental perimeters. An echo of this one-to-one correspondence comes in chapter 17, which makes up all of Part Seven. In a final tribute, White lets her hold the stage alone in the book's last scene. Her behavior implies that this prominence has embarrassed her. With her usual modesty, Ruth Godbold dwells on others. She believes that her three fellow riders have taken the fiery chariot to heaven, where they live reborn, all their hurts healed, alongside the Risen Christ. The book's shrewdly chosen last word, "live" (p. 532), dares us to gainsay her belief.

III

Its moments of affirmation, together with its outstanding knowledge of Kabbalism and Merkabah mysticism, make us wish that *Riders* were a smoother, more sustained performance. White's problem in controlling his materials arises from his having too many of them. *Riders,* says Argyle, "contains enough material for several contemporary novels,"[11] and he is right. Congestion hurts the work. Like the later *Solid Mandala* and *Fringe of Leaves, Riders* begins casually, recounting the gossip of two local women. But, unlike its successors, the work fails to build momentum after its slow start. For all its geographical sweep and temporal depth, *Riders* lacks a sense of motion and change. Its people seem posed; when meant to look fresh and spontaneous, they only mystify. A one-note book, *Riders* doesn't solve the serious questions it raises about the nature and practice of literature. White's attempts to smooth the anomalies in *Riders* usually fail. The book's effects are too rigged and its plot too diagrammatic. John Colmer supports his claim that *Riders* is White's "most programmatic novel" by asserting that the work's "interlocking profusion of detail" is "more reminiscent of an unfinished jigsaw puzzle than the mystic unity of a sacred mosaic."[12] Almost everything appears based on a preordained design, robbing the characters of their autonomy and causing the symbols to speak too loudly. As the resemblances between Himmelfarb after he leaves Germany, and Christ show, the New Testament parallels in the book are rigid and codified. Other characters also hew too closely to the Christ myth: Mrs. Godbold and Mary are obviously the two Marys of the Pietà; Dubbo is Judas and Peter; Rosetree plays both Judas and Pilate. But these forced parallels don't explain all of the novel's faults. Distressingly, White sometimes flubs his facts. Mary Hare claims to have put out milk for a snake and then to have watched the snake drink, but as readers of the Sherlock Holmes story "The Adventure of the Speckled Band" have suspected, snakes don't drink milk. White also claims that Himmelfarb studied at "the University of Oxford" (p. 115); the institution to which this Cambridge graduate refers is known as Oxford University.

These factual errors mar the novel less than does White's prose. White embarrasses himself more in *Riders* than in any other work, largely because of the book's range of stylistic quality. Had *Riders* not achieved such splendors of expression, its infelicities would attract less notice. The novel's lusterless, rambling sentences incorporate all kinds of puzzling linguistic formulations. Substituting manner for clarity and freshness, White robs a good action verb of its power by casting it in the passive voice: "As the man continued along the road, the stones were crunched steadily" (p. 63). He often misuses nouns as badly as he does verbs. The following sentence ascribes different meanings to the same noun: "The son resumed relations with relations" (p. 123). Earlier, he had referred to Norbert Hare's "shooting match" (p. 48) when recalling Norbert's destruction of his drawing room chandelier. Norbert participated in no match because he had no opponent, nor was he competing for a prize.

By all rights, the slipshod phrasing and punctuation of *Riders* should have doomed the novel. Its ability to survive its rhetorical failings bespeaks a powerful vision. The most boldly and grandly conceived of White's novels, *Riders* nonetheless cries out for an editor. The book's mannered, muffled prose implies that he may have been trying to wrest beauty from ugliness in the same way that his freakish characters disclose internal beauty as they make themselves known to us. Alas, no such alchemy takes place. Nor did White's attempt to transplant Victorian amplitude to Australian soil work, either; too often his earnestness results in doggedness, and his gestures toward solidness and size produce cryptic or spongy rhetoric. How badly can a good book be written and still remain a good book? *Riders in the Chariot* makes us wonder. White's own recognition of this imponderable shows in the trimmer design, the smoother texture, and the relative shortness of his next novel, *The Solid Mandala*, which he rates a personal favorite.

8. Deeper than Blood

WHITE LIKES *The Solid Mandala* (1965) because of its welding of vision and craft: "It's a very personal kind of book, I suppose, and comes closest to what I've wanted,"[1] he said in 1969. Several familiar motifs helped him approach his ideal. Shifting time as freely as he did in *Riders,* he oscillates between the present and the world of remembered experience. *The Aunt's Story* and *The Eye of the Storm,* though published twenty-five years apart, indicate another crucial similarity. Whereas three of the four riders in White's 1961 novel live alone, the main characters in *Mandala* live together as a family. White may well have been thinking of his own childhood when he called *Mandala* a personal kind of book. In 1980 he referred to his father as "an amiable accommodating husband" and to his mother as one who "seemed to rule the roost."[2] His description fits Theodora Goodman's parents and also Bill and Elizabeth Hunter. (With small modifications, it would also describe the Furlows of *Happy Valley* and the Golsons of *Twyborn Affair*). But rather than studying marriage, as he does in *Tree,* the White of *Mandala* focuses upon the sibling tie, as he will do again in *Vivisector, Eye of the Storm,* and *Fringe of Leaves.* By making the Brown brothers twins, he alludes to both the strength and the depth of their tie. "I don't think . . . I could live without my brother. He was more than half of me" (p. 303), says the seventy-year-old Arthur Brown. Both as a boy and as an old man, Waldo finds himself breathing in unison with Arthur. First seen walking hand in hand, the brothers travel together toward the same goal. One of them may wander from the path, delaying their joint progress. More often they define progress differently and prefer to walk down different paths. Whereas Waldo likes the busy commercial streets, Arthur, who tires easily because of his weight and who doesn't need the buzz of crowds to feel complete, prefers the side roads, where he can look at the fennel. He will even stop to call Waldo's attention to a crumbling, sunblanched dog turd. Such whims infuriate the cold, methodical Waldo. *The Solid Mandala* gives one of White's fullest pictures of love—that dark, deep impulse which shows that life can't be lived without the beloved, and that life can only be lived without the beloved.

The near-maniacal power of brotherly love obeys no controls. Waldo's calling Arthur "the brother who looked almost right inside him" (p. 33) rests less on reason than on instinct. Arthur's power to read Waldo's heart never wavers; go where he may, in his fantasies or on his social calls, Arthur is close by. The mystical tie joining him to Arthur finds expression in two of the book's epigraphs, "There is another world, but it is in this one" and "It is not outside, it is inside: wholly within." The laws governing life are intrinsic, not imposed. Dormant for years, they awaken quickly and assert their might at key moments. The Brown's longstanding neighbor, Mrs. Poulter, walks effortlessly into the lives of the twins after an absence of years, as did Mrs. O'Dowd with the Parkers in *Tree*. *Mandala* deals with the appalling privacy of private experience, and with the unconfessed bonds and loyalties that shape us, often against our wills. That these ties resist our wishes and control doesn't make White a determinist. He still believes in divine disclosure and the possibility of redemption, as he did in *Riders*, but now he seats his belief in the family, as he will in the next three novels. Looking back to the marriage of Else Godbold and Bob Tanner at the end of *Riders*, he has George Brown, the twins' father, install a classical pediment above his modest veranda; a simple weatherboard shack takes on classical grandeur if it houses people who love each other.

The idea that buildings have souls isn't new in White, nor is the notion that spiritual truths dwell in remote, tumbledown places and touch unlikely people. Only by becoming the lowest of the low did Mary Hare acquire the insight that later made her a nature mystic. In *Tree* White wondered whether "the purposes of God are made clear to some old women, and nuns, and idiots" (p. 218). The enlightened freaks of *Riders* lacked beauty and, except for Alf Dubbo, practiced no special skill; Hurtle Duffield fulfills *his* artistic promise in old age, after the years have sapped his youthful vim and a stroke has warped his painting arm; Elizabeth Hunter, whose inward growth matches that of Hurtle, is a woman of eighty-six lying on her deathbed. Appearances mislead in White. The dimming of the mandala's outer radiance often signals internal activity. The softening of Arthur Brown's harsh red hair with the passage of years reflects the mellowing of his soul. As if touched by the holy fire of Yeats's "Byzantium," he brightens spiritually while fading physically.

Setting conveys White's democratic belief that all may partake of this process. Part One, in which the Brown brothers are introduced, is called "In the Bus." At least one of the characters who discuss the twins, Mrs. Poulter, feels the magic emanating from the Browns' creaking home. Her conversation with Edna Dun aboard the Sarsaparilla bus hews to a familiar curve in White. Important relationships often start in public, commonplace settings: Mrs. Flack and Mrs. Jolley also met on a bus, as will Sir Basil Hunter and Mitty Jacka in *Eye of the Storm,* a work in which another character, Snow Tunks, is a bus conductor; Alf Dubbo meets the woman who helps cure his syphilis and becomes his landlady in a public park; people who influence Hurtle Duffield come into his life in a park, on a harbor ferry, along a breakwater, and in a neighborhood grocery; finally, Eddie Twyborn talks to his mother for the first time in some twenty years while in a London churchyard. Their conversation, involving two Australians but taking place in England, touches on an idea featured in *Mandala,* that of incongruity and love's ability to transcend it. In the decade or so following World War II, during which most of *Mandala* takes place, a great wave of immigration from southern Europe and the introduction of new industrial machinery made Australia conscious of itself as a burgeoning world power. White turns away from this new prosperity to look at those who stand apart from its clamor. Waldo and Arthur Brown, retired librarian and grocer, boast no great feats and add little to the ferment generated by recent changes. Like Happy Valley, their locale has been excluded from recent developments. The commuter train no longer stops at their once-booming suburb of Sarsaparilla, making the name of their street, Terminus Road, both a misnomer and a sad reminder of the neighborhood's decline. What is more, the "disintegrating wooden box" (p. 165) where the Browns live is surrounded by leaves and rubble. It stands over a rancid, overflowing grease trap, and it consists of building materials that have gone faded, chipped, or rusty. On the other hand, the classical pediment fronting this sagging wreck discloses the attempt to transform the tired and the tawdry into something sublime. This attempt impresses White as much as the achievement. Even though Terminus Road is a neglected cul de sac, it constitutes no dead end for him.

The perfection symbolized by the mandala asserts itself in everyday life. No dream or wish projection, it appears in the Chinese wheel tree, in Dulcie Feinstein Saporta's Star of David, and in the weave of her husband Leonard's carpet. The transcendent permeates the finite. Like all metaphysicians, White sees the material and spiritual worlds as one. The interaction of spirit and matter reveals itself negatively in Stan Parker's act of spitting out God just before his dying revelation. Although Stan learns that "One, and no other figure, is the answer to all sums" (p. 497), he dies within moments of his discovery. Spitting out God was a mistake. Spirit needs the concreteness supplied by flesh and other matter. Like the ruined Xanadu in *Riders,* it may shake and sag, droop and decay. Just as Dubbo's destructiveness interacted rhythmically with his creativity to serve higher ends, so does the mingling of decay and growth and of the psychic and the palpable extend limits. The dusty, unkempt path along which the Brown twins stub hand in hand during their daily walks sprouts a rich array of blossoms and fruit.

I

The harvesting of this rich yield demands courage and independence. The Australia of *Mandala* is phallocentric, puritanical, and ruled by the middle-class creeds of utility and practicality. White demythologizes this traditional masculinity, removing its Calvinist props. Rather than equating maleness with dominance and aggression, he sees sexual roles as elastic and interchangeable. His view refers to Jung's belief that everyone has masculine and feminine components which must be accepted and developed if the personality is to become whole. The man who derides his softer tendencies and the woman who discounts her aggressiveness both suffer deprivation. According to Zen, which includes the mandala in its system, the One Mind transcends all definitions and identifying marks. Analogously, speculation and sentimentality both miss the unity of experience. To intuit the harmony between the mind and the external world is to dissolve into the oneness of things.[3] Familiar with the Hindu belief in the *prana,* or life breath (p. 232), Arthur transcends dualities. Waldo's calling him "a big fat helpless female" (p. 222) and Mrs. Poulter's view of him as an "aged man or crumpled child" (p. 304) reveal him combining different stages of human development. Whereas the neatness provided by solid surfaces and squared-off corners comforts Waldo, who dreams of living in a texture brick home, the more harmoniously constituted Arthur tends toward roundness and shagginess, with his silken mop of uncombed hair, his rotund build, and large, encircling arms. He adapts so well to circumstances that he feels comfortable anywhere. His ability to admit, resolve, and transcend opposites entitles him to keep the mandalas, those four marbles of different color and design he carries in his pockets for many years.

Arthur's voluntary stewardship of the mandalas expresses his belief that myth and symbol pervade life. In contrast to his renegade Baptist father, whose ethic of striving and achieving excludes the intangible, the less literal-minded Arthur gains strength from musing about mythical figures like Demeter and Athena. His ability to yoke myth to life enriches him. By not accounting strictly for their factual existences, he responds to these figures from his heart. His mandalas convey his warmth and inclusiveness of vision. A.P. Riemer calls the mandala a "symbol or image of divine harmony."[4] Buddhism explains it as a cosmic diagram which helps meditation. Because meditation opens a path to the oneness of things, the mandala often accompanies Buddhist worship. Such formalism and utility barely graze White's artistic intent. Like the chariot, his mandala lacks a fixed meaning or purpose. Often a network of straight and curved lines, like the circle and overlapping triangles in some representations of the Star of David, it symbolizes the universe. The encyclopedia definition that Arthur reads explains it as a principle of being: "The Mandala is a symbol of totality. It is believed to be the 'dwelling of the god.' Its protective circle is a pattern of order super—imposed on—psychic—chaos" (p. 229). As in Plato's formulation of the chariot in *Phaedrus,* the mandala's outer plane doesn't negate the energy within so much as contain it to stop its running to waste. The mandala orders itself intrinsically. What looks like a flaw enriches the design and enhances the system of internal stresses and balances. It may also mirror a truth external to itself; the knot in the marble, or mandala, that Arthur identifies with Waldo refers to Waldo's being born with his entrails twisted. It also prefigures the cramp in his nature that causes Waldo's death—from spite, says Mrs. Poulter, or from hate, according to Arthur.

A mandala may combine and recombine elements. Waldo's eyes are of the same cloudy blue color as the marble that Arthur chooses for Dulcie. It is typically ironic that the faithless Waldo is given eyes of a color traditionally symbolizing faith, religion, and loyalty. Both he and Dulcie have inherited the skepticism of their atheist-rationalist fathers; their meeting at a tennis party symbolizes the competition of their fathers' secular-capitalist society as vividly as Arthur's playing a piano duet with Dulcie at first meeting bespeaks harmony. Because Mount Pleasant, the name of Dulcie's parents' home, has a sexual ring that heightens Waldo's joy at the prospect of being entertained there, he rages inwardly when he finds Dulcie and Arthur sitting together on a piano stool just after being introduced. Along with the penchant for harmony that led her father to open a music store and that restored her husband to the Judaism of his forebears, the cloudy blue mandala of faith stabilizes and supports Dulcie (Saporta). Her acceptance of it when Arthur offers it to her helps free her of deprivation; she faces and comes to terms with her needs. Waldo's refusing *his* marble constitutes a denial of the truth about himself and makes his deprivation more hateful.

Waldo defeats himself many times. Having been born with his innards twisted, he now ties himself into more knots. On the surface he and Arthur complement each other, bestriding the little world of Sarsaparilla. Whereas the bulky, shambling Arthur dispenses food as a grocer, Waldo, a thin, meticulous librarian, nourishes minds and helps kindle souls. In his way each brother sustains life and thus fends off death. But Waldo's work brings more frustration than fulfillment. Rather than ordering, cataloging, and shelving other people's books, he would prefer to write his own. His failure to do so has jaded his literary tastes while hardening his heart. He turns down invitations to the homes of published writers, and, while he lectures to a book club on the work of one Barron Field, he denounces Goethe as "a disagreeable, egotistical man and overrated writer" (p. 122). Arthur, on the other hand, is in tune with both his job and the times. Right after coming to Australia as a child he started to speak Australian English. A first-rate grocer, he learns the store's stock, and he adds up the customers' bills so quickly and accurately that he amazes his employer. Adapting to industrial change in his science-dominated society, he feels just as comfortable in the gasoline station which later stands on the site of Allwrights' grocery as he did in the grocery itself. His first long walk with Waldo, during which the brothers pass the filling station, points up a major difference between them. Waldo's aesthetic sense recoils from the utility and mechanization called forth by the steel-and-concrete filling station; the less fastidious Arthur jokes with the mechanics, who had given him candy and simple jobs to do on the cars they were servicing. As they walk past the station, Arthur's warm, enfolding hand, which kneads dough for bread and has milked cows, holds the thin, cold one of his librarian brother, whose job centers largely on flat, dry, lifeless paper. The outdoor garb worn by the brothers is also thematic. The deep pile of Arthur's shaggy, moth-eaten tweed may pick up stains and smells, but its companionable warmth also provides comfort, both psychic and physical. The same claim can't be made for Waldo's flapping oilskin raincoat. Smooth, shiny, and stiff, it will never fade, snag, or smell like Arthur's tweed, but it is too thin and untextured to provide warmth. Its association with rain, clouds, and sunlessness also makes the yellow slicker a pessimist's garb; to wear it is to be attuned to nasty weather, perhaps to nastiness itself.

Expecting and thus helping to bring on the worst typifies Waldo, who lives at such a great distance from his feelings that he perforce defeats himself. The association of his name with that of Ralph Waldo Emerson, American champion of self-reliance and the gospel of self-trust, makes his egoism and nervous striving all the more pathetic. "I don't like to ask favors, be beholden to anybody" (p. 19), says this thin-blooded prisoner of duty, conscience, and self-discipline—who, ironically, owes his professional career to a well-wishing and influential friend. Inconsistency bedevils him. "You're the coldest fish I'll ever hope to meet" (p. 116), one of his fellow librarians tells him when he suddenly withdraws into his aloofness during a chat about sex. The co-worker is right. The cautious, self-absorbed Waldo is too guarded to achieve Arthur's simplicity or goodness of heart. He also lacks ordinary humanity. If a friend can be defined as somebody you don't mind troubling yourself for, then he has no friends. He musters the excuse of a long homeward trip in order to keep distance between himself and his co-worker, Walter Pugh. That they work together, write poetry, and share the first three letters of their first names make Waldo's denial of his double a self-denial. Nor does he redeem himself after Walter's death at the front in World War I. When Walter's sister gives him her brother's literary remains, a handful of poems, Waldo quails; because he recognizes "the nobler rage" (p. 122) irradiating Walter's poetry as beyond his own creative powers, he feels reproached just as he did when Walter enlisted. The traits he dislikes most about himself have come to the fore. Mortified and angered, he suppresses the poems.

The only constant in his dealings with people is his doggedness in keeping them at bay. Included in his fantasy about marrying Dulcie is the wish to have his own bed. But he'd never have married Dulcie even if given the chance, for all his relationships outside the home are official and impersonal. When someone tries to get close to him, he freezes. Saving himself for some undefined higher calling, he renounces love and friendship. Imputing sexual motives, he turns down two friendly invitations by women. He pretends to be out when a former schoolmate, now a middle-aged M.P., knocks on his door. That Johnny Haynes's father built the house where Waldo still lives and that Johnny once rivaled Waldo academically and tempted him sexually reveal Waldo to be in hiding both from the past and from himself. He blanches at the overtures of others, including his brother, throughout. Unless he is in charge he feels menaced. But the control he craves keeps eluding him because it lacks a solid base. The faith he places in reason, money, and property and the pride he takes in his mother's highborn English blood can't sustain him. He has defined life too narrowly. Failing to see people as ends in themselves, he wonders if a rich local widow, Mrs. Musto, has included him in her will. He also wonders why his brother has been inflicted on him, and he tries to shake off their bond. His own friendly overtures he mismanages so badly that they can only bring embarrassment and emptiness. Although he'd like to make friends with his neighbors, the Poulters, he doesn't know how to. His never having had a male friend prompts him to approach Bill Poulter, an uneducated laborer from upcountry. But he doesn't approach Bill on his own terms. Not only does he offer him a book, but that book is the Everyman edition of James Fenimore Cooper's *The Deerslayer*. The length, wooden prose, and small print of the volume would probably alienate, rather than win, Bill even if he were a reader. His response to Bill's statement that he never reads—"Then there's nothing I can do for you" (p. 135)—spells out Waldo's own failure, not Bill's. His friendly overture to Bill's wife some years later is even more clumsy and thoughtless. "I lugged this thing all the way down Terminus Road, and think you had better have it as—well, there isn't anybody else" (p. 177), he blurts out while offering this childless woman a lifelike plastic doll. He is too obtuse to notice whether his offer of a baby substitute shocks or offends her. This offer occurs within three or four pages of his cowering inside his house as

Johnny Haynes knocks anxiously without; thus readers see him failing twice in short order on his own turf, validating the grief that will soon flatten him.

Waldo has been flattened before. In 1934 he was hit by a car in downtown Sydney after learning that Dulcie had named her son after Arthur. He was nearly hit by a semi-trailer during the long walk with Arthur that opens the book. His lack of emotional reserves and poor moral balance have always made him vulnerable to upset, especially regarding Dulcie and Arthur. Soon after the end of the First War, he comes to the Feinsteins both to console Dulcie over her mother's recent death and, in view of her shakiness, to offer the security of marriage. Nothing works out as expected. He finds her speaking confidentially to Arthur; he hears that her mother's death has gladdened her; he learns that she is already engaged to Leonard Saporta. Because he clings so stubbornly to his ego, he couldn't foresee any of these developments, which drive him deeper into himself. His practice of disguising or suppressing his feelings has nullified the security of selfhood. He can face neither himself nor the normal demands of life. Whereas Arthur sleeps well, bad dreams plague Waldo. He also fails to act like a son. He discovers his father dead but steals away because he's too cowardly to face the death and to announce it to the family. He denies that his mother drinks too much, he refuses to discuss her breast surgery, and he stays away from her funeral. His problems can only worsen. His showing only a thin edge of himself, rather than facing life squarely, engenders denial elsewhere; he flusters easily and can't shake off his guilt. Guilt, not sexual excitement, grips him when he sees Mrs. Poulter naked at her washstand basin, and then, he tries to drive her naked image from his mind. Unable to cope with problems, he ignores them and hopes they will go away. In some cases he wishes death on a person whom he identifies with a problem.

He goes to pieces most quickly when goaded by impulse and spontaneity. Having neglected the implications of the truth that *Wald* means "forest" in German, he has tried to bury his dark animal side. He has fought himself in vain. Because he can't let himself go, he never finds his true character. His failure haunts him. Arthur accepts the family's dogs without trying to change them, use them, or rationalize their behavior: "The poor buggers . . . are only dogs. I love them" (p. 172), he says, stroking them, nuzzling them, and rolling with them on the floor. Conversely, Waldo shies away from the dogs, approaching them only to shoo them away with a kick. His failure to love or to win the love of the dogs that he lives with for many years gauges the gulf between him and his animal self. What most nettles this creature of habit and fact is his androgyny. Waldo responds sexually to other men. Noting the cleft chin of a chief librarian, which he takes as "the sign of a lover" (p. 167), he sees the man as a sexual force. The last time he sees Wally Pugh, another librarian and perhaps a brother substitute, before Wally ships overseas, he admits that he could love Wally and embraces him "furtively, though affectionately" (p. 121). This show of vulnerability could explain both the coldness with which he treats Wally's sister and the ruthlessness with which he suppresses the poems she brings him after Wally's death. Wally's role as a brother surrogate identifies Waldo in his own mind with Wally's sister. The aptness of the identification dredges up Waldo's lost hopes, self-contempt, and unspoken fears.

The sexual attraction that Waldo feels for Johnny Haynes provokes a still stronger response. When he read a schoolboy essay, Johnny's presence in the room made breathing a problem for him. Sexual provocation also colored Johnny's bullying of Waldo when school was out. If Waldo didn't enjoy the provocation, he nevertheless accepted it, and reacted angrily when Arthur rushed in to protect him and split Johnny's lip. Like his resentment of Arthur, Waldo's attraction to Johnny lingers. Prodded by envy and spite, he wonders years later whether the woman accompanying Johnny on his visit to Terminus Road has syphilis. More dramatically, he puts on his mother's old dress after not opening the door to Johnny. His female nature has won out: Johnny still makes him feel like a girl. Arthur's comment, years later, that Waldo is afraid of having a baby hits home. Putting on his mother's dress uncovered a rich vein of creativity in Waldo. But, shrinking from his true heart, he lacks the courage to mine it. He hides and then throws away the dress, the source of his greatest self-insight. His novel-in-progress, *Tiresias as a Youngish Man,* he stashes in two different hiding places as his worries about security mount. Of course, it is never completed. How could it be? Waldo's obsession with hiding reveals a man hiding from himself.

Waldo needn't have bothered to conceal his manuscript from Arthur, who has always read him perfectly. Waldo can't keep anything from Arthur—his friendship with the Feinsteins, especially Dulcie; the library where he works; the writing of poetry. Round Arthur keeps bouncing into areas Waldo views as his sacred preserve. Dismissed by Waldo as subliterary, he probes deeply into his psyche to write about the disturbing subjects Waldo has tried to shut out—the wives he carries inside his body and the primacy of pain in all love and all creation. Reading Arthur's poetry shows Waldo that, in avoiding pain, he has bypassed life; the person who can't feel pain can't feel anything else. Confused and angered by the nakedness of what he has just read, he destroys Arthur's poem. Then this enemy of life burns his own papers, which are no longer tolerable to him now that Arthur's purity and honesty have exposed their poverty. Wherever he turns he is forestalled or surpassed by the brother he has always tried to undervalue. Now that the force of Arthur's imagination has shown him the weakness of his own, Waldo must die. He is a destroyer, not a creator. Fittingly, he dies immediately after burning the unfinished literary works he had hidden in his mother's old dress box. Both he and his writing, with which he identifies, perish together after emerging from their hiding places, ridding the world of two shams with one stroke.

Waldo's death shatters Arthur so badly that he never recovers; the brotherly tie Waldo always discounted, Arthur cherishes. The scene describing most vividly the moral contrast between the twins occurs at the library. Seeing his shambling brother among the other patrons infuriates Waldo; he isn't even safe from Arthur at his city job. Although Waldo has gone to the library every working day for years, Arthur seems more relaxed and reasonable when he and Waldo meet there. He has come primarily to read *The Brothers Karamazov*, a book whose searing home truths threatened the scrawny humanist soul of George Brown so much that he burned his copy of it. A hive of contradictions, Waldo, as has been seen, got his first librarian's job through influence, even though he has always claimed that he doesn't accept favors. Now, some forty years later, not merely does he deny Arthur his right to use a public library; his deafness to Arthur's words about Dostoevski's Inquisitor also show that, despite a career among books, he can't relate literature to life. He has spent his career dispensing books to people without understanding the connection. Fragmentation and futility occur elsewhere. His calling Arthur "sir" (p. 191) as he orders him out of the reading room is the ultimate insult to Arthur, denying the bond joining him to his twin. But Arthur survives the insult better than Waldo, to whom the library had become a second home. Feeling less secure than he should, Waldo drives Arthur away because he is afraid that somebody will connect him to Arthur. Such a discovery would shame him to his colleagues. Thus his anxiety isn't moral, a matter of conscience, but social and pinned to appearances. Unlike him, Arthur doesn't care how things look or what people say. Though ugly and clumsy, he has a firm sense of himself; other people's reactions can't hurt him.

Chuffing Arthur serves wholeness. Whereas Waldo leads a splintered life, going to pieces when his family encroaches upon his work, Arthur has intuited the organic continuity between himself and the universe. He is as soothing as the milk and bread he distributes to his neighbors. Comfortable with his mystical knowledge, he doesn't feel obliged to make it productive. Possessions mean as little to him as do the opinions of others. He would give up his favorite mandala if asked. Having responded to it from the heart, he needn't own it; it is already his forever. Judging correctly, Hadgraft puts him in a literary tradition which includes Lear's Fool and Ahab's Pip, that of the inspired idiot who has the truth: "Arthur appears more complex than his frustrated twin. The glass marbles that he carries symbolize him, the mandalas, religious and magical figures of circle and square, signifying both unity and totality. He has, for instance, a gift for mathematics; he possesses an intuitive understanding of motives; he can distinguish unerringly between the trivial and the important. And— the essential difference from Waldo—his core is love.["5] Since he sees love as the highest law, his foibles can be overlooked. What he lacks in social amenities he more than recoups with his ability to touch and win hearts. He calls upon people uninvited; he asks embarrassing questions; he corrects his elders and betters when they misspeak themselves. At the Feinsteins he takes an ill-bred interest in the furniture, asks for food, stuffs himself, and falls asleep. This rudeness offends nobody. Mr. Feinstein calls him a "spirit of enlightenment" (p. 100), and his daughter soon tells him, "I think . . . you may be able to tell me a lot I shall want to hear" (p. 102). Earthy and sustaining, he keeps friends as easily as he makes them. Nobody can quite dismiss this slobbering, bovine man, unsavory though he may be. Rather, all suspect him of harboring special insights; the more time people spend with him, the more their surmises are rewarded. As regal as his name, he follows his impulses without needing to justify himself or to feel useful. Those impulses are usually reliable. Gainsaying distinctions, he finds as much beauty in weeds as in flowers. While crossing Plant Street, indicative of health and growth, he says that sickness is an access to reality: "when you are ill . . . you can get much farther in" (p. 51). His beliefs also inspire activity. Going straight to the music itself, he plays the piano without bothering about musical theory. He makes up songs, writes and enacts a tragedy, and dances the mandala. "The creative aspect of Arthur's path is evident when he dances the mandala," says Paul M. St. Pierre. "When Arthur reaches the center of the mandala . . . his mouth is a gateway to permanence, 'a silent hole.' "[6]

Arthur's policy of letting the world's sunshine pour through that hole helps him dance the mandala; the joy conveyed in the rhythmic movement of the dance needs no words. Indeed, words interfere. He learns the secrets of his four mandalas through light and touch, not through language, and he enjoys a deep wordless bond with Dulcie's father, bolstered by touch, right before the old man's death. Arthur's love is not derived or abstract, but firsthand, concrete, and often sensual. He can quell a crisis by dint of his mere presence, his spongy mass absorbing and neutralizing terror. When he hears of Dulcie's mother's death, he goes to the Feinsteins' house immediately and comforts the mourners; so deeply touched is Dulcie that she doesn't notice Waldo when he comes into the room and starts talking. Years later, after her father's death, Dulcie finds Arthur such a spiritual force that she asks him, "Are you, I wonder, the instrument we feel you are?" (p. 269). She also credits him with having given her the strength to face the truth about herself. His own father's death also reveals Arthur as a fount of spiritual faith. Without saying anything, his mother goes straight to him for consolation as soon as she learns of George Brown's death. He proves himself equal to her trust, even looming huge to Waldo. The love he bestows has expanded him. He soothes and comforts his mother, making sure that she eats, and arranges the funeral. Then his mood lifts. "When the doctor gets here I'd better be making tracks" (p. 67), he says, becoming breezy and going to work the same day his father dies. His business-as-usual manner softens the impact of George Brown's death on his mother. Arthur can be counted on to see that life survives pitfalls and reversals.

His ability to respond intuitively to the needs of others calls forth godlike associations. Tallying with his uncanny intuition is his openness to experience. Only a person who lives fully can delight in trifles like ringing a doorbell and also react viscerally to Dosteovski's Inquisitor. After sailing from England as a boy, he never leaves greater Sydney. His wresting value from what is nearest shows him embodying the Emersonian belief, stated in "Self-Reliance," that the wise man avoids travel because he has all he needs at home. Again repelling distinctions, he reveals traits of male and female, child and old man, all at once. This happy spread of self over the local landscape enriches others. All of his intimates, except for the resisting Waldo, profit from knowing him. Wilkes judges well to say that he becomes Mrs. Poulter's saint and her surrogate child in the final scene.[7] Her calling him "my pet" and "my love" (p. 308) suggests that he also becomes her substitute husband. The man-child of this taut scene had earlier acted as her priest; when he exclaims, "Why did you marry Mr. Poulter?" (p. 248) she surprises herself by answering him honestly and then feeling refreshed. People unburden themselves to him because they feel at ease. Because his tactless questions invite answers that will relieve stress, his boldness comforts more than it offends. He catches Mrs. Musto off guard when, after delivering her groceries, he strolls through her house and finds her standing in her underclothes in an upstairs room. Biting back an impulse to scream, this rich hoyden relaxes as soon as she recognizes her intruder. "O dear, Arthur ... it is you! I am sure you will understand" (p. 227), she says, sinking into a soft chair and telling him her troubles.

His visits to Mrs. Musto help explain his priestlike activity with Dulcie. As a boy he sees a bottle of perfume called *L'Amour de Paris* belonging to Mrs. Musto; its label shows Pierrot balancing on the moon. When he later sees Pierrot on a piece of sheet music the parallel between him and this traditional figure of romance, beauty, and unrequited love is strengthened. Pierrot, that sad clown from French pantomime who wears a floppy white suit, never gets the girl. But he's still a *Pierrot d'amour* because he helps the girl win love and happiness with someone else. White's modifications push the role close to the religious sphere. Arthur is no drooping harlequin, and he can only be said to want Dulcie in that Waldo, whom he calls "more than half of me" (p. 303), once wanted to marry her. But just as he

completes Mrs. Poulter by becoming her unborn child, so does he give
Dulcie the strength to marry and have children of her own. Appropriately,
she invites him and not Waldo to her wedding and later names her first son
after him. Just as appropriately, he dreams about giving birth to Dulcie in
the form of a tree. She is his spiritual creation, rooted in the rich hum-
mocky soil of his love and branching out, through her children, to an
assured future. Her rejection of her father's atheism in favor of the formal
Judaism of her forefathers restores religious faith to her bloodline. The last
time Arthur sees her, as he looks in unobserved through her dining room
window, she and her husband are conducting a religious rite with their
grandchildren and other relatives. Though outdoors, he nonetheless fills
the room and ritual with his spirit. Standing outside and looking in satisfies
him, as it satisfied Dubbo when he watched Mary Hare and Ruth Godbold
tending a dying Himmelfarb. Artist-priests, both men intercede on behalf
of a life they never partake of directly.

II

Nor did Arthur attend the wedding which helped make possible the
religious gathering he witnesses many years later. Both the wedding
and his rejection of Dulcie's invitation to it come to light in Part Three,
"Arthur." Arthur's section follows Waldo's, first, because Waldo prede-
ceases him and, next, because seeing the action from Arthur's standpoint
reveals him as more magnanimous than Waldo had imagined. Part Three
repeats some scenes already recounted in Part Two, like Waldo's first visit
to the Feinsteins and the death of pompous, innocent George Brown.
Some of the dialogue is even repeated verbatim (pp. 67, 201). What makes
this material worth repeating is the loving kindness supplied by Arthur's
point of view. Part Three shows the moral genius with which Arthur rises
above jealousies, rivalries, and grudges. Only in Part Three do we learn
that Arthur saw Waldo wearing their mother's blue dress on the day of
Johnny Haynes's visit. Though he is neither shocked nor upset by what he
sees, he spares Waldo's feelings by keeping his discovery to himself. His
mention of the hermaphroditic Adam after his discovery stands as a gentle
attempt to get closer to Waldo; Waldo's dismissal of the reference as filth
and madness deepens his self-alienation. No wonder he puts his head on a
table and cries.

  If the events of Part Three illuminate those of Part Two, they also
prefigure those of Part Four. Arthur declines Dulcie's wedding invitation,
not because his presence at the wedding would vex Waldo (which it would)
but because he can't imagine attending such an important event without
Waldo. He accepts what Waldo constantly kicks against—the closeness of
their bond. But perhaps the bond is even closer than the accepting Arthur

knows. Although the Brown twins aren't meant to represent opposite sides of the head-heart dualism, Waldo's death robs Arthur of the control and balance he needs to survive. Foolishly, he blames himself for the death; he reels around the city for days, racked by cold, hunger, and fatigue in addition to his emotional burden. After turning up at Mrs. Poulter's and becoming "her little boy, her old, snotty man" (p. 305), he goes to a mental home, no more able to look after himself than was Theodora Goodman at her own trail's end. His acceptance of his fate constitutes a recognition, both by him and White, that he can't survive on his own. As lovable as White finds Arthur, he portrays him objectively rather than sentimentally and withholds his total assent. Arthur seems immune to judgment. Like God, transcending finite dimensions, he leads a pure existence. Much of him is untouched by experience, and he seems incapable of learning. What he knows he seems to have known all along, and what he is ignorant of, like social graces, he can never be taught. The last chapter finds him having come full circle, back to infancy. Referred to several times as a baby, he fondles his one remaining marble with childish absorption, and he reminds Mrs. Poulter to bring him orange jujubes on visiting day. Finally, his being called "young fuller" (p. 308), a term used at least once to refer to him as a boy (p. 214), confirms either his purity or his appalling opacity.

The book's time scheme suits the continuous present in which Arthur lives. White shifts time freely to deliver him and Waldo from a cramped linear chronology and thus to convey the interior flow of both their joint and private lives. Besides causing Waldo's brief pangs over the enlistment and, later, the death of Walter Pugh, the First War barely touches the Browns. The Second War is reduced to a gala in downtown Sydney marking its end. The postwar boom that both heartened and puzzled Australians is symbolized by a new phone, frying pan, and television owned by the Poulters. Although White may include such details to document the passage of time, even mentioning a birthday now and then, he prefers to convey truths closer to home. Sometimes he will cut to the brothers' childhood, other times to a recent event. At one point in Part Two the twins look at the passing bus containing Mrs. Poulter and Dun, from which they were seen in Part One. The fragmenting of the novel's time scheme sharpens the continuity of the brothers' values, attitudes, and personal styles.

If the gliding chronology of *Mandala* recalls that of *Riders,* the later novel's cleaner, tighter style brings a welcome change. The prose of *Mandala* is controlled without being thin; a few details such as the Poulters' telephone, frying pan, and TV can do the work of pages of brooding analysis. White writes about things you can touch, feel, and smell, giving his prose tactile values missing from or buried inside a mound of words in *Riders.* Physical details, buttressed by a sound grasp of anatomy, account for the vitality of the book's finest moment—Arthur's dance of the mandala. Arthur both withers and swells as he honors the real and the ideal, the spirit and the flesh, and what never existed in his wordless tribute. That Mrs. Poulter watches the dance with her hair spreading lavishly on her shoulders indicates her receptiveness to it. That her husband, who knows nothing of the dance, forbids her to walk alone with Arthur after the dance outing captures the incongruity of experience.

White's ability both to balance the incongruous and the rhapsodic and to distinguish between plenty and excess helps shape the fresh, hopping data comprising *Mandala*. The book has a precision and an economy missing since *The Aunt's Story*, but it surpasses the latter by portraying two characters in depth, rather than just one, and by exploring their relationship, which runs deeper than any enjoyed by Theodora Goodman. Although the variety of narrative modes he displays as he moves from book to book makes White's development hard to trace, the superiority of *Mandala* over *Aunt's Story* shows outstanding artistic growth. This same growth will characterize the much longer *Vivisector*, which shows, like its two immediate predecessors, that life may be served in many ways. Writing *The Solid Mandala* showed White that he needn't be trapped in a style. His art had attained a distinction that could compensate for his having fathered no children. In it, he had created something that was his and no other man's. Like him, the main figure of *The Vivisector* is a bachelor artist whose important relationships bypass traditional definitions. Hurtle Duffield's overcoming of limits symbolizes White's confrontation with himself. The excellence of *The Solid Mandala* enabled White to probe the meaning both of his career and of his commitments within the roominess of the long novel.

9. Knives of Light

Do WE NEED another novel about an artist after reading about Joyce's budding author in *A Portrait* (1916), Cary's painter in *The Horse's Mouth* (1944), and Mann's musician in *Dr. Faustus* (1948)? Yes—if the novel says something new and important about the artistic process, the artist's personality, and the tie joining the artist to his background. *The Vivisector* (1970) shows how and why Hurtle Duffield's artistry was formed, why he stayed with it, and what price he paid. It also conveys both the agonies and the rewards of imaginative creation. Vulnerable and self-critical, Hurtle dramatizes the superiority of instinctive arousal. He is by no means impervious, cool headed, or immune to setback. But his suffering promotes faith; in anguish, his spirit comes to life, glimpsing eternity and infinity. In that his creative flair stays in step with his self-creation, he resembles a work of art in his own right. His ability to wrest inspiration from people as different as Boo Hollingrake, a rich, accomplished socialite, and Cecil Cutbush, an uncouth homosexual grocer, makes him the artist of both androgynous and democratic sensibility. *Vivisector* clears a midway path for the artist between highbrow and lowbrow and between the formal and the popular. To the Freudian, Hurtle exemplifies the sublimation of instinct in art; although he doesn't want to supplant his father, his childhood trauma of being sold by his parents to a rich family has made him distrust both authority and intimacy. The devotee of Australian themes could explain him as the artist who confers poetic truth upon local materials without trumpeting national ideals or pressing for social activism. An interpreter of a new world, Hurtle Duffield is vast and contains multitudes.

The rich variety of the Australian nation-continent mirrors this vastness. Having severed himself from both family and social class, as his country did from England, Hurtle has a clear sense of self and place. His stint in the back country shows him to have inherited the rough masculine urge for freedom and adventure associated with Australia's pioneer heritage. His land's bond with the sea shows in his living in such nautical-sounding places as Sydney's Cox Street and Chubb's Lane. White also links him to a national tradition of painting by giving him a name whose initials recall Australia's greatest painters, Hans Heysen, Russell Drysdale, and William Dobell (whose painting, "The Dead Landlord," inspired *The Ham Funeral*); Hurtle's voluptuous nude women and his brief residence in a primitive shack up the line, recalling Norman Lindsay, further strengthen the book's tie with Australian art. But the Australian artist who never leaves home dwarfs himself. White takes Hurtle from Australia three times because his imagination needs the stimulation provided by England, France, and Greece. His time in the Old World helps build and refine his sensibility.

Having knocked about with Paris's bohemian set after his army discharge, Hurtle returns home to develop his creativity. He supports himself as a kitchen hand, janitor, and factory worker while continuing to paint. Never does he question the wisdom of having returned to Sydney; the artist is embedded in his nation's traditions, landscape, and people. While visiting Greece in midlife, he vows never to leave home again. Not only does he keep his vow, spending the whole second half of his life in greater Sydney; he also spends more and more time walking Sydney's streets, involves himself in the life of his neighborhood, and renews a tie with his adoptive sister, Rhoda, that had languished for forty years. This immersion in home truths deepens his artistic vision while activating his heart. Like Alf Dubbo, he gravitates progressively slumwards as he probes his vitality. His painting joins the dark blaze of creativity to the common light of day.

White doesn't describe the process by which Hurtle's imagination seizes upon and transforms the external conditions of life. The artist's secret remains hidden because imaginative creation is mysterious. Just as Hurtle is arrogant, ambiguous, and tender in his dealings with others, so is his painting oblique, ethereal, and agonizing. Whereas peace and stability lull the mind, unrest brings on the recklessness and then possibly the violence that quickens it. White's refusal to demythologize the artistic process almost betrays him into claiming that the artist's burden is only slightly lighter than the Cross. On the other hand, his refusal to dissolve Hurtle in a sociological formula, a Freudian paradigm, or an aesthetic theory insures both Hurtle's uniqueness and commonality. The Flint Street home where he lives virtually his whole adult life stands on a corner, facing two ways and having entrances on two sides. Most of what goes on nearby falls within his range of vision. Furthermore, his imagination gives this abundance new life. The artist extends and refines his options, rather than limiting them; Hurtle can serve both as Kathy Volkov's spiritual father and as her lover. The positioning of the doors leading into his corner house, like the eye symbolism connected with him, strikes affinities with Janus, the all-seeing pagan god of doorways and arches. The parallel is revealing. The legends about the gates of Janus opening only in times of war invoke the artist's struggles. The more Hurtle claws and scrapes, the closer he comes to the mystery of the divine; the more he draws upon his capacity for evil, the more he exploits his creativity. The notion that Janus is related to Diana, chaste goddess of the hunt, while keeping bloodshed and cruelty to the fore, also makes claims for the deformed Rhoda which further enrich our appreciation of her artist brother.[1]

I

Hurtle's relationship with Rhoda is the most important of his life. His reunion with his adoptive sister helps him grow both as an artist and as a man. Except for the feelings roused in him by Rhoda and, later, by Kathy Volkov, he had parried all emotion other than what could be conveyed within the formal medium of painting. His having painted Rhoda as both a pythonness and an octopus shows that he has remained constantly if indirectly aware of her during their long separation. His aesthetic preoccupation with her lunges into the moral sphere and soon overtakes all. John Docker mistakenly describes the process as destructive: "Rhoda . . . is the 'Octopus': tentacular in her insidious possessiveness; suppressive in her presumed intuitive understanding, without any flow of inner natural and sexual life. Rhoda comes finally to represent in the novel Hurtle's own social self. . . . Hence she is potentially the most destructive of his creative life."[2] Though a hunchbacked dwarf scraping along on a diet of bread and cheese, Rhoda is the book's toughest, most independent character. Her self-imposed job of feeding the neighborhood cats horsemeat from her go-cart satisfies her enough to rule out the need for anybody. Such eccentricity would hardly motivate this near-sociopath to tame and socialize Hurtle. Rather than stifling his creativity, she whets it; rather than trying to possess and consume him, she resists him. He is moved much more deeply by their reunion than she is. He reaches out for her hand, offers her food, and leads her tearfully to his home. When he says, "We could be a help to each other, couldn't we?" (p. 401) she responds by taking her hand from his. She will not live with him until begged, and she only comes on her own terms—that her fifteen cats come, too. She doesn't need to corrupt or stifle him. Her descent from her parents' elegant mansion to the shabby night world of the alley is complete; she has pared life to the bare necessities of food, shelter, and work.

Hurtle, on the other hand, sees his need for her immediately. Kathy has already shown him the importance of opening his heart, although, either gifted or afflicted with the artist's personality, she sidesteps most of his romantic overtures. Perhaps she sees that he isn't ready for love, that he must first sort out his life and his art. He makes headway quickly. He refers to Rhoda as "a moral force, or booster of his conscience" (p. 404), and he believes that her reentry into his life will provide a focus and a unity beneficial to his painting. His artist's concern with design has responded to her as a chance for completeness and wholeness. By looking to be served, he approaches her selfishly. His exceeding his selfish hopes certifies his humanity. She teaches him about the self he has denied for so many years in the alleged service of his art. By sharing his life, he uncovers both the tenderness and the need to give first awakened in him by Kathy. This rich flow of humanity rouses his imagination quickly; his creativity awakens with his heart. Soon after he receives Rhoda in his home, he begins experimenting with a new art form, that of colored paper cutouts arranged in a collage. (The reference, extending the range of comparisons between him and other notable painters, recalls Matisse, who also took up collage-making in his maturity.)

Hurtle needs her more than she needs him; her deformity has deprived her of compassion for so long that she has learned to do without it. With her sharp chin, pointed nose, and ratlike eyes, this twisted old frump makes his late creative spurt believable. She thinks clearly, speaks plainly, and, having stripped her life to essentials, avoids vanity and affectation. Her resistance to his offer of a fur coat shows Hurtle the difficulty of giving. When his patronness, Boo Hollingrake, had offered him a car, he had turned her down with a sneer. Rhoda's stubbornness teaches him compassion, patience, and tact. He acquires the imagination needed to deal with her effectively. As a result, the new life he helps instill in her constitutes a rebirth equal to his own. White's numerous references to her as a rose foreshadow her taking on a new softness, delicacy, and grace that make her final years with Hurtle an adventure for both of them.

Some of the book's best passages (and some of White's most effective incursions into domestic realism) dramatize this adventure. Rhoda and Hurtle shout, argue, slam doors, eat together, and nurse each other as they age and tire. They also share moments of tenderness all the more touching because of their silent agreement to shun each other's vulnerabilities. They have come to know each other well enough to conduct the most vital parts of their relationship in the realm of the tacit and the surmised. The Biblical Rhoda was a New Testament Christian. In Acts 12, she opened her door to Peter after his release from prison; so shocked was she to see him that she slammed the door in his face. Rhoda Courtney's knowledge that her ugliness led her parents to adopt Hurtle had often tempted her to shut him out of her own life, and his crotchets and vagaries have often made her regret her adult decision to open the door and readmit

him. The social poise and heart knowledge she displays at the end show
that she did well to maintain her tie with this modern spirit of doorways
and arches. Her ability to put aside her accumulated resentment in favor of
sharing her life with Hurtle shows real growth.

Hurtle must also surmount barriers before he can make a home with
Rhoda. His apartness from others both haunts and helps him. The artist
can't always afford candor. Because, as a vivisector, he trades on pain and
loss, he must wear a mask and keep his purposes to himself: "You,
Hurtle—you were born with a knife in you hand," says Maman, quickly
correcting herself, "No . . . in your eye" (p. 129). The artist's accurate,
unrelenting eye sees deeply and mercilessly. In his search for the truth he
respects no creeds, institutions, or persons. Nor does he cloud his percep-
tions with sentiment. He will use people, then discard them. The money
and the sex that the Sydney prostitute Nance Lightfoot gives him mean less
to him than the inspiration she provides. Even this inspiration may drown in
the light of a more pressing need: when Nance asks for her share of the
commission he earns on the sale of a painting, he glances at his watch and
changes the subject. A later lover, Hero Pavloussi, attempts suicide because
she feels so neglected. The guilt welling up in him because of such damage
means that he works secretly, even furtively, practicing his art as a vice.

He learned this steely-eyed detachment as a boy. Prizing utility over
beauty, his natural father wanted him to learn a trade. Though Mumma
always stressed the importance of "edgercation" (p. 8), cleaning a church
to pay for Hurtle's French and Latin lessons, she also frowned upon his
reading of the Bible. Her first reaction to his drawing, "You and yer
scribbles. . . . I'll have Pa take the belt to you if it ever happens again"
(p. 8), proves that his biological parents can't help him develop his sensibility. Nor does he find help and encouragement after the Courtneys adopt
him. Perhaps reflecting the Saxon distrust of brilliance, his first teacher
(aptly named Miss Adams) accuses him of showing off and throws away
his sketch of death, which he represents as an elephant draped in a lion's
skin. Later "his pretended father" (p. 88), Harry Courtney, whips him
with a riding crop for painting on his bedroom wall. The whipping both recalls and extends several motifs from Joyce's *Portrait*—
the physical suffering of the artist, the artist's lonely pride, and his ability
to detach himself from his own pain. (Just as Stephen Dedalus thought of
his stinging, burning hands as belonging to someone else, so does Hurtle
see that Harry Courtney feels the lash of the riding crop more keenly than
he.) Another legacy from Joyce is the artist's sense of outrage and self-
disgust. The brutality depicted in his wall painting makes Hurtle shiver
with horror. He accepts without flinching the whipping he knows he
deserves. Ironically, had he portrayed his Latin tutor's suicide less effectively, he'd not have shocked himself so much.

Self-division continues to dog him, his art prospering at the expense of his well being. The pattern can be traced to his early childhood. *The Vivisector* presents these years honestly and accurately, without sentimentality or moral purpose. The action begins when Hurtle is four or five years old, probably because small children have a sensitivity that most of us non-artists shed with the passage of years. His laundress mother, Bessie, and his father, Jim, who sells empty bottles, have made him feel secure and whole despite the shortage of money and abundance of children in the noisy, crowded Duffield home. His questions bring predictable answers, especially when they concern the old family papers and photographs preserved by his father. That Hurtle's perusal of these treasures usually takes place on Sunday endows it with ritual force; the photos and papers communicate a sense of family tradition that deepens with each celebration. This innocent, orderly world cracks. Beginning in an atmosphere of warmth, security, and intimacy, chapter 1 ends on a note of irrevocable exile. Because of his exceptional beauty and intelligence, Ma Duffield is able to sell Hurtle to the well-to-do Courtneys, in whose home she does laundry twice a week. "You're what Pa and me knows we aren't" (p. 15), she tells him, knowing that he will stand a better chance to develop his skills amid the splendors of Sunningdale than in his parents' slum shanty.

By sending Hurtle to the Courtneys, she believes herself to be acting in his best interests. She is only partly right. The sacrifice that opens new vistas for him also saddles him with a separation anxiety that will stay with him forever. He becomes self-divided; what hobbles him as a man helps him as an artist. He never comes close to marrying, joins no political or social clubs, plays no team sports, and resists male friendships with the steeliness of a Waldo Brown. Being peddled to the Courtneys angers and confuses him. The unpredictability of adults also teaches him distrust. Rather than risking commitment to another person, he turns inward. Rather than going into business, which would be tantamount to endorsing the marketplace ethic that ripped him from his home, he develops his flair for painting. Art protects him from a middle-class consumer mentality that sanctions the sale of children. Art also gives him an important foothold. Instead of immobilizing him, his childhood upheaval makes him feel tentative enough about himself to work out his own place. This place excludes all women until he rediscovers Rhoda. His defensiveness makes sense, because women either banish him or try to smother him. Whereas Bessie Duffield drove him from the family hearth, Alfreda Courtney keeps him on a tight rein. She jams his head into the "scented silky darkness" (p. 77) of her wardrobe to teach him her smell and thus to win his loyalty, just as she would with a puppy. Her act recoils on her. Hurtle doesn't want to suffocate in a wardrobe or be swallowed with the chocolate she sucks out of his mouth. To avoid being engulfed by her, he enlists in the army (by falsifying his age, as did Oliver Halliday in *Happy Valley*). Women continue to threaten him. The cool, accomplished Boo Hollingrake stuffs her tongue into his mouth at Sunningdale and again, twenty years later, at Flint Street. The sight of her deliberately licking a postage stamp (as Vic Moriarty did in *Happy Valley*) in Sydney's William Street Post Office heightens his fears that she wants to lick him into shape before presenting him to her rich friends. His first reaction to Nance Lightfoot casts her in the same threatening, dominating role. Again, the orally transmitted threat endangers his ability to breathe: "suffocated by fur and brandy, he'd had enough of Nance" (p. 163). His decision to paint rather than to become the head of the Courtney family, now that Harry is dead, has strengthened him, and he can't let his new resolve be shaken. Standing by a breakwater shortly after his return from Europe, he dreads being washed into the sea, that powerful symbol of femaleness and, to him, of the devouring mother.

His fear of being absorbed by women stays with him. Although they remain important to him throughout his life, he protects himself from them by dealing with them in pairs: the self-canceling force of Mumma Duffield and his sister Lena gives way to that of Rhoda and Maman in his youth, and then to that of Nance and Boo; Boo continues to befriend him after Nance's death, which allows Hero Pavloussi to step in as his lover. These women need protection more than he does. The two who try hardest to win his love and the only two he is seen to have sex with, Nance and Hero, both die. Nor do their deaths change the pattern of his female bondings: during his last years he divides his heart between Rhoda, with whom he never has sex, and Kathy Volkov, whom he only makes love to once, during her adolescence and while he has adopted the passive, traditionally female posture.

The negation he feels toward men runs in different channels. As an authority figure who demands obedience, the father exerts as much menace as the stifling mother. Each of Hurtle's foster parents tries to mold him, and each must be escaped. His rejection of Harry Courtney's wish to turn him into a rancher motivates him as much as the fear of suffocating inside Maman's warm, padded rooms. Only *he* can determine the quality of the air he breathes. But whereas he resists his outdoorsman-father as an authority figure, he loves Harry Courtney the person— the solid, decent wearer of tweeds who has a stroke, ages quickly, and dies. Courtney wins Hurtle's love by falling from omnipotence. No such descent happened to Jim Duffield, Hurtle's natural father. None was necessary. Adept only at siring children (Mumma is carrying her eighth when Hurtle leaves Cox Street), Pa never attained any height from which to fall; he is ugly, earns little money, and Mumma keeps stressing how his lack of education kept him below the social and intellectual levels of his gentleman-father. His failure to talk Mumma out of selling Hurtle to the Courtneys, within the boy's hearing, depicts him once again as a flawed father, one whom a talented, ambitious son wouldn't emulate or identify with.

But he still exerts force. Though Hurtle despises him intellectually and rejects him as a role model, he can't drive his natural father from his heart. The figure of the absentee father rules others in the book, too, as their sexual responses show. Hurtle reminds Nance of her father, and Kathy speaks of Hurtle as a surrogate father after they make love. Hurtle's reaction to Pa is more complex, because of his heterosexuality and his angry individualism (as a boy, he tears up a drawing after seeing in it the influence of Goya). But he can't detach sex from his view of his father any more than Kathy and Nance could. The influence burns briefly but brightly. He and Pa may have both enjoyed Nance, even though he rejects the possibility the moment it presents itself. When he sees a bottle on her dressing table, his tongue thickens and his throat tightens in horror. But he regains control, letting pass her statement that the bottle came from a junk dealer-customer. Instead of wondering about the junk dealer, he turns his mind to the bottles Maman used to keep. His mental acrobatic is clearly an evasion tactic. He was so eager to escape Maman, whom Robert S. Baker rightly calls "the archetype of the threatening female,"[3] that he lied about his age to get into the army; he never answered her letters; he has made no effort to reach her, now that he has returned to Sydney. The riot wrought by Nance's bottle refers less to her than to stringy, ineffectual Jim Duffield, whose genes both animate and define him.

A much more potent father figure—and thus one more easy for Hurtle to defy—is Hero's husband, Cosma Pavloussi. Although lusting for Hurtle, Hero continues to worship Cosma. Her reverence leaves her unsatisfied. Cosma's complacency when he hears of her affair is just one example of his inscrutability. Knowing that Hurtle must withhold love from her, Hero can live no more fully with him than she can with the husband who denies her sexually. Cosma's great power and money, his stocky peasant build and ancestry, and the many business deals that take him all over the world and thus give the impression of ubiquity liken him to a god—a cruel god, invoking the words from *King Lear* (a work seminal to White's next novel): "As flies to wanton boys are we to th' gods;/ They kill us for their sport" (IV, i, 36-37). Destroying life on a whim, he orders a sackful of cats drowned; the act disturbs Hurtle deeply enough, given his sister Rhoda's kinship with cats, to inspire one of his most searching paintings. Cosma continues to rankle Hurtle, almost as if he were directing his apparently random depredations to the main themes of Hurtle's life. His adopting a little Aboriginal girl and then sending her back to her mother on the reserve, along with some money for the mother's trouble, reminds Hurtle of how money and power cut across his own family tie. Both Hurtle and Sosa have been deprived of families; both have also been treated like merchandise, Sosa more grievously than he, since she was sent back when her rich buyer no longer wanted her. Hurtle never snaps his childhood tie or outgrows his childhood trauma. What better way to avenge the wrongs dealt Sosa, himself, and the cats that remind him of Rhoda than to steal the wife of the symbolic head of the world that perpetrated them?

The mystery of unity set forth in works like *Voss* and *Riders* deepens in *Vivisector*, where the creator Hurtle rivals God and defies his earthly surrogates. The rivalry makes psychological sense. If he can hope for no more help from God than from his parents, Hurtle must then create himself. A major step in his drama of self-creation comes in early middle age, when he flies with Hero from Australia to the Greek island of Perialos. She has come to this "island of saints and miracles" (p. 297) to redeem herself; she wants to atone for her adultery. The trip fails her. Summoned by spirit, she can't escape the flesh and other manifestations of matter. Her plight is foreshadowed by the sight of a man urinating into the wind. Then she learns that an epidemic has sickened many of the island's inhabitants; the convent she visits with Hurtle lodges orphan-whores; the abbess of the convent has a cold and seems trite, mundane, and mercenary. Hero's spirits sink again when she visits a chapel in hope of talking to the hermit-monk who lives there. Not only is the monk gone, but a pile of human excrement is also seen decaying alongside the abandoned chapel's altar. While saddening Hero (who never reappears after her hapless Grecian pilgrimage), the trip to Perialos teaches Hurtle that he can't find answers to his problems outside himself. The bread he chews hungrily the morning after the outing to the chapel and the convent symbolizes his taking of the Eucharist and marks his formal dedication to himself as his own creator and arbiter.

A key statement on his policy of self-trust comes in a comment of Hero's made just outside the empty chapel: "I think we have lost our faith in God because we cannot respect men. They are so disgusting" (p. 355). People are so dim, bent, and corrupt that they whet the artist's malice. To look at a hunchbacked dwarf like Rhoda or a fat homosexual like Cecil Cutbush is to understand the cruelty of a Cosma Pavloussi. But the artist must resist Cosma's drive to crush and degrade. The great artist is embedded in his culture, not divorced from it; Hurtle invites Rhoda to live with him, extending the idea of culture and society into the home. Other affirmations brighten Flint Street. Hurtle affirms his belief in the richness and the shimmering goodness of the world in paint; as Alf Dubbo showed, to paint God's creation is to worship it. Such reverence requires genius. Whereas anyone can worship beauty, splendor, and success, only a truly creative imagination can love the nastiness and frailty that constitute humanity. Hurtle possesses this godlike sensibility. The novel's epigraph from Ben Nicholson links painting to religion; both activities aspire to infinity. In line with Nicholson's idea, the action begins on a Sunday when a formal ritual, Hurtle's weekly inspection of his family's history, is celebrated, and it ends with the words "indi-ggoddd" (p. 567). As in *Solid Mandala*, the color blue symbolizes religious faith and heavenly truth. In Hurtle's dying vision art has moved from the realm of contingency to that of divinity, sweeping the artist's spirit along with it. Though Hurtle does die, White's eliminating a full stop after the book's last word certifies the immortality of his spirit. Richard N. Coe has shown how the artist effects this miracle. First, Hurtle's common birth, puts him close to the folk spirit of his people and thus gives him an intuitive grasp of its sanctity: "The role of the artist in a democratic society is to steep himself in the vulgarity of the mass, and yet at the same time, remaining still inexorably himself, to transmute it into something unique and everlasting."[4]

One challenge set forth by the artist's transmuting role consists of adopting means inconsistent with his ends. Although he strives to wrest radiance and joy out of common human clay, he must rely on an insight so detached and merciless that it resembles the cruelty so damaging to his redemptive goals. The novel's title refers to the creative necessity he sometimes describes as an inner deformity or wound. Vivisection enters the novel directly with Maman's anti-vivisectionist campaign. A moral crusader and charity worker, Alfreda Courtney recoils in horror from the model of a vivisected dog in a London taxidermist's window. The plaster model also stirs Hurtle deeply, but in a different way. The vivisected dog tells him that no artist can afford to make exclusions or to limit his spirit. The artist enacts the boundlessness of divine grace by arrogating absolute freedom to his imagination. Maman's antivivisectionist campaign denies a source of inspiration, the creativity of destruction; the burning-away of slag in a refinery leaves strong, malleable steel. Vivisection can also teach valuable lessons; a scientist can't see a muscle in action, like a heart pumping blood, in a dead animal. Ugliness and brutality activate Hurtle. Besides being moved by the taxidermist's model, he reacts strongly to Nance's smashed body, the seizure of an epileptic girl at one of Boo's parties, and the spectacle of Rhoda's twisted, defenseless nudity in a Brittany hotel. The excitement he feels when witnessing female devastation includes but goes beyond his revolt against Maman. "The painter is cruel. Why do painters have to deform everything they see?" (p. 287) he is asked at a dinner party. His polite answer bypasses the spirit of the question. The artist is no copyist. Rather than reproducing photographic replicas, he distorts in order to capture a reality beyond appearances. Sometimes an inner truth lies in the mangled and the deformed. Ugliness can convey truths beyond the ken of sanity, reason, and politeness.

But doesn't his walking in darkness damage him more than any imposition of restraints? Using methods both criminal and crippling, the artist pays a heavy price for his inventiveness: "He becomes beyond all others the great Invalid, the great Criminal, the great Accursed One—and the Supreme Knower," says Rimbaud in one of the book's epigraphs. The artist resembles a vivisector because he slices through people's defenses in order to probe their weaknesses. His practice reflects shrewd judgment; in our vulnerabilities lies our reality. The artist's brush, writer's pen, or orchestra conductor's baton resembling a scalpel, he captures people in those moments in which their vitality asserts itself unchecked. He can't act otherwise. The artist must portray life on the wing if he is to capture its shimmer and dancing vibrancy. But what animates his art makes his subjects wince. We don't like being caught off guard, preferring instead to keep private our obsessions and those other loyalties by which we define ourselves. The artist menaces us in other ways, too. By baring our naked impulses, he sometimes peels away raw flesh along with protective interfaces such as social rank, property, and titles. He must sacrifice us to his gimlet eye, even to the point of indulging cruelty, if he is to catch us when most alive and thus disclose the heretofore unknown.

II

Working at top form, the artist combines purity of vision with driving detachment. His creativity ebbs, flows, and bubbles into new channels, as Hurtle's different phases of artistic growth show. A viewer of his paintings remarks astutely, "They're so different from one another. . . . Not all by the same person" (p. 393). Like the different narrative modes reflected in White's novels, Hurtle's constant experiments with line, color, and density reveal polystylism as the hallmark of the artist. The artist uses different techniques to reach the truth. By fleeing success, which counts less than the truth, he avoids hardening into a manner. He also grows. Hurtle's series of paintings of Nance, Rhoda, the rocks near his outback retreat, and his furniture convey his refusal to take refuge in a single style. They also hone his vision and technique for the huge God paintings, those "savage and mysterious pictures"[5] of his late maturity. His method isn't inductive, the patient, accurate translation of observed phenomena to canvas. Nor is it elitist and intuitive, a highly subjective process only accessible to those sympathetically attuned with him. Combining inspiration and drudgery, Hurtle works single-mindedly. He doesn't wait for the divine afflatus. Only after the mechanical plodding has taken place will the imagination respond with the stroke that magically transforms an entire work.

The artist's genius and his craft rest on his sensuality. Though not tempted by the church or politics, as was Joyce's Stephen, Hurtle insists on relating to life intimately and immediately. He learns the value of touch as a small child. He will touch and brush against his mother when he wants a favor from her. He will tear a flower to bits to study its makeup and taste the rusty flakes he peels from an old weatherbeaten stove. The same curiosity that leads him to push a horsehair into the rear end of a fly or to break a tuberous begonia makes him want to touch, or even lick, the surface of a beautiful painting. His rage for beauty knits with his urge to damage and destroy. In each case he wants to know at first hand the texture, consistency, and tensile strength of sensory objects. He needs to know the surfaces of a thing before he can touch its animating core. The first thing he does after entering his new room at his adoptive parents' home is to feel the walls. The clamoring participials and finite verbs in the following description show how life thrums and crackles for him, the description's strong concluding image expressing the primitive force of his sensuality: "The heaped branches of the uppermost trees blazed in the last of the bonfire, a wind rushed in to douse: there was a hissing, a spitting, and clapping, and lapping, as the stream poured . . . the engulfed trees swaying, and tugging at their roots like submerged weeds, the gorge moaning its fulfillment" (p. 204).

The severity of his lifestyle follows from his need to be in sensuous contact with reality. Abrasive, gritty surfaces dominate his life. The names of the places he lives—Ironstone and Flint Street—convey his self-imposed harshness. Like an athlete, he keeps physically fit without mortifying himself. The artist must give rein to his full range of sensuality. The same person who delights in the rainbow shudder of the Courtneys' chandelier and wears fine English tweeds can build a makeshift shack in the bush and sleep on potato sacks. "He no longer knew whether he was an artist, an ascetic, or a prig" (p. 203), he notes in a self-questioning moment. The eye he paints as a boy symbolizes the ruthless detachment and truth-probing that become his artistic ideal. He wants to penetrate the reality of material things in order to find an in-dwelling principle. Artistic objectivity in White stems from immersion in the concrete, palpable world. Among other gains reaped from this philosophy of participation is the ability to show things in the process of becoming other things. As a boy of twelve, Alf Dubbo painted a tree bearing dreams which had not yet been dreamt. Like him, Hurtle wants to catch experience that has not yet been experienced. He blurs frontiers between different orders of being to discover new truths. When he tells Cutbush that some buildings on the horizon remind him of unlit gas fires, he shows his imagination at work; the upshot of his talk with Cutbush is his frightening "Lantana Lovers Under Moonfire." Other fresh fusions of normally unrelated forms include his androgynous self-portrait; his painting of a sackful of drowning cats, who take on human traits as they near death; and the early "Animal Rock Forms." His rocks aren't hard, cold, and jagged but "big, pink, cushiony forms" (p. 206) that resemble sleeping animals as they float in "a shower of milky seed or light" (p. 206).

The artist mirrors his art, his blood sometimes reconciling different strains or cultures just as his imagination combines and recombines opposites. By nature he is working class, a slum brat; by nurture, a plutocrat. Both upper and lower classes can claim him. Though he lives in a near-slum, he has retained traces of the aristocratic bearing and temper inherited from his clergyman-grandfather and later cultivated at Sunningdale. The smooth, widely traveled Boo Hollingrake (who has the breeding and aplomb to get away with calling herself Boo) spends as much time with him as he will permit. He also speaks courteously and gently to strangers. When the printer Mothersole asks him if he's a successful artist, he answers modestly, "I'm said to be" (p. 365). His reply to little Kathy Volkov's abrupt, "Aren't you the painter?" is spoken simply and quietly: "Yes, I do paint" (p. 386). Nor do his gentlemanly ways bar him from the middle class. His regular work routine, fixed residence, and need to support himself make him as middle class as any other rate-payer. Like most artists, he is classless—but like all good ones, he belongs to everybody. And he knows it. He isn't so steeped in the ether of imaginative creation that he has forgotten the crude energy throbbing both within and around him.

His name conveys his origins and purposes. Hurt, which he is called by several friends, reminds us of the artist's anguish, both physical and emotional. He can't escape pain. Having served in the army during wartime, he metes out pain all his life. White refers to him as a vivisector with good reason. As a small child, he throws a stone at a cat, splits a school-mate's lip, and routs a mob of larrikins. His very presence at Sunningdale throws up Rhoda's handicap to her; her parents wouldn't have adopted him had she pleased them. He angers Maman constantly; he frustrates Hero Pavloussi so much that, after her suicide attempt, she travels to Greece to confess her sins; he may even have driven Nance to suicide.[6] Much of the hurt he generates stings him more keenly than it does others. His creative throes, his nightmares, and the guilt he feels over exploiting people describe him as a battlefield; no serene, all-forgiving Olympian, he. The art that drains off some of his aggression covers a broad range. As his two last names imply, he belongs to both the field and the court; because the artist can't make exclusions, he draws sustenance from both realms. The process is instinctive and unconscious. If he inclines toward the fertile earth, as opposed to the artificial glare of the court, he would agree with Rhoda that his stint under the chandelier helped him. But neither the court nor the field strictly pertains to him. He lives most of his life along Sydney's pavements. Also, White's account of his life has a rude urban vigor, abundance, and atmosphere which make *Vivisector* his most metropolitan novel. Though his artist-hero does hurdle the field (White won't let us overlook the pun), he doesn't forget that Australia's wide prairie offers a source of hope. His experiences in the outdoors show that, like Harry Courtney, he believes in doing a man's job in the heart of a man's country.

Like Kathy, whose last name, Volkov, testifies to her rootedness in the yeomanry of her nation, he views his career as an Australian drama. He speaks favorably of "an Australian instinct he hoped he possessed" (pp. 194-95) when he sets out to build his crude bushland shack. His interlude up the line, during which he lives like a hermit, has a cohesive effect, in addition to the obvious separating one. He learns a great deal about his nation's history. The time and energy he spends building the shack isn't wasted. His efforts deepen his understanding of both homesteading (as practiced by untold Stan Parkers) and the frontiersman's belief that the good life inheres in going into the bush or the outback.

His involvement in the fellowship of Australia deepens after he comes back to the city from Ironstone and moves to Flint Street. He spends more and more time riding buses and walking Sydney's busy streets; he develops a growing affection for his neighbors; an increasing number of his pictures treat local scenes or people. His brief encounter with Mothersole in chapter 7 means so much to him because of Mothersole's ordinariness; as in Thomas Mann, the genius in White yearns for the commonplace. "Boring, decent" (p. 365) Mothersole shows Hurtle that loving can hurt; considering the artist's name and his proneness to hurt, the printer's example puts Hurtle in closer touch with his own reality. Mothersole lost his wife; his son died in the war; his sister is a cripple. Viewing the ferry ride he takes with Mothersole as a symbolic sea journey, Hurtle attunes himself to the similarities between himself and Mothersole. He and the printer, a literary descendent of the Dyer of Holunderthal in *Riders*, are about the same age, have a deformed sister, and served in the First War. The vigor he gains from recognizing these similarities discloses both his own renewability and the sinew of the middle class. Before he met Mothersole, his world had gone flat and his paintings seemed lifeless. The chance meeting with his alter ego represents a rebirth through love. Without it, he'd never have invited Rhoda to live with him when chance materializes her in the next chapter. His heart quickens immediately. As his name implies, Mothersole awakens Hurtle's femininity. The time of the ferry meeting is fortunate. At fifty-five or so, Hurtle has reached the point where he has become woman-ish. But the stilling of his male hormones promotes fertility. As soon as the "spinsterish air" (p. 373) of his parlor and "the skirt" (p. 373) of his robe are noted, his spiritual-child-to-be, Kathy, appears on his doorstep. His virility and his art then renew themselves thanks to his newfound ability to love. In fact, only when he invites his own femaleness do his art and his long-dormant male sexuality reawaken. His passiveness during sex with Kathy shows him the limits of male aggressiveness and dominance. As he learned aboard the Manly ferry, sometimes a person profits more from going with the tide than from fighting it. He does well to let life happen to him. He could have found no better restorative for his sagging spirits than

Mothersole, even if he had searched all of Sydney. His enacting of the female role helps create the most memorable erotic experiences of his life.

As this experience proves, he can do no better than to reach into the yeomanry for an infusion of pep or purpose. When he returned to Australia after his army service, he lacked ballast. But he also wanted to stop drifting. The outset of chapter 4 shows him primed for rebirth, eating fish and chips while leaning over a breakwater: "The young man beside the sea-wall stuffed into his mouth handfuls of the limp chips and encrusted fish" (p. 152). The reference to Stephen Dedalus' humble breakfast at the start of chapter 5 of *A Portrait* after his epiphany alongside another body of water is one of several Joycean motifs in this important scene. What follows Hurtle's impromptu meal is his recollection of letters he received in Europe, mostly from the family he has since renounced. Although he has returned to Sydney, he lives at a great distance from his townsfolk. He only knows that he does *not* want to be a Courtney. His life lacks positive thrust. Standing near the slapping sea, he resembles something formless that has washed to shore. Then he collides with the prostitute Nance Lightfoot. Stephen Dedalus's epiphany by the Irish Sea, crowned by his soul's cry of "Heavenly God"[7] at the end of chapter 4 of *Portrait*, finds a rough parallel at the start of the fourth chapter of *Vivisector* in the exclamation, "Holy *Moses!*" (p. 162). But the yelp of astonishment comes not from Hurtle but from Nance. Hurtle will go home with her, paint her, and give more of himself to her than to any other woman to date. Whereas Stephen's encounter with the bird girl (Stephen, too, visited prostitutes) is sexless, Hurtle's with Nance reeks of sex. Having just pondered unanswered letters written to him months and years ago, Hurtle needs the physical contact Nance offers. She walks into him to begin with because she mistakes him for a lamppost bereft of its lamp. Unready, he puts out little light or heat in the following hours. His awareness of the textures and masses of Nance's body make this time more of an aesthetic than a sexual experience. But sex primes his artistic sense. Thanks to her, his vocation leaps to life. He gives up his menial job in order to live off of her and to have more time to paint. His tie with Nance has given him the force and direction he needs by welding the sexual to the artisitic instinct. But while he grows, she droops. He exploits her, painting her, spending her money, and taking her love for granted. Having sacrificed himself to his obsession, he doesn't quail at sacrificing her. Her reference to Moses when she first meets him proves apt: though she leads him to the promised land of imaginative creation, she can't share it with him.

The death of Nance, who represents the raw material his inventiveness uses and transforms, saddens Hurtle. But it doesn't stop him. Again he recovers strength and hope from a person both ordinary and special. His chance meeting with Cecil Cutbush, the masturbating homosexual grocer, on a park bench reasserts his belief in the flesh. Cutbush inspires him even though Hurtle spends as little time with him as he will with Mothersole. The creative spirit needs no extended encounter or deep personal tie to respond to the prose of every day. Baker misses the point in his reference to Hurtle's "curious preoccupation with either sexually neutral or feminized males, with homosexuals, widowers, hermaphrodites, and androgynes."[8] Ruled by intuition rather than by morality or conscious choice, the artist must go where his spirit bids. The sympathetic tie joining Hurtle and Cutbush is based on a need that neither man can understand or control. Reason fails to explain why Cutbush stirs Hurtle's imagination and then lodges there. Hurtle can't escape the grocer, even though he meets him but once in early middle age and doesn't see him again for some thirty years. Cutbush not only inspires an important painting; he also helps Hurtle when the artist has a stroke outside his grocery, and he has known both Rhoda and the Volkovs for years. Having suffered a stroke himself, along with having had sex with an adolescent, Cutbush may be said to inspire, collaborate with, and reenact some of Hurtle's most dramatic moments.

The mystery of the artistic process decrees that Cutbush can't be dismissed. The artist doesn't select all the materials of his art, nor does he know to which materials his imagination will respond. Unless he experiences all of life, even perforce imaginatively, he can never reach the unknown. He both soars and grovels; he transforms ugliness. His need to rivet on elements ignored and despised by others accounts for the preponderance of feces in the novel. The same artistic creativity that joins hands with sex and religion can also take root in decay and filth. All is grist to the artist's mill. White's concept of the artist resembles Whitman's idea of the poet. The world throbs and gleams for Hurtle; encompassing all, this mystic sensualist finds artistic inspiration in everybody and everything. Toilet functions dominate the Courtneys' visit to St. Yves de Tregor in Brittany, where Hurtle is inspired to paint his nude pictures of Rhoda. The family stops in St. Yves because they're too exhausted by diarrhea to continue their trip. Rhoda finds a dirty chamber pot under a hotel bed. Noteworthy, too, is the manure tub in Sunningdale's garden which streaks Rhoda's dress and alongside which Rhoda and Hurtle feel the first impulses of mutual love; the shit that Hurtle rubs into his self-portrait after Nance's death; the mound of dung in the empty Grecian chapel; and the used toilet paper that blows in the face of a woman on a Corfu-bound steamer. The fertility symbolized by the wind, the vagina-like gorge down which Nance falls to her death, and the androgyny of the dung-smeared self-portrait all spell out the aliveness of the sensory world.

His ability to confront reality so livingly insures his continued growth. The process perpetuates itself, his inventiveness transferring development in one area of activity to another, albeit erratically. Beatson has shown how a broken rhythm of collapse and renewal describes the flow of Hurtle's creativity more accurately than does a smooth, even curve: "A period of spiritual or emotional depletion seems to be necessary to the regenerative process. . . . This necessary black night of the soul occurs to almost all of White's major characters, and is summed up in Hurtle Duffield's pitch black painting that he is forced to execute before his final affirmations."[9] By giving him someone to love, the rebirth of his tie with Rhoda gives these affirmations a sound underpinning; the artist creates with his whole self, not just his mind. It also dramatizes White's belief that the blood tie can be overrated. Family feeling in White depends more upon need and choice than upon genes. Others beside Hurtle learn this lesson. Rhoda claims, "Parents and children, I think, are only accidentally related" (p. 453), and Mrs. Volkov describes Kathy's paternity as a chance encounter with a near stranger.

Perhaps dramatizing White's drive to compensate for not having begotten any children of his own, Hurtle and Kathy act together as if the blood tie imposes limits, rather than conferring solidarity and belonging. The union of the painter and the concert pianist is based on but goes beyond sex. Kathy gains knowledge, control, and self-esteem from Hurtle. Whereas her piano teacher polishes her technique, Hurtle, her father-lover, provides the vision upon which that technique is based: "It was you who taught me how to see, to be, to know instinctively" (p. 494), she tells him in a letter from Europe. Her letter also mentions "the things we haven't said" (p. 493). She and Hurtle have overcome an age gap of some forty years to become lovers, patron and protegée, and spiritual father and daughter. Much of their deep, many-sided love dwells in the realm of the unspoken. In his last decade Hurtle scarcely talks to Kathy. Perhaps their love doesn't lend itself to speech; remaining silent may keep their appetite for speech alive. Perhaps, too, their wordless bond throbs with possibilities too fearsome to face.

In any case, White believes that progress in human relationships comes from encounters like theirs, inchoate and ill defined though they may be. The progress made by the two artists during the time they know each other testifies to the vitality of their spiritual cross-fertilization. Kathy acquires the mastery to become a world-famous pianist, and Hurtle paints the freighted, potent God paintings. D.J. O'Hearn described *Vivisector* accurately in his [Melbourne] *Age* review by calling it "a portrait of the artist from one childhood to another."[10] By touching Hurtle deeply, Kathy transforms him. His assuming the passive role during sex teaches him what Docker calls "the receiving and life-giving qualities of the womb."[11] Kathy's ability to shatter his adult defenses also redeems him. By becoming childlike, he allows himself to be led by a child. His last years bristle with new beginnings. He strengthens his loyalty to the moiling, banal street life that primes his imagination. As that imagination grows wilder and bolder, it sinks its roots ever deeper in the commonplace. Avoiding the rich, the chic, and the academic, he delights in the ordinary. He comes to life in crowds. The pungent, the earthy, and the fleshy make his blood sparkle: "The smell of streets made him alive: warm pockets of female flesh; lamp-posts where dogs had pissed; fumes of buses going places" (p. 476).

A major breakthrough comes at the retrospective exhibition of his work at the New South Wales State Gallery. The exhibition does honor him, but not as intended. Refusing to harden into a monument, he makes the exhibition more of a fresh start than a celebration of past accomplishments. "I'm just beginning. I'm only learning" (p. 536), he says at the fête. Much of the freedom and genius of his last years consists of his manifesting several stages of human development at once—baby, apprentice artist, lover, spiritual father, and truant schoolboy. Knowing that the formality of the exhibition could sap his strength, he protests by fleeing just before the official dedication. He refuses to serve as a corpse at a state funeral.

The Gallery provided the setting for a prior event that helped him pierce the skin of time. His accidental meeting with his sister Lena, whom he hadn't seen since leaving Cox Street at age five or six, whips him backward and forward simultaneously. Lena's reappearance in his life revives his suppressed past. Though he acts heartlessly by fleeing her, his heart is deeply rocked. He is also carrying a blue (prefiguring the indigodd) plastic bag, in which he is to take home a sheep's heart for one of Rhoda's sick cats. His errand to the butcher reminds him, as did Lena, of being sold like a slab of meat in the butcher's shop of life. Like Kathy's mother before him and Cec Cutbush after him, he has a stroke—he is "stroked" by God and thus reborn. His first vision of the indigodd, believed by William J. Scheick to represent the *god*like nature of the *ind*ividual,[12] accompanies the stroke which flattens him. The stroke continues to affect him, both giving and taking away and thus duplicating the shuttle rhythm that carries him backward and forward in time during his most highly charged moments. While deepening his vision, the stroke impairs his power to communicate it. Thus his teaching his unafflicted arm how to paint constitutes a real rebirth through pain. Having been honored for a long, distinguished career, he starts working afresh in a new medium. His expanded sensibility requires a greater painting surface; his last works, the God paintings, are done on huge boards. His subjects, half invented and half recalled, come unbidden from his subconscious, giving him "a curious sense of grace" (p. 564).

His last work pushes into the religious sphere. Following Stephen Dedalus, a writer who leaves us in the act of writing in *A Portrait*, Hurtle dies in his studio, busy at his easel. The last scene shows him active and acted upon, painting the same indigo, interpreted by Morley as "truth, heaven, and heavenly love,"[13] that flashed before him during his stroke. His painting joins the human to the divine, combines process with product, and yokes his achievement to his undoing. The artist-creator fuses with his creating medium as the hairs on his head mingle imaginatively with those in his brush. Faced with death, he acts instantly, intuitively, and freely. His moment of naked enlightenment resolves all differences. But it occurs just when he is swept into eternity. White's eliminating a full stop after the book's last word shows that Hurtle dies before he translates his supreme revelation into paint. Although the artist's intimations open a path to the divine, they don't take him to path's end. He can't attain the celestial radiance he envisions during his lifetime.

III

This truth unfolds in its own good time, *Vivisector* finding its own unforced pace and design. Though the book includes external movement, much of its action happens inside Hurtle. Its rigor and complexity of description convey unusual power and subtlety, even for White. Stylistically the book is clean, orderly, and, with its Joycean excavations into Hurtle's mind, exciting. *The Vivisector* is written in several stylistic registers, all of which show vigor and concentration. The numerous letters in chapter 4, written in antiphonal voices, convey information quickly. Without wrenching narrative structure they explain changes that took place, mostly in the Courtney family, while Hurtle was serving overseas. The letters also reveal White's sensitivity to the social ramifications of speech. Included in his portrait of the energy and bounce of Sydney is his reproduction of the city's street talk. The working-class onlookers who comment upon Hurtle's stroke display the guarded shabby-genteel malice overheard in pubs or bus queues the world over. But White is salon smart besides being street wise. In some of his most devastating social comedy he represents the shallowness, pretense, and bitchiness of antipodean pseudo-chic. The gaudy patter of the guests attending the Retrospective Exhibition, reported as snatches of overheard cocktail party conversation, discloses a new and corrosive feather touch.

More impressive, because more sustained, is White's unified picture of Hurtle's disordered interior world. In middle age Hurtle's early life revives, as he moves back into the dirt-strewn, shouldering city he had left as a small boy. He returns to the core realities of his life with new insight and command, rejecting those aspects of his past which will hobble him. His character forms through his dreams, his paintings, and his unspoken thoughts. To maintain balance and tempo, White also shows him through the eyes of others. White's longest and most sensuous novel, *The Vivisector* shows remarkable self-detachment. Enriching this poise is the book's humor. Brains are served at the first meal the Courtneys feed their new genius-son, and before they agree to adopt him they make him read. He must prove he can give value for money. *The Vivisector* isn't "the weakest of the major novels,"[14] as Adrian Mitchell claims. Rather, its fun, wisdom, and verbal range make it a memorable and enduring work and also lift it to the upper register of an important writer's oeuvre.

10. Jaws

NOTHING BEFORE *The Eye of the Storm* (1973) could have prepared us for the book's new maturity in subject, approach, and procedure. Here White demonstrates his appreciation of the incongruity of experience, and especially of unlooked-for turns in social behavior. A morsel of unchewed pear that shoots out of a distraught mouth can incite a little drama of its own. Relying more on accurate observation than on technical virtuosity, White adopts a rich, supple Jamesian idiom. The touch that seems quicker and lighter than before chimes with artistic intent. *Eye* is a long, complicated novel written in long, complicated sentences. Like James, White at his best doesn't wag a finger to make his points, instead letting them emerge incidentally from the action. His allusive, polyphonic style displays the splendor of brilliant, socially accomplished people; one woman says to another, while pinning an expensive jewel on her dress, "See? I haven't altered you. . . . Only heightened a mystery which was there already, and which is too valuable not to respect" (p. 167). Such diction permeates both dialogue and narrative. The cadence and word choice in the following formulation of male elegance depend on a carefully developed Jamesian precision: "Freshly shaven cheeks giving off gusts of an aggressive, though not disagreeably pungent lotion; hair cleverly trimmed to within an inch of Romantic excess; clothes pressed or laundered to a degree that the man of the world demands, then ignores." (p. 410). That this grooming, though carefully noted, isn't mentioned by those witnessing it helps give the book a sense of subtext that sometimes enforces and sometimes undermines the action. An event will often count less than the feelings of its participants. Moreover, these feelings may disclose a surprising aspect of what is being said and done, as an apparently minor concern leaps to the foreground. White's controlling vision lends consistency to the drama of minute discriminations. Updating James's international theme, *Eye* features the pursuit of money and power by two Australians, both of whom can boast European titles. But the novel does more than study upper-class manners. The Australia that forms the bedrock of *Eye* prizes equality over authority and hierarchy. White contrasts early-century rural Australia with the affluent, urbanized Australia of the 1960s, and he records the impact of working-class energy upon this change. Beaky, wiry, uneducated speech helps convey the pervasiveness of the impact. Rather than aping the Jamesian idiom, White tunes it to a contemporary register. He may even ridicule it. Of a jammed toilet, someone notes inwardly, "It was nothing and everything" (p. 303).

Jokes can backfire, and, as the paradox implies, the White of *Eye* sometimes labors small points to the detriment of narrative flow. He subordinates life to literature most often in his descriptions of working-class characters. Neither the minor figure nor the action he undertakes in the following passage deserves such rhetorical flourishes. Despite his admiration for simplicity, White refuses to let the farmer Rory Macrory take another slice of mutton because Macrory likes the taste or because he (whose thick eyelashes typify White's Irish Australians) is hungry: "Cocking his head, lowering his eyelids, his lashes so thick they looked as if they were gummed together, or fringed with flies, he agreed delicately to accept another helping of mutton" (pp. 410-11). *Eye* manifests its literary self-image in other ways. White affects elegance by using the word masticate instead of chew and saying cleanly instead of clean; he could also be reflecting the aesthete's disdain for physical science in his erroneous reference to sciatica (a disorder of the sciatic nerve, one of the largest and longest in the human body) as a "superficial pain" (p. 578). Happily, such flaws rarely pit the richly marbled surface of *Eye*, perhaps White's best-controlled and sustained work.

Besides helping us know and judge White's characters without authorial intervention, this well-tempered abundance moderates the negativity fretting the book. Doggedly unsentimental, *Eye* belongs to the hard-headed, militant branch of modern fiction of which malice forms the underpinning. The beached black carcass of a dead dog in chapter 7 symbolizes the absent deity, or loss of faith, as in the "Proteus" section of *Ulysses*. This horrible portent climaxes a series of a sordid images accompanying an outdoor luncheon taken at Watson's Bay. A businessman falls through a chair amid gales of boozy laughter; the restaurant then degenerates into a shambles of "disordered tables, crumpled napkins, lipstuck glasses, the skeletons and shells of fish" (p. 351). Squalor soon dominates the once-festive area: "Scum, and condoms, and rotting fruit, and rusted tins, and excrement" (p. 352) litter the beach adjoining the restaurant where the dead dog appears. This ugliness tallies with the Hunter children's visit to Sydney, which culminates in incest, death, and isolation. Its force is felt elsewhere as well. On her way out of the restaurant, the book's most saintly character, a nurse, trips and falls. Her dining companion falls several times during the action. Earlier his sister had hissed (p. 268) while opening an envelope containing a large check. Supporting both this primitive imagery and the idea of depravity the imagery puts out is the recurrence of worms in the action. White consistently juxtaposes worms with something delicate and fragrant. As the nurse's fall at the end of chapter 7 showed, ancient evil threatens all; it has already engulfed the Hunter family. A worm invades a peach at the end of an elaborate dinner party in chapter 2; "lashing themselves into a frenzy of pink exposure" (p. 209), worms defile a rose garden. Dorothy Hunter, the Princesse de Lascabanes, worries that her mother will "worm out" (p. 216) a secret she has been harboring. Finally, one of the book's most dramatic scenes, in which Elizabeth Hunter tries to pry some sleeping pills from a nurse, contrary to doctor's orders, takes place with Mrs. Hunter sitting on the same toilet where she will later die.

The moral decay symbolized by the toilet and the worm attains dramatic expression in the book's scathing descriptions of Australians socializing. Blanket judgments in White are usually carping. Because man can best know and save himself while alone, people in groups vex him. Dinner parties and other social gatherings bring out their vanity, pretensions, and affectations. The worm in the peach served to Mrs. Hunter at a fancy dress dinner prefigures the adultery she will commit only hours later. The coincidence of her rut with her son's fall from a tree hundreds of miles away shows the worm burrowing deeply into Australia's homes and gardens. So pervasive is it that once it shows its pink, featureless face, it can work its way on family members miles and a generation apart. Evil reverberates, even when White's purpose seems more satirical than metaphysical. Dinner parties don't succeed because the men fart and talk shop, ignoring their overdressed, heavily made-up wives, who pass the time in malicious gossip. Australian *haute monde* suburbia lacks the civilized graces needed to throw a proper dinner party. Substituting ostentation for breeding, a suburban family in *Eye* serves too much food and drink, fogging the conversation of the diners: the hostess, already about to pass out, offers a guest "a brandy balloon, more than half filled" (p. 295). Her conduct typifies White's recent work, which often makes vacuity and nastiness a function of bad table manners. Characters who misbehave around food will commit worse gaffes elsewhere. A luncheon guest in *Vivisector* refused to go home until he has filled a manila envelope with lobster salad. During a dinner party in *Twyborn Affair*, food falls on the floor, champagne bottles overturn and spill, and a socialite tries to undo the trousers of a younger man while talking to him on a couch.

If White ridicules his bit players, he magnifies and intensifies their foibles in his leading figures. None of the characters in *Eye* likes each other, and all feel ill used. All *are* ill used. Elizabeth Hunter doesn't want to have sex with the marine ecologist Edvard Pehl on Brumby Island, off the Queensland coast; she only flirts with him to score a point off her daughter, Dorothy. Fifteen years later Dorothy and Basil unite to reduce their dying mother's retinue. Money lust has created this partnership of a brother and a sister who haven't seen each other for years. Each needs the other for support, yet each despises the other both for mistreating their mother and for being so blatantly mercenary. Each, too, sees his/her faults reflected the other. Because they have taught each other that the grubbiness of self is inescapable, they try to enlist a third party to do their bidding. They hope the family solicitor, Arnold Wyburd, will move their mother into a nursing home where she can die at moderate cost. Exploitation has been thriving to the side of this plot. Mrs. Hunter and her housekeeper, Lottie Lippmann, have been using each other to whet their respective appetites for cruelty and masochism, and one of Mrs. Hunter's nurses, Flora Manhood, uses Basil as an unsuspecting stud.

I

White's metaphor for the destructive woman is the loveless mother. A stranger to compassion and charity, she will damage her children by devouring or suffocating them, as did Amy Parker and Alfreda Courtney; to compensate for Maman, Harry Courtney took up the maternal office by providing masculine gentleness. She can bully them (Austin Roxburgh's mother in *Fringe*), favor one of them over the other (Julia Goodman), neglect them (Shirl Rosetree), compete with them (Doris Bannister of "The Night the Prowler"), or exploit them (Mumma Duffield). Eadie Twyborn gainsays maternal love by becoming a lesbian and a drunk. Characters like Theodora Goodman, Mrs. Poulter, and Ellen Gluyas Roxburgh imply that sympathetic women in White are sympathetic only because they have been spared the burdens of motherhood; mothers in White's fiction inflict damage. Bypassing only the vagaries of Eadie Twyborn, Mrs. Hunter denies her children in each of the ways indulged by her counterparts. It is plausible that Dorothy and Basil have left Australia, that they avoid their mother during their time in Sydney, and that they prefer staying in hotels rather than in their childhood home. They deny her the satisfaction of playing the caring, sheltering mother; nor do they want to stop one of her barbs should she revert to her former destructiveness. Their resentment over her dying so expensively also makes sense. Dorothy's solitary life in genteel semi-poverty and her actor-brother's rejection of life in favor of a theatrical image of it describe pathetic shadow existences alongside the fierce splendor of their mother's brilliance, age-wrecked as it is.

This brilliance cows Dorothy more than it does Basil, and it could cow her even more if she were to know all it has done. Her mother did in fact what Dorothy only does in fantasy—have sex with the family solicitor, Arnold Wyburd. Moreover, she embraced Wyburd when he was young and vital, whereas Dorothy's fantasies only begin when he is elderly. Even though Mrs. Hunter didn't seduce Edvard Pehl on Brumby Island, she kept him out of a willing Dorothy's bed. So assured is she of her dominance over Dorothy that, fifteen years later, as she lies on her deathbed withered and blind, she reminds Dorothy of the Brumby Island incident at the precise moment Dorothy has come with Basil to talk her into a nursing home. Not only has she intuited the purpose of her children's visit; her reference to Brumby Island also serves notice that, feeble as she is, she welcomes the worst they can throw at her. The comparison between her and Shakespeare's Cleopatra, inferred by a description of a dress she wore at age seventy-one, captures her magic: "Age had not tarnished its splendor, nor blunted its fluting" (p. 420). Obviously, the wearer's virtues have brought out the virtues of the dress.

These, bound up as they are with her faults, are less easily assessed. Like Alma Jugg Lusty in *The Ham Funeral*, she both creates and destroys. Thanks to her beauty, her riches, her subtlety, and her nonsense, she moves at a grander level. Elizabeth Hunter is as paradoxical, unpredictable, and full of meaning as a piece of holy writ. Her age (eighty-six) has made her both frail and, because of her strong will, frightening. White stresses her decrepitude not to belittle her but to contrast it with her inner strength. The description of her drinking—"The lips suggested some lower form of life, a sea creature perhaps, extracting more than water from water" (pp. 22-23)—suggests both a ghoulishness and a wisdom that has set her apart from the other characters. Like his sister, Basil feels intimidated by this primordial energy; he wouldn't have dared to broach the subject of a nursing home without Dorothy alongside him. Also like her, he wants Mrs. Hunter to die so he can have her money. His survival, he claims, depends on her death. Nor can she complain of mistreatment, since she has used people her whole life. In trying to hasten her death, Basil is merely applying a morality learned from her. Besides, turnabout is fair play. Referred to as "a great baby" and "an almost chrysalis" (p. 9), Mrs. Hunter regresses to infantilism before she can be a parent. Having denied her children the maternal benefits of love, tenderness, and protection, she can only offer them money. She withdraws her will to live in order to give Dorothy and Basil her only remaining treasure. Everything tallies. If money is her only bequest, it is all her children want from her. Again, she can't complain. Dorothy and Basil don't know how to love because she has never taught them how.

The single-mindedness of their fortune-hunting shows Dorothy and

Basil living up to their last name (which is also the name of the valley in
New South Wales where White's family has owned land for four
generations).[1] The name Hunter applies even more vividly to their mother,
whose spotless white dresses and elusive personality suggest Diana, or
Artemis, the moon goddess and huntress of classical mythology. Mrs.
Hunter's arrows, like Diana's, hit their mark, as is shown by her verbal
accuracy; both her humor and her malice have wounded many. What is
more, she searches out her quarry with skill, like any other good hunter. As
a young socialite she rode horses, a hobby indulged in by other proud,
destructive beauties like Sidney Furlow of *Happy Valley* and Madeleine of
Tree of Man. People still fear her, yielding to her demands for obedience
and worship. These demands take many forms, as befits her strong will. If
permitted, she would disturb an off-duty nurse for a trifle. Such an imposition fits with her practice of demanding good value from her retainers.
Besides doing their assigned jobs, her cook dances, her cleaning woman
tells stories, one nurse, a trained cosmetician, applies her makeup, and
another gives spiritual instruction. In the first chapter three nurses, her
cook, a doctor, and a lawyer flock to her bedside to do her bidding. She has
become the still center of a moiling, racketing world during a time of
upheaval. Her having instigated great activity in others while remaining
motionless herself defines her as a spiritual force. In additon to meeting
Eliot's definition of God in *Four Quartets*, she suits the Zen philosopher
D.T. Suzuki's qualifications for the attainment of enlightenment: "The center
of life-gravity remains immobile, and . . . when this has successfully taken
hold of all the life activities . . . whether in a life of quietude and learning or in
one of intense action, a state of self-realization obtains, which expresses itself
in a most exquisite manner in the life and acts of the person."[2]

Most of Mrs. Hunter's acts refer to herself. She is enlightened, irradi-
ated by an inner gleam that gives her mastery over the young, the mobile,
and the sighted. Hers is a case of the blind leading the blind in this work
about degrees of blindness. White demythologizes her internal strength at
the same time that he raises it to the religious dimension; she is to be seen as
a person, rather than as a goddess. Her sumptuous material surroundings
bespeak vanity and selfishness. The many mirrors hanging in her Moreton
Drive home aggravate these traits, as does a comparison between the
pictures of her and her husband adorning the dining room. The picture of
decent, simple Bill Hunter is smaller than that of his widow; Bill's ego was
smaller, too. He died quietly on his farm, where he would least distress
those who loved him. From the large, elaborately carved bed where she
lies, his widow attracts retainers and relatives; those buzzing around her
all serve vanity, which naturally both blinds and confines.

What helps give her vanity a metaphysical *frisson* is her having endured
a cyclone on Brumby Island by herself. Eschewing simplified moralities,

White portrays the storm both as Mrs. Hunter's punishment for betraying Dorothy, who had flown from France to be with her after her marriage broke up, and her honor, because she emerges from it renewed. The big storm frees her inner self, negating the ego and opening new inlets of perception. She calls her pelting by the storm "the utmost in experience" (p. 414) and "the highest pitch of awfulness the human spirit can endure" (p. 424). This terror flattens and trivializes everything else that has happened to her. It releases her spirit from her body. Torn, hammered, and recast, a new self comes to life amid the smashed, soaked furnishings of her hosts' cabin. Being whipped into the still center of the wild storm has taught her the universal parity of existence. In this moment of oneness she merges with nature, identifying both in her thoughts and her feelings with the surrounding wreckage. Her identification defies reason. As always happens to White's characters at the moment of revelation, the tempering of her spirit is a function of her physical battering. She is soothed by her belief in her oneness with the shambles of dead fish, horsehair, and iron as "the most natural conclusion" (p. 425) of the storm. The contingent has grazed the absolute. If her mighty ordeal won't improve her ethics, it will nonetheless steel her for all future trials. Surviving the cyclone helps her fend off the voracity of her children, White interrupting the visit in which Dorothy and Basil rehearse the alleged virtues of a nursing home (in Chapter 8) with a long flashback to Brumby Island. Mrs. Hunter connects these two events, and so should we. The self-presence that carried her through the cyclone will help her weather the gusts set in motion by her children's greed. Her strong will, her trial by storm, and her queenly first name all put her as close to Shakespeare's Lear, a role that obsesses Basil, as their greed puts her children to Goneril and Regan.

Lest we make too much of the equation, we must recall that the inwardness of White's vision blurs the objectivity of factual experience. Mrs. Hunter's past and present, her memories and feelings, all exist on a par. Her life can't be judged objectively; the quality of life depends upon how a person sees it. Because a person's life is what he/she makes of it, Voss expands into the greatness he intuits within himself, and Hurtle Duffield grows artistically at a time when a stroke, the infirmities of age, and a retrospective exhibit of his work all tell him to slow down. Given her venom and her vanity, Mrs. Hunter's deathbed thoughts occasion a more complex self-inventory. Her great years, her thunderclap experience on Brumby Island, and the wavering of her mind have not put her beyond self-justification or self-blame. She needs the deep reservoir of self-knowledge the years have created if she is to sink the strong sense of guilt which keeps surfacing. This guilt is a byproduct of success. After a life of winning and owning, she suspects that she has nothing. She is right. Riches impoverish, and success divides. Her beauty, her social rank, and her

cunning have won her many prizes, but they have also made her fatally
selfish. She has lived fully, and she hasn't lived at all. Specifically, she has
never learned how to give. What is more, her insight into this failing is
sharpened by the belief that no one in her circle merits her generosity or
self-sacrifice, and by the suspicion that she has crushed any worthiness
capable of being crushed. Human debris surrounds her. The skiapod, a
legendary sea beast with whom she indentifies and whose jaws open so
wide that it can swallow larger fish, has devoured or dismembered
everyone.

This rapacity has tarnished all her trophies. She might well ask, on the
day of her death, "Haven't I been sleeping all my life?" (p. 442). Despite
her many triumphs, she fears that reality has escaped her. Her never having
touched her husband's penis, her vivid recollections of her two adulteries,
and her inability to breastfeed her children explain her problem as a failure
to love. Her heart is strong but insensitive. Bullying and manipulating
people has drained the vitality from her. How to restore it? She expects no
love from her children; their wrecked marriages, their avoidance of her,
and their enthusiasm for her money as opposed to her welfare all show that
they have no love to give. For this lovelessness she feels responsible, if not
guilty. She doesn't need to receive love so much as to extend it. She nursed
her husband in his last sad days out of duty, not out of love; she never saw
Basil act professionally, even though he was performing in a play while she
was in London; she tormented Dorothy when she came to Brumby Island
for motherly comfort. This ex-socialite who charmed, fascinated, and
thrilled hearts over a long and brilliant career has never opened her own
heart to another. Instead, she has worn herself out reaching for hollow,
trivial prizes. Having imposed her iron will, she has blocked the flow of
spontaneous life. Her refusal to let life happen to her constitutes a lack of
faith. Ironically, the strong will of this dilapidated queen has brought
about her undoing, not her fulfillment. Lying on her deathbed, she clutches
greedily at her few remaining scraps of life, a Hunter stalking new game.
As her remarkably strong pulse indicates, she wants to grace her life with
love before it ends.

A difficult job: the power she has gained over a lifetime of getting what
she wants impedes the selfless outgoing of love. It also hides her vulnerability. One of her favorite cover mechanisms consists of brewing trouble.
Whereas more prudent souls shrink from embarrassing or painful subjects,
she welcomes them. She seems to relish the discomfort of others. One of
her cook's song-and-dance routines ends when she, Mrs. Hunter, opens
her rheum-gorged eyes as wide as she can and stares at the onlookers.
Earlier she had stunned her solicitor and onetime lover, Arnold Wyburd,
by referring playfully to Basil as "our son" (p. 280). But the main target for
her malicious mirth must be Wyburd's prim, retiring wife. Envying Lal

Wyburd's sane, orderly routine, Elizabeth Hunter has been shocking and torturing her for years. Not content merely to seduce her straitlaced husband, she constantly snipes at Lal's unstylishness and her freckles. One of the book's funniest scenes shows Lal visiting her on the day of her death and being reduced to flatfooted dismay by her flashing wit. Looking in another direction as Lal enters her room, Mrs. Hunter accuses her of neglecting the possibly cancerous freckles mottling her hands; she denies Lal food and makes the denial sound like Lal's idea; she taunts her by referring knowingly to Arnold. But even then she hasn't finished scoring off her visitor. After grazing the most intimate realities of Lal's life with her non sequiturs, half-truths, and manufactured solicitude, she gives Lal a turquoise chain. The reason for the gift emerges only after Mrs. Hunter dies. Wyburd notes on his return from the funeral that the chain has made Lal's neck look red, shriveled, and heavily freckled. Blind Betty's last joke on Lal was to give her the chain because she saw with her inner eye that it would accent Lal's worst features. In mitigation, she pays for the joke that her blindness and her death stop her from relishing first hand, bequeathing Lal $5,000 as back wages for being tormented, precisely the same amount she presented to both of her children upon their arrival in Sydney. The equality she bestows upon her victims signals an acceptance of responsibility for her misdeeds.

If her wrongs to Dorothy on Brumby Island and elsewhere are righted at all, the righting comes at the moment of Mrs. Hunter's death. The mother withdraws her will to live while sitting on the toilet; she literally prefers to die than to be stowed in a nursing home. She will give her children what they want and deserve, but in her own way. The style of her death mocks them, expressing her disdain for both them and their greed. Does White approve of this parting shot? He judges his brilliant heroine shrewdly but also sympathetically. Her last recorded conscious thought is a prayer to her husband which acknowledges his goodness, her love for him, and her sorrow over having failed him. It may be her greatest, because her most selfless, moment. Her death, which follows shortly, is described as a union of two infinities, her spirit drifting into the spirit world. Also central to White's judgment of her is her dying in a sitting position. Whereas her children fall from grace by violating both the Fifth Commandment and one of the Western world's strongest taboos, incest, she dies without falling. Even in death she needs no foreign titles or honors to prop her up. That she dies on the same night, perhaps at the same moment, when Dorothy and Basil are committing incest makes her death the grisly fruit of their rut. Any such connection made by her children between the two events might have made her smile ruefully.

Beyond help or hurt, this bringer and destroyer of life outshines all her counterparts. She wets and soils her bed; her bones creak; her mind wanders. Like Hurtle Duffield, though, she withers and blossoms at the same time, having cultivated other senses to offset her blindness. She notes the "fatty laugh" (p. 74) of her doctor, and she says inwardly of Wyburd, "He smelled old. He sounded dry" (p. 25). Her amazing mind, though unsteady, remains sharp "on its better days" (p. 85). She speaks Flora Manhood's innermost thoughts as Flora is thinking them; she upstages Basil when he plays his grand homecoming scene; the intuition, or second sight, she has cultivated to make up for her loss of eyesight helps her score at will upon both Dorothy and Lal Wyburd. Though she may confuse present events, claiming to have just heard a doorbell that rang hours before, she accurately recalls events from long ago. Though fixated on the past, she won't romanticize it: "They were walking . . . beside this great river. No, it wasn't: it was the shallow and often drought-stricken stream which meandered through everybody's place" (p. 23). White's entering her stream of consciousness to select events from her long, colorful life nearly puts her beyond blame and guilt; yet it also deepens blame and guilt in the way that only first-rate psychological realism can. The conniving Betty Hunter would rage, pout, or coyly produce a dimple to get what she wanted. She would also destroy. Reared in a broken-down farmhouse, she wrecked both her own cheap dolls and the prettier, more numerous ones of her little friend Kate Nutley. Because dolls meant more to her than anything, they had to be destroyed. The knowledge that her own poor assortment of dolls could never equal Kate's fine collection sparked her hatred of all dolls everywhere. Other recollections of the past maintain a consistency between her many acts of spite and envy. In old age she is still, intriguingly, very much herself. *Eye* sets her past and present lives before us simultaneously. She sees in her mind's eye (and we see, too) her younger incarnations doing things that will form her character. In a passage that prefigures her dying attempts to redeem herself, she seduces Wyburd the same day the nervous young solicitor brings her her will to sign. Being faced with her mortality has whetted her greed for life. Besides signing her will, she works her will—as she'll do many times in the future. In retaliation, Wyburd steals a sapphire from her just before her death; she owes him that much after decades of having manipulated and bullied him.

White's time-shifting within the stream of her consciousness brings her before us as a legend and a person, a great beauty and a haggard husk. At all phases of her life she discloses the same capacity for good and evil. She may wince while being tended to by a nurse, but the cause is the pain brought about by a recollection, rather than the nurse's touch. This polyvalence rests on White's nonlinear portrayal of her. She refers to "that state of pure living bliss she was now and then allowed to enter" (p. 24), a level of being where she neither sleeps nor wakes and where distinctions like past and present disappear. In this semi-consciousness she reorders time, her will relaxes, and her inner eye takes charge. Experienced on the inward planes of perception, things reveal their unity, their stillness flowing into that of their perceiver. Elizabeth Hunter's blindness, frailty, and guilty self-knowledge lose their sting. She has transcended judgment and division. Existence itself has become active, even imperative. To partake of this miracle suffices for her. The spiritual equilibrium she attains is mirrored by her supine immobility. She comes even closer to perfect union with the indigodd than did Hurtle, who was also more demonic than angelic. The difference between the two characters is attributive. Whereas Hurtle's divine intimations came from his inventiveness, those of Mrs. Hunter bespeak her whole self.

II

Both of Mrs. Hunter's children have titles; both live in glamorous European capitals. La Princesse de Lascabanes and Sir Basil Hunter embody an important feature of the middle-class push to get ahead. They have inherited both the drive and the dream from their mother, a poor farm girl who acquired money, property, and social rank. So triumphant was she that her children aimed even higher and succeeded more wildly. But outdoing their mother in the scramble for earthly prizes has undone them. With their European establishments, they have scored high in Australian terms. Seen as people rather than romantic exile-aristocrats, they look futile and empty. Their inner fears, longings, and frustrations, so out of keeping with their shiny public images, surface quickly. Having been denied maternal protection, support, and nourishment (as has been mentioned, Mrs. Hunter couldn't breast-feed her children), they bring a heavy charge of anger with them to Moreton Drive. Their anger they unload. It has already been seen how neither one of them spends much time with her, stays at her home, or disguises his/her disapproval of the cost required to maintain her. Dorothy even pinches her nose while cleaning it, the memory of Brumby Island still rankling her. After serving notice that they plan to move her into a nursing home, they never see her again. Nor do they attend her funeral. Her request for sleeping pills, which she doesn't need, coincided with their arrival. Aware of their long-standing resentment, she prefers death from an overdose to the neglect and cruelty they have learned from her.

They don't need to see their mother after telling her that she is to be moved from Moreton Drive. They have said the final word on the topic that brought them to Sydney, to begin with. Wasting no time, they interview the director of the local nursing home into which they want to book their mother as soon as the death of a present occupant creates a vacancy. They try to heal freshly opened psychological wounds in the interim. Smarting with guilt and feeling fragmented by denying their mother, they go to their childhood home in the back country to trace other ancestral roots. These roots drive more deeply than they had imagined. Seeing "Kudjeri," their father's property, makes them feel as if living in Europe has severed them from their vital sources. But Europe has also infiltrated their bloodstreams; observing psychological accuracy, White assures that the Hunter children bring post-childhood conditioning with them to Kudjeri. Basil, for instance, declaims a speech from *The Merchant of Venice* and thinks of acting the role of Richard II, another exile who returns to his homeland to find himself dispossessed. Dorothy, whose European tenure has sagged after its brilliant start, harks back to the mother she has just denied as a role model. Dorothy imitates Mrs. Hunter, wearing the white dresses that were once her mother's hallmark and flirting with the Macrory children in the same way that her mother did with the Warming children fifteen years before. But the self-renewal she attains is wholly her own. For the first time she feels at home. She sews, cooks, peels potatoes, and arranges cupboards "as though she had taken possession of the house" (p. 487). The solidness that comes from immersing herself in the routine of the Macrorys, the present owners of Kudjeri, affirms itself quickly. She feels strong and useful. Anne Macrory says that the family can't manage without her. Basil's references to her as Dorothy Sansverina (p. 484; after a character in Stendhal's *Charterhouse of Parma*) and Dorothy Cahoots (p. 592) pay further tribute to her growth.

The visit to Kudjeri affects Basil differently because he undertakes it in a different spirit. Unlike the strident, priggish Dorothy, he can let himself go, and he looks hopefully to the future. What he wants most is wholeness. The job of separating what he is from what he does presents obstacles, though. He feels out of place amid the rural simplicity and traditional family values of Kudjeri. The career that has elevated him professionally, even winning him a knighthood, has dwarfed him emotionally, and the smoothness of his rehearsed responses sometimes appalls him. Yet the trip to Kudjeri was his idea, and it touches a sensitive nerve. Like Dorothy, he responds in ways that he never does elsewhere; he savors the sensation of mud curling around his toes, while the scents exuded by the local flora give crisp new meaning to long-dormant memories.

Some of these memories refer to Dorothy. All along he, Dorothy, and their mother have been denying the importance of their bond. In fact, Mrs. Hunter is so excited to see her daughter for the first time in fifteen years that she wets herself; Basil she won't even receive in bed, insisting that she be propped in a chair wearing full makeup and a lilac-colored wig. Dorothy's Parisian veneer cracks at the sight of the mother toward whom she claims indifference. Basil's nonchalance in stating that he hasn't seen either his sister or his mother in half a lifetime is refuted by his failing at sex and then vomiting from drink during his stopover in Bangkok. Despite his breezy tone, the prospect of a family reunion has jarred him.

The only Hunter who accepts the meaning of the family is decent, kindly Bill. An outdoorsman whom White treats more gently than his earlier incarnation, Harry Courtney of *Vivisector,* Bill sees his son act on the London stage. The same simple dignity that later silences any complaints about the liver cancer that is destroying him keeps him from both asking his wife to join him at the play and visiting Basil backstage. A man of quiet purpose, he needs no fanfares to advertise his comings and goings. His dying with the onset of winter on the acreage he loves attests to his harmonious nature. He deserves the statue put up in his honor in the town of Gogong, near Kudjeri. That his widow misses the unveiling of the statue also rings true. Ashamed of having dismissed his tenderness and generosity, she has buried her guilt under a glittering cosmopolitan facade. Her children would have suffered no such qualms had they bothered to learn of the unveiling. Bill Hunter's decency always bored them; neither of them budged from Europe either to console him in his last days or to attend his funeral. Adopting a tone of self-congratulation, Dorothy cites important obligations in Paris, even though others with the same obligations (like her truant husband) have been neglecting them; Basil's letter of regret carries the same claim of martyrdom. So mean-spirited are the Hunter children that their very neglect of Bill (Basil says that he doesn't think about his father for years at a stretch) supports White's indirect request that this local hero be viewed as a moral exemplar.

Their stay at Kudjeri makes this mean-spirited pair sharply aware of their pain. Fear, need, and the iron grip of the past drive them into bed naked. Dorothy's chittering words uttered weeks before, upon her arrival at Kudjeri, "I've never felt more frightened . . . not even on my wedding night" (p. 473), have taken on a prophetic ring. They also sound the note of ambiguity that peals through all of White. Dorothy's coupling with her brother shows a willingness to defy one of society's strongest taboos for his sake. At the same time they are declaring their faith in each other, she and Basil are getting closer to their own feelings and thus to themselves. Their incest is an act of mutual self-acceptance, clearing a path to self-being they couldn't find in Europe. Yet both lack the patience, the goodness of heart, and the self-respect to profit from their act. Each has always seen in the other a reflection of his/her greed, ineffectuality, and treachery. From the outset they have joined forces reluctantly. These uneasy allies-to-be meet for the first time in the book in a solicitor's office. The "steel and concrete cell" (p. 258) where the meeting occurs symbolizes the lovelessness of their union, the resurrection of which both delay by coming late. This reluctance lingers. Though their union brings them closer than either party had wanted or thought possible, it creates no permanent healing. Basil and Dorothy have sex in the same bed in which they were conceived because, in usurping their parents' roles, they believe they can wipe out the past and start anew. Their act backfires. They can't negate their parents, the most vital part of a common past that has been saturating their spirits for the past weeks, without negating themselves. Lear's infamous proposition, "Nothing will come from nothing" (I, i, 92), has done its work on them. The offspring of their sexuality is death, their mother dying at perhaps the exact time they are coupling.

More will come to grief than Mrs. Hunter. The damage her children incite begins to surface immediately. Having just shown them abed, chapter 10 ends in darkness; unwarmed and uneasy, Dorothy and Basil lie awake amid the "frozen ridges" (p. 527) of their parents' bed, the full moon fixing them in its stark, sterile glow. The opening words of the next chapter, spoken by their mother, "Is it cold, sister?" (p. 528), could easily have come from Basil, given the chill surrounding him at the end of the previous chapter. Only in the next sentence does White let on that the scene has shifted. But Mrs. Hunter's death later in the chapter and her dream about Dorothy and Basil as unborn twins both show that the shift is only spatial. The action of chapters 10 and 11 is continuous, as were the Australian and European interludes of the Hunter children. The mystery of unity swathes all. Upheavals jolt whole families in White's fiction, as the death of Waldo Brown in *Solid Mandala* and Hurtle's rediscovery of Rhoda Courtney in *Vivisector* showed. Manfred Mackenzie describes the incest at Kudjeri as "suicidal": "It is as if Basil and Dorothy would accelerate their mother's death by black magic,"[3] he says of their self-defeating exorcism. The death rattle set in motion by her children's bed-springs reverberates in Mrs. Hunter's dream, as the cold weather that gripped Kudjeri forces the summer athletes in the park fronting Moreton Drive to dress in warm clothing. This same chill marks her children's response to her death. In prepared-sounding cadences, Basil refers to her vanity and (twice) to her materialistic values, probably to hide his lack of feeling. An equally ungrieving Dorothy cries briefly, but only for the bereavement of her hostess, Anne Macrory, who loved Mrs. Hunter after meeting her but once. Dorothy has never loved anyone enough to bewail a particular death. Embarrassed by their hypocrisy, she and Basil avoid each other's eyes during their mourning session with Anne.

The split between them widens. Ironically, the mother whose death they craved had been holding them together by giving them a common cause. They reject her gift. Their last encounter begins in the same solicitor's office where they first met, brought there once more by money rather than love. They will never meet again. Their final separation squares with skipping their mother's funeral. By passing up this last goodbye, they fail to put closure on the most vital and most rankling relationship of their lives. They have learned nothing. Avarice has whittled them down to nothing. And nothing will come from nothing.

The Hunter sib drawn more deeply into the abyss is Dorothy. A dry stick who worries about cancer, she neither fits nor belongs anywhere: "Dorothy Hunter's misfortune was to feel at her most French in Australia, her most Australian in France" (p. 49), White says of her after she laboriously clears customs at Sydney International Airport. Alienation and displacement have been dogging her. After marrying a foreigner from a different generation, nationality, and social class, she found herself abandoned. The old-world patina on her French prince had tarnished and chipped. Hubert de Lascabanes, a sham aristocrat, presumably ended a long career of dalliance (which included a Venetian gondolier) by discarding Dorothy for a Cincinnati margarine heiress. The Catholicism Dorothy had adopted in order to marry Hubert has stopped her from divorcing him. Her pride, still smarting from the Brumby Island incident, stops her from returning to Australia, even though Paris offers her only a doubtful claim on a smudged title and a leaking gas stove in an underfurnished flat. Her reversals have soured her and left her nowhere to turn. She doesn't even know *how* to turn. Whereas her husband censured her for controlling her feelings too well, her mother censures her for indulging them. She has become so emotionally knotted that she won't dent the $5,000 check her mother gives her to buy a good dress. As mean with others as with herself, she also roots in the garbage bin of her mother's kitchen to see how much food the servants have wasted, listens in on telephone conversations, and stands just outside open doors in order to eavesdrop.

Some hundred years after Christina Light, the future Princess Casamassima, appeared in Henry James's *Roderick Hudson* (1875), this heiress of all the ages has descended to eavesdropping and garbage-mongering. Everything ennobling is wasted on her. She is too brittle and stingy to profit from her revelation on the flight out. She lacks the simple warmth to accept Basil's luncheon invitation after seeing him for the first time in decades; her moral cowardice moves her to spurn his overtures of love after their mother's death. Her booking a flight to Paris without telling him typifies this devious, sly Regan figure. Although she introduces the subject of nursing homes to her mother, she speaks vaguely and briefly, leaving the details to Basil. Then there is her habit of defecting without giving notice. She left Brumby Island in a pique and without saying goodbye. Her exit from Sydney, again undertaken at the earliest possible moment, constitutes a denial of her tie with Basil. Joining forces with him to get their mother's money and then sealing their union incestuously has hardened the shell encasing her. But problems can't be solved by bouncing them off a shell or by running away from them. The meaning of what she and Basil did will continue to bedevil her. She couldn't need him any more than she already does, even if she were his embryonic twin of their mother's dream.

Veronica Brady has called her sagging peacock of a brother "the hollow man of artifice whose life is a tissue of insincerities and lies and whose main concern is to escape the truth of himself."[4] She is partly right. The similarities between Basil and Dorothy do make him his sister's spiritual twin; he is Dorothy writ large. He spends less time than Dorothy with their mother, and he tries just as hard as Dorothy to convince himself of their mother's unfitness, emphasizing her materialistic ways so that he can fleece her with impunity. Also like Dorothy, he worries about not belonging. His legal daughter was probably sired by another man. (He and Dorothy could both be sterile—their mother's joke and legacy.) His sleeping on Mitty Jacka's couch in London, in Janie Carson's hotel room in Bangkok, and in a Sydney hotel point up the homelessness of this man. About his living arrangements in London nothing is said. He lives among shadows. The artifice of the stage has dulled his responses to the outside world, including himself; his four-hour delay in Bangkok makes him aware of his inability to provide himself good company. His clumsiness is another sign of his being out of step with reality. Acting more like a clown or a slapstick comic (which could be his true calling) than a tragedian, he trips, flops, and stumbles through the action. This "victim of knobs and corners and low-hung lintels" (p. 477) fell from a tree and broke his arm as a boy; he slid on a banana peel that a playgoer had thrown onto a Glasgow stage; he almost overturns a bar stool in Bangkok. Nor does returning to Australia improve his bearings—he trips on the steps outside his mother's home after having been in the country only a few hours. At Kudjeri, where he goes to find a foothold on life, he cuts one foot while padding in mud, and he catches the other in a moldy old boot.

Before Basil can walk with practical feet, he must first acquire moral balance. He knows that he has no time to waste. Having been knighted by the Queen for playing the title roles in *Richard II, Hamlet, Lear,* and *Macbeth,* he has seen his career start to flag. His theatrical airs have also started to irk him. Lacking simple conviction, he turns everything he does into a bravura performance. The letter in which he tells his dying father that he can't come to Kudjeri shows him at his most theatrical-contemptible. Despite his joviality, he tries to give the impression that Bill Hunter is lucky to get so much as a letter, given his son's busy schedule and the superficiality of their relationship ("We scarcely ever spoke to each other, did we?" [p. 202]). During his father's decline he is rehearsing *Macbeth,* a play that treats the denial of basic human values. Ironically, the vanity-ridden Basil will play his most important role unconsciously, when his mother's nurse, Flora Manhood, singles him out to sire her baby. Performance becomes reality, as both her acting and her sense of mission outpace his.

His punishment for denying basic human values follows as remorselessly as Macbeth's. Judged on his own terms, those of the theater, he has failed. Greatness in acting often consists of an actor's ability to step outside of himself in order to become another person. Having inherited his mother's ego, he can't let himself go. His great private sorrow inheres in his having failed at King Lear, a role he deems nearly unplayable but within his artistic ken. To play Lear he would have to depersonalize himself with the utmost severity, given his belief, at age fifty, that the role can only be acted by an old man with the build of a young one. But while he dreams of playing Lear, he comes across an even greater artistic challenge—Mitty Jacka's Drama of the Unplayed I. Life grows knottier but perhaps also more rewarding with age, as Stan Parker and Hurtle Duffield learned. An independent London producer, Jacka wants Basil to play himself in her nonplay. Rather than working from a script, he will use material from his own life. He will present his own feelings, not those of a character created by someone else. Because his identity won't be caged by a role, he will enact his whole self, rather than just a part of it. Basil fears this challenge, having long ago substituted dramatic technique for sincerity. Better to fail as a performer, he reasons, than as a person. But the news of his mother's stroke fuels his waning resolve. After visiting Jacka in London's Beulah Hill (Beulah is the land of peace and rest visited near journey's end in the Bible), he goes to Australia to raise money for the nonplay. He soon finds that both his life and his livelihood depend on his mother's death. In view of his desperation and the warmth connoted by his many overtures to Dorothy, he bids well to succeed. If he fails to make it in his prescribed terms, he will do so in a way consistent with his dramatic flair and newfound honesty. Revisiting the countryside where he grew up has strengthened him. Furthermore, his ability to shake off Dorothy's many rejections shows that he's not stopped by setbacks. Unlike his sister, he'll gamble on his feelings.

But perhaps Flora Manhood, the nurse of twenty-five who finds Mrs. Hunter dead, garners the most from the drawn-out deathbed ordeal. Brady judges well to fault this hoyden who carries a gaudy plastic handbag, cadges free lunches, and prefers artificial over natural flowers: "Sister Manhood ... lives by an ideology, the religion of a hollow, materially-oriented culture. Vulgar and ignorant, she is terrified of pain and of everything she cannot control for her own pleasure."[5] This pleasure Manhood rates highly but defines narrowly. She resents her lover, Colin Pardoe, a pharmacist who reads Unamuno and listens to Mahler, because his self-improvement program stands as a reproach to her laziness. Easily bored, she speaks often of quitting her job at Moreton Drive, where she despises everybody but Mrs. Hunter. This unmoving mover has sparked a bonfire of activity in Flora: "I don't seem to have control over myself" (p. 278), the nurse whines; so powerful is her patient that she has robbed Flora of her ability to act on her own. Flora's disparaging references to "the old witch" (p. 86) and "a geriatric nut" (p. 304) express her resentment of the older woman's grip upon her interior life. But even though she

resents Mrs. Hunter, she cannot deny her, as did Dorothy and Basil. In
fact, she admires her so much that she connives (unsuccessfully, it turns
out) to have Basil's baby; she wants to play a vital role in her dying
patient's rebirth. Yet she is also the only member of the Moreton Drive
retinue who defies Mrs. Hunter. She knows she can risk surliness and
defiance because she applies Mrs. Hunter's makeup and thus preens her
ego; vain and selfish herself, she knows how much her cosmetic skill means
to her patient. She refuses Mrs. Hunter's gift of a pink sapphire because of
the conditions that accompany it, and, immediately detecting her patient's
purpose, she turns down her request for free access to her sleeping pills.

Mrs. Hunter's death changes Flora more than it does anyone else, this
common flower blossoming psychically if not physically. Flora acts as if
Mrs. Hunter's spirit passes into her at the moment of death. Inspired by her
patient, who, like her, grew up on a poor farm, she responds with perfect
tact to the sexual overture of the attending physician: "Dr. Gidley . . . if
you've forgotten your wife, I haven't forgotten my patient. I'd like to treat
her respectfully" (p. 565). Respect and tenderness continue to rule her, as
devotion replaces duty in her hierarchy of values. Usually anxious to bolt
Moreton Drive the moment her shift ends, she works long past her time to
expedite final details with appropriate reverence. The hours following her
departure from Mrs. Hunter's house reveal her as whipped and weary. She
has no job; her scheme to become pregnant has failed; she walks away
from her cousin, her only living relative, after the latter suggests that they
live together. According to her last recorded words in the novel, "I'm
nothing" (p. 573), she is like a hollow vessel. But she can be filled. Going
against Lear's claim that nothing will come from nothing, her hollowness
constitutes the state most friendly to spiritual activity in White.

Mary de Santis, the night nurse or "the archpriestess" (p. 19) of Mrs.
Hunter's sickroom, needs no such hollowing out. She sets no store by the
self. Asking nothing, she has always lived to serve others. What was
drudgery to Flora sustains her. The humbler the job the better, she believes.
Mrs. Hunter's statement that Mary is complete comes close to being true.
She will invent jobs both to test her faith and to keep herself in that bare,
unaccommodated state where she is most sensitive to a patient's needs.
After Mrs. Hunter's death she prepares to nurse an even more difficult
patient, whom White introduces six pages from the end to affirm the
strength of Mary's goodness. White also lets Mary hold the stage alone at
book's end, showing that self-negation may be the best instrument for
survival.

III

On duty, significantly, in the book's opening scene, Mary closes the action
by feeding the birds on Mrs. Hunter's dawn-lit lawn. This symbolic

reference to St. Francis of Assisi (Dorothy visited Assisi with her husband) gives her devotion a religious coloring that sets her apart from the other characters. Australia's industrial middle class is puzzled by its own comfort. Though it has inherited the egalitarianism and independence of the frontier, it also enjoys the ease and privilege that upward mobility brings. *Eye* accounts for this unsettling change. Others besides Mrs. Hunter and her children improve their material lot but droop in other ways. Rory Macrory marries above his station; Flora Manhood goes from a banana farm to Sydney, where she trains as a nurse. Yet each retains a stubborn charge of working-class truculence. Flora resents Col Pardoe's efforts to improve himself, and she stands up to Mrs. Hunter. Macrory, the gruff, up-country farmer, refuses to be impressed with Dorothy and Basil's titles and honors when they visit him at Kudjeri. Moreover, he outdoes them in tact and breeding by turning them down when they offer to pay for his hospitality. Like Bill Hunter, Kudjeri's former owner, Macrory helps spell out White's moral preference for the country. Again, the infusion of rural values into his cosmopolitanism becomes Basil's best hope for rebirth. This indirect criticism of the urban inferno adds to the novel's persuasiveness. Timely references to women in Mia Farrow haircuts, pantsuits, and miniskirts, to Vietnam, and even to the silent majority (p. 331) reveal *Eye* to be keenly sensitive to contemporary language, styles, and attitudes. This sensitivity is thematic. A work in which two people fly 12,000 miles within two days *should* describe the world in which such rapid, wholesale change occurs.

Continuity, though, exerts as much force as does change, lending both dialectical rhythm and historical depth to the book's stylish intelligence. The country-born Elizabeth Hunter, who spent her adolescence and early youth in the nineteenth century, evokes Australia's frontier tradition—as does her junior, Arnold Wyburd, to a lesser degree. Then there are the literary references which evoke Australia's European heritage. (Australia's aboriginal heritage will be featured in *A Fringe of Leaves*, White's next book.) The most outstanding of these references is to *King Lear*. Brian Kiernan noted some tie-ins between Shakespeare's play and *Eye*: "Basil's ambition to play the most difficult of tragic roles, and his and Dorothy's ingratitude to their mother, the centrality of the storm incident all suggest that we are invited to consider a parallel with Lear."[6] His running parallel is richly thematic. If Dorothy's sly treachery invokes Regan and if the more flamboyant Basil's comparisons between himself and Goneril make sense, then the cook's reference to the Hunter children as murderers (p. 488) invites another issue: the absence of a Cordelia surrogate. Our vain search for Cordelia amid this band of Hunters calls forth both the disrepair of the Hunter family and the menace building around Elizabeth, an octogenarian preparing to divide her spoils while clinging to life. Wyburd's popping a button from his shirt and Basil's fondness for quoting Lear's request that his shirt button be undone help make Cordelia an imaginative presence; only when stripped of all does Lear appreciate Cordelia's goodness. Mrs. Hunter's granddaughter, Imogen, is named for a Shakespearean heroine as virtuous as Cordelia, but she lives in distant England and has never met Mrs. Hunter. That her namesake appears in *Cymbeline*—a work, like Lear, centering on an early English king—makes her inability to soothe her grandmother all the more regrettable.

But Mrs. Hunter rarely needs to be soothed. Her first name (which is also that of England's most illustrious monarch), her long life, and her magnanimity, all echoing Lear, suggest the means by which she defeats her enemies. Further parallels with Lear focus her remarkable powers still more sharply. Although Basil covets the role of Lear, he sees his mother as Lear's true-life counterpart. Her dying on the commode, which she calls her "throne," conveys her strength and wisdom. She rules to the last with a serenity that can ennoble something as improbable as a toilet. In a drunken reverie which takes place while Basil is flying back to England, members of his circle fuse and overlap with Shakespeare's people. His mother is always the king; such power does she wield that the audience must help the whole cast stamp her into her coffin at play's end. Such wit has she exerted over the years that he feels foolish and deprived of a role to play. Her fusions of wisdom, humor, and senile nonsense make her a better choice for the role of Fool than Basil, to whom she even materializes as Edgar, a good son, in a parody of the Dover scene (*"Poor Mum's acold"* [p. 493]) he enacts near Kudjeri. Finally, her blindness invites a parallel with Gloucester, loyal parent and servant to the king. This dominance explains Basil's wish that his mother die. Her material existence, marginal as it is, robs him of space in which to grow and to be.

The wish to overthrow and supplant the mother also resonates with the Freudian overtones sent out by the generational conflict. The Eye of the novel's title teases out Oedipal associations amply justified by the action. Corresponding to Mrs. Hunter's physical blindness is the moral blindness of her children. As in Sophocles, blindness in *Eye* refers most pointedly to family trouble; problems outside the home in both Sydney and Thebes stem from problems within. The family touches all. Dorothy marries a man old enough to be her father; she fantasizes about having sex with Wyburd, her Australian father surrogate; after looking incestuously at Basil the first time she sees him in the novel, she sleeps with him. Basil already knows the Oedipal orbit. In Bangkok he had tried to mount the actress Janie Carson, who looks like and who attended school with Imogen. The Bangkok incident takes the incest motif back to the stage, where Oedipus first lived, as Janie hopes one day to play Cordelia to Basil's Lear.

Janie will never play opposite Basil, if he has any say in the matter. The futility of merging life and art recurs in *The Charterhouse of Parma*, the favorite novel of both Bill and Dorothy Hunter. Bill so admired Gina Pietranera, the subtle, vital, and beautiful Duchess of Sanseverina, that, in marrying Elizabeth, he felt he could become one with her real-life counterpart. The many years he lives apart from her and her inability to give him the love she knows he deserves both describe a failure as dismal as her son's stage-ridden behavior. Stendhal's 1839 novel sheds other revealing light on *Eye*. The total effect is one of depth, drive, and effortless flow. More inventive than managerial, *Eye* deals with profound, timeless emotions in a craftsmanlike way, and it gives them contemporary relevance. The ease with which the narrative elements join show in the book's undersea references. "Over there you look like something underwater" (p. 532), says Mrs. Hunter to Lal Wyburd; the idea of death by drowning comes to Flora; Edvard Pehl specializes in marine ecology; the skiapod, that carnivore to which Mrs. Hunter likens herself, inhabits the sea. Besides evoking the mysterious unity that permeates all White's work, the ocean metaphor presents unevolved characters daunted by problems as ancient as the immortal, rolling sea.

The divisions in the book capture this rhythm. Like Part One of the bipartite *Happy Valley*, the first half of *Eye* covers one day. Repetitions both within and between its two time settings establish a flow that controls the later book. Some of the repetitions and variations count more than others. Mrs. Hunter married at age thirty-two, the same age as Mary De Santis's father; Mary, who has been a nurse for thirty-two years at the time of the novel, used to give pain-killing injections to her dying father, as did Mrs. Hunter to Bill in his decline. These repetitions reinforce existing patterns. All along the undersea logic of the novel has fused the husband with the father and has also raised ambiguities between the roles of healer, life-giver, and destroyer. Some of the repetitions gain more from accretion than from ambiguity. Basil gets his foot jammed inside one of his father's old boots while prowling around on old shed. Later he wears his father's boot in another sense by having sex in his parents' bed. Dorothy is again with him, rocking back and forth in the same anguished rhythm displayed in her attempt to remove the boot. Their sexuality will hobble both of them. They couldn't have hoped to destroy their mother without destroying something vital in themselves.

Moments like this make *Eye* one of the best novels of the 1970s. Brady's praise both typifies the reception the book received and explains the critical eminence it enjoys: "If the story of civilization is the story of the growth of consciousness, then White's achievement here is to make available areas of awareness hitherto out of range of all but the most ambitious artists."[7] White does display a heightened sense of artistic purpose in *Eye*, aiming for truths and effects beyond the grasp of realism. The already quoted description of Mrs. Hunter drinking water imparts a primitive dread and endows Mrs. Hunter with an ancient wisdom; it also makes us wonder if her children don't have more to fear from her than she does from them. And it comes at a good time, on page 22. The opening pages of *Eye* make the reader worry whether he can slog through the next 600. White has drawn the vastness of Australia tightly around himself by seating his opening scene in the cramped, static confines of a sickroom. The son and daughter of the patient create a symmetry that also bids to block outlets for the plot. Nor does the dying old patient promise to lighten the languor that looms ahead, judging from the adverbs in the book's brief opening paragraph: "The old woman's head was barely fretting against the pillow. She could have moaned slightly" (p. 9). Mrs. Hunter's head is so wasted that it hardly frets, or makes an impression on, the pillow supporting it. Yet this same head also heads a family, and it will vex and fret other heads as it comes to life in the course of the book. White has both direct knowledge and an intuitive grasp of the effects of Mrs. Hunter's resurrection. Observing the dramatic ideal of Mitty Jacka, he will not use plot or thesis to cage his characters. The people in *Eye* are seen from both inside and out, at the moment of dramatic enactment and in historical depth. Instead of becoming simple, the reality they portray grows complex. The technique of *The Eye of the Storm* imparts depth, grandeur, and mystery to the dark fire of its theme. Only a handful of English-language novels of the century can boast such a blend of form and content.

11. Castaways

A Fringe of Leaves (1976) returns to the question which underlay *Tree* and *Voss*, White's two novels of the 1950s. Again White asks: What is the Australian? How did he become the way he is? And where is he heading? Like the European prospectors who camp near the goldfields of Ballarat, Victoria, in Henry Handel Richardson's *Australia Felix* (1917), the English characters in *Fringe* get a stronger dosage of Australia then they had bargained for. Beyond the symbolic fringe of White's title lies a world indifferent to human needs and goals. The waves created by this indifference break over a wide coastline. Only a ragged fringe divides the civilized from the savage. The idea of living right up against nature also refers to Australia's demography. A strip of civilization extending from Brisbane to Adelaide, called the Boomerang, occupies less than 5 percent of Australia's surface while supporting nearly 75 percent of the population. Symbolizing the thinness of civilization, this suburban fringe also divides two mighty, mysterious forces, the ocean and the outback. *Fringe* both extends and refines the insights set forth by *Voss*, a fictionalized account of Ludwig Leichhardt's doomed crossing of Australia's desert interior, but it differs in approach. Rather than unfolding in the outback, most of *Fringe*'s action takes place at sea and in the bush bordering Queensland's southern coast. Whereas *Voss* featured a German bachelor, *Fringe* takes as its real-life model an English wife, Eliza Fraser, whose husband's ship crashed and sank on the Great Barrier Reef in 1836.[1]

The nineteenth century matters to White not only because it was the great age of Australian exploration, migration, and population growth but also because it gave rise to the fictional mode that he has called his chief literary influence.[2] Victorian in shape, pace, and tone, *Fringe* leans on different conventions of nineteenth-century storytelling, if only to bend them to its own purposes. In the robust Ellen Roxburgh and her wan husband, Austin, White reverses the Gothic pattern of the brave adventurer-hero and the sickly, hypersensitive heroine. The novel portrays law-breakers but no villains, and, rather than contrasting virtue and vice, blurs the outlines between them; often no moral difference obtains between the gentry and the convicts seen in prison camps in Moreton Bay and Van Diemen's Land, or Tasmania. What is more, the heroine does have sex with the crypto-villain—at *her* instigation. From the pattern of the saltwater saga of adventure come the storm and shipwreck, followed by the sighting of land, the beaching of boats, the capture and death at the hands of natives, and the main figure's miraculous escape and return to civilization. Underlying this derring-do is that later development of Victorian fiction, the Conradian journey into the self's own heart of darkness. To her dismay, Ellen finds in herself the same capacity for betrayal and bloodshed she condemns in her savage captors. The prominence of Aboriginals and convicts also touches two raw nerves in the Australian body politic—the nation's convict heritage and the abuse of Aboriginals by white settlers. Like *Tree* and *Voss*, *Fringe* recounts issues and incidents that reflect the sometimes painful growth of Australia, "the lucky country."

Some of this pain is symbolized by distance. Australia's remoteness from the world's cultural centers has fostered a sense of isolation and displacement ever since the country's origin as a convict depot.[3] Nearly everyone in *Fringe* is adrift; nearly everyone would rather be somewhere else. The note of estrangement rings out from both the Aboriginals, with their migratory habits, and the dateline on Ellen's first recorded diary entry, "*At sea*" (p. 69). Poor health sent Austin Roxburgh to Cornwall, where he met Ellen some fifteen years before the present action; his brother Garnet lives in Tasmania, where he went to escape arrest, trial, and possibly, jail. Jack Chance, who rescues Ellen from the natives and restores her to civilization, embodies displacement more dramatically, surviving alone in the bush with the natives providing his only human contact. His escape from the penal camp at Moreton Bay, Queensland's only European settlement at the time, has put him at a double remove from home; besides having been exiled to Australia for life, this Londoner has forsaken the fellowship of his kind. Expressive of his alienation is his tongue-tied stammering when Ellen asks him his name: his ordeal has cut him off from his native language. From her lonely Cornwall childhood to her convalescence at the penal camp, Ellen has never felt at home. Her sailing down the Brisbane River aboard the *Princess Charlotte* at the end makes her homelessness the norm of the novel. She is still adrift. A ship's passenger, she is being carried by others to a destination, and she lacks the security of solid earth under her feet.

It is plausible for one so powerless and bereft of controls to seek comfort in superstition; frustrated by people, she turns to the spirit world.

This believer in the legendary magic connected with Cornwall's St. Hya's Well and Tintagel later threads her wedding ring into a skirt of vines in an effort to maintain a link with English respectability. The mysterious disappearance of the ring within hours of the time she sights the Oakeses' farm proves that she can't return to civilization until she has shed every scrap of her English past. To be reborn she crawls naked and filthy to the Oakeses' farmhouse. If her dung-smeared nakedness recalls the violent self-naughting of Theodora Goodman, Hurtle Duffield, and Elizabeth Hunter during rebirth, her wedding ring harks to the red curving of glass coveted by Ray Parker, Jr., and to Arthur Brown's mandalas. White's characters believe in charms and talismans (as did Joyce's Leopold Bloom, with his potato and bar of soap). Despite the "radical formal differences"[4] in narrative technique between *Fringe* and *Eye*, a technical breakthrough for White, *Fringe* squares well with the rest of the canon. It begins in the same way as *Solid Mandala*: White introduces his main characters indirectly, using minor figures to discuss them (from a moving vehicle) rather than projecting them center stage. The ending of *Fringe* resembles that of *Voss* even more markedly. In both works a government official questions a woman about the brutal outdoors ordeals that form the works' central actions. In the characters of Albert Judd and Pilcher, second mate of the shipwrecked brig *Bristol Maid*, White surprises the reader by introducing survivors of the ordeals. The downbeat last sentence in each work also undercuts an affirmation White had been building toward but wants to qualify for the sake of moral balance.

I

The same realism marking the finale of *Fringe* governs White's portrayal of the mystery of unity. The metaphysical principle that makes sense of life's diversity will emerge briefly and then vanish. Chaos will triumph over order. The unknowability and unpredictability of the universe comes forth in the name Jack Chance, in the *Bristol Maid*'s accidental ramming into a coral reef, and in the mishap that splashes Mr. Jevons's tea on Ellen's dress. Yet order has been making inroads of its own. The novel's formalized nineteenth-century diction controls or at least counterpoints the anarchy, as does the elaborate network of cross-references and foreshadowings. The network sends out its lines of force early. The riders in the carriage leaving Sydney's Circular Wharf at the outset are "rocked together and apart . . . as seaborne passengers . . . by the waves" (p. 9). Chapter 3 describes the flapping of canvas, the groaning of timbers, and the mewing of gulls as the *Bristol Maid* puts out to sea amid high winds. White has drawn a parallel between sea and land travel. Other parallels have already begun to take form. Delaney the emancipist, at whose property the carriage had stopped in chapter 1, tells of a shepherd found dead in the barrens with his leg missing. Later Ellen will find the corpse of the *Bristol Maid*'s second mate, Ned Courtney, its leg removed at the hip and presumably eaten by Courtney's Aboriginal slayers. The motif gains force. Its final manifestation shows Ellen happening upon the close of a cannibal feast. More participant than observer, she gnaws on the thighbone of the young woman who had supplied her tribesmen's shameful meal. White doesn't always order his repetitions to produce a crescendo, a succession of dramatic peaks numbing, rather than rousing, the reader. Tasmania, called in William Hay's *The Escape of the Notorious Sir William Heans* (1919) "a wild island at the bottom of the world,"[5] reminds Ellen of rugged Cornwall. Later the roughness with which she is handled by her native captors rouses in her the same helpless wrath she felt as a bride in Cheltenham, where her new husband and his circle were all older and better bred than she. Her connecting these far-flung social milieus bears out White's belief in the oneness of experience. An event recurs because it expresses an important truth.

White often seats truth or even necessity close to the animal world. The frequent presence of horses, birds, and snakes creates a running parallel between human motives and animal impulses. The capacity for animal cruelty that the wilderness brings out in Ellen prompts her denial, to the commandant of the penal camp, that the Aboriginals abused her. She claims no moral superiority over her ex-captors. She has also seen brute impulse driving into the sphere of social justice and making nonsense of moral distinctions. Garnet Roxburgh may have sinned worse than the prisoners confined near his property. In fact, sin may have won him the property, which had belonged to his older, widowed wife. The property comprising Dulcet came to Garnet, his wife's sole heir, after the wife fell from a gig Garnet was driving. And perhaps she, a rich heiress at the time she married Garnet, acquired Dulcet through means just as suspicious. White won't let us rule out a long regress of foul play. His characters don't bear close moral scrutiny. Undetected and unconfessed sinners if not already in chains, they are all capable of evil.

This drift toward vice and guilt creates a rich tapestry of motives. Though physically close, from being jammed together in the longboat used to flee the shipwreck, Ellen and Austin are light years apart psychically. Their habit of concealing truths can also make for fun; at one point aboard the sinking *Bristol Maid*, each keeps the same secret from the other. Consistent with this doubleness is the fluidity of their tie. At the end of chapter 4 Austin, who is twenty years her senior, reminds Ellen of her father, but moments later he stirs her maternal instincts; she bares her breast to his sleeping mouth just before covering up and going to her own berth. The figure of the baby son remains active with this childless woman who has already miscarried and then lost an infant boy. A stillborn son, delivered by Austin in the leaking longboat, is put to sea inside the glory bag of Oswald Dignam, the brig's recently drowned cabin boy and Ellen's doting surrogate son.

That Ellen looks like the shipwreck's only survivor reflects White's appreciation of women. That the two ships on which she is seen to sail have feminine names—the *Bristol Maid* and the *Princess Charlotte*, whose prototype, Captain Fraser's *Stirling Castle*, lacked womanly associations—conveys his belief that women can provide support, along with tenderness and sympathy. Ellen's sturdiness and renewability show in her outliving people she has mothered, like Oswald, Austin, and a pustular, snouted Aboriginal girl she is ordered to nurse. To call attention to her vigor, White reverses his usual practice of allowing mothers to survive fathers. Whereas mothers outlive their mates in *Aunt's Story*, *Tree*, "Clay" (1963), "Dead Roses" (1964), *Riders*, *Solid Mandala*, and *Eye*, White kills off Clara Gluyas earlier than her violent, drunken husband to leave Ellen unprotected. The chic Meg Bosanquet of *Big Toys* (1977) also overcame both her hard beginnings and a widowed laborer-father who tried to force her. Meg, Mrs. Hunter, and Ellen, the heroines of White's major works of the mid-1970s, reflect the era's sensitivity to women. They also fuse elements of the yeomanry and the gentry, having risen to privilege from poverty. Ellen's early rural training helps her survive in the bush. The refinements she learned later as a lady, comprising no survival manual, have made her self-righteous and censorious, as is seen in her first question to Jack: "Are you a Christian?" (p. 280). Her telling the chaplain of the penal colony at the end that she doesn't know if she's a Christian (p. 385) shows how her pilgrimage has schooled her. She has been humbled. Like any good educational program, her bush trek has sensitized her soul while teaching her intellectual honesty. It has also eased the pain of not belonging; pulled out of an uncouth world, yet confused and uneasy among the gentry, she rivals Dorothy Hunter de Lascabanes in feeling displaced. Her pilgrimage resurrects the natural self she had submerged in order to become socialized.

Whereas Mrs. Hunter was selfish and seductive, Ellen is outgoing and sensual. Her survival represents the triumph of the ordinary. Like Vic Moriarty with her cyclamen in *Happy Valley*, Ellen takes as her totem a flower—the teasel, a wildflower that blooms despite drought and harsh salt winds. Ellen and Austin find it at Sydney Cove and keep it in a jar in their cabin aboard the *Bristol Maid*. Although it looks dead, it lives, demonstrating Ellen's own will to endure against odds. At times Ellen exists only marginally. *Fringe* portrays female passiveness relative to male power. Adapting to each culture and to each man that claims her, Ellen testifies to the idea that women live in a borrowed light. She has always aquiesced to men less able and less noble than she, as a farm girl, a lady, and a slave. Like her patronizing husband, the Aboriginals treat her as their creation. They see her as a "work of art" (pp. 251-52, which is exactly how Austin referred to her in England [p. 61]) after hacking off her hair, pressing a wax helmet into her raw scalp, and rubbing her body with charcoal. They use her as a nurse, a pack animal, and a food gatherer. They pinch and punch, slap and scratch her. For fun they make her pluck possums out of their nests in high trees by prodding her bottom with firesticks. She survives these indignities because she has known others like them.

What she has not known is self-worth; she has never been accepted for herself. Instead, people have prescribed for her, dressed her in unfamiliar garb, spoken to her in an alien tongue, and tried to change her. Before enjoying the privileges appropriate to her station as Austin's wife, she had to prove herself worthy of them. She started keeping a diary, and she agreed to undertake the course in social etiquette deemed necessary by her new family. Labor before rest, decrees the prevailing Puritan-industrial morality—even in bucolic Cheltenham, which she finds as regimented and repressive as her author would when he attended college there a century later.[6] Having lived her first thirty years in England, she knows what to expect from a male-dominated culture. Her father-ridden girlhood gave way to a husband-ridden adulthood, making her adjustment to Aboriginal culture less onerous than might be thought. Having been rescued by Garnet Roxburgh after a would-be rapist attacks her in Hobart Town, she has also known the plight of using the bad to spare herself from the worst. She stands a better chance of survival with the Aboriginals than on her own in the wild, unfamiliar bush.

She married Austin to avoid facing the world alone after her father's death. This whining intellectual with his upper-class crotchets and spin-sterish ways has given her good cause to rue her choice. Although he studied law, his poor health stopped him from practicing. His status as a permanent invalid or convalescent has also cast her in the role of nurse-maid. Characteristically, he first appears sitting, rather than standing, and reading a book with his back to a door. He is unhappy with his dry, passive intellectual life; he frays the edges of the pages he turns and dogears the corners, expressing his frustration. His impluses lack outlets. Like many of his nineteenth-century fictional counterparts, such as George Eliot's Mr. Casaubon in *Middlemarch*, he needs drive and discipline to offset his laziness. He gives up a novel-in-progress after struggling through three chapters. Raking leaves blisters his soft hands, forcing him to sit down despite his belief in the "sacramental function" (p. 54) of work. The reek of medicine and musty old books conveys his faintheartedness. He flinches from the prospect of seeing a calf slaughtered for market. Whereas Ellen knows farming, having experienced the intimacies of birth and death directly, he filters it through a screen of literature. But finally the screen caves in. Ironically, this hypochondriac who sees death as an intellectual conceit will die brutally.[7]

With his aloofness and sniffing superiority, he condescends to Ellen. He will turn a compliment into an act of self-praise; after telling her over tea that she looks "uncommonly nice" he adds, "I was right in advising you to wear green" (p. 60). He has forgotten how she protects and sustains him. Besides viewing her as a pet project, i.e., a rough gem he must trim and polish, he is embarrassed when she displays a tearful red face at a funeral. Typically, he has forgotten that she is crying for *his* dead mother. He has never tried to know her heart. Expecting her to be sexually submissive, he recoils in shock at her one show of ardor. On the other hand, this dry stick will bend. He hasn't limited her range of acceptable responses to obedience and gratitude. During their courtship each treads on the other's turf, however cautiously; she reads part of a book he loans her, and he goes exploring with her along Cornwall's rugged lanes. The storms they experience together also humanize the contrast between them. So do her two pregnancies by him, their undertaking the long, hard voyage to Tasmania together, and his numerous intuitive flashes. White carefully avoids facile polarities in his portrayal of their marriage. Austin's frailty doesn't bar him from enjoying the sight of a ship under sail, and his soul freshens in the sailors' world of rope, timber, and canvas. Like Ellen he shows courage under duress. After the *Bristol Maid's* fatal mishap, he goes back to his waterlogged stateroom to fetch his Virgil. He doesn't care that the copy is a crib or that he has read it many times; nor does he retrieve it to show off to his wife. Heretofore clinging and whining, he acts decisively. He prizes the book enough to risk his life for it. The thrashing storm has inspired him, rather than making him quail. It doesn't matter that his heroism goes unnoticed. Once roused, Austin becomes active and useful, unloading supplies from the brig's hold and stowing them in the longboats. The knowledge that nature can be harsher than Virgil describes it in the *Georgics* hasn't buckled his spirits. He won't dope himself with literature during a crisis as Ellen's former protector, her father, had done with drink.

Austin wins Ellen's loyalty for having rescued her from orphanhood and poverty. She offers him protection, obedience, and honor without expecting much in return. Although she embroiders him a bookmark for Christmas, during their time in Tasmania, she doesn't complain when she gets no gift from him. This oversight means little within the larger picture of her unconfessed disappointment. Prodded by an inner demon that rules her better feelings, she wants more than he can give. Her capacity for sensual indulgence, for instance, keeps surprising her. Playful and imaginative, she also has a flair for adventure that verges on the strange and the terrible. White makes her Cornish to accentuate this flair, which her

husband never understands. The men and women of Cornwall have con-
tributed proudly to the formation of Australia. Many Cornish miners dug
for copper in South Australia in the 1870s and 1880s,[8] their descendants
later scattering to different parts of the country. The Cornishman William
James Trewhella in D.H. Lawrence's *Kangaroo* (1923) lives near Sydney,
and Ellen's faith in local legend reflects Trewhella's zest for a new start.
Her first great wish is to visit Tintagel, a cape in West Cornwall where King
Arthur was supposedly born. She also bathes in St. Hya's Well nearby, to
ward off evil, and she retains an affection for talismans and tokens. Her
vision of Cornwall, land of great boulders and heroic legends, as an island
gives her romantic isolation a wild dynamism. Islands foster chaos. Gold-
ing's young island castaways in *Lord of the Flies* (1954) ignore mainland
law. Pointing to the damage caused by the rock of Scylla in the *Odyssey*,
John Fowles equates islands with seduction and murder.[9] Now Scylla is
female (as is the rocky bulge in the Rhine called the Lorelei); *Bristol Maid*,
which also has a feminine name, breaks up when it rams a reef, perhaps a
distant female cousin of Scylla or Lorelei. Ellen, who is linked to treachery,
deceit, and death in the presence of water, also proves that the magic
conferred by islands can bewitch and destroy. "You'll always hate me. I
bet tha's stuck pins in me and throwed me to the fire" (p. 65), says her
father, speaking more wisely than he knows.

Exulting in freedom and movement, she constantly seeks new limits.
She prowls forgotten corners of her husband's estate; she will walk the
deck of the *Bristol Maid* by herself in weather so foul that she is ordered
below by the captain; at Sydney Cove she neglects her husband's frailty by
insisting that she sees what lies beyond a certain knoll. The roomy outdoors is her milieu. "She was only at ease when received into the countryside" (p. 92), notes White of her at Dulcet, Garnet's property near Hobart.
During a rainstorm that pelted her and Austin years earlier in Cornwall,
she had put her body between that of the spindly patrician and the gust. No
need to protect herself; though often drenched by mist, rain, and sea spray,
she never gets sick. That many of the key moments in her life occur
outdoors also shows that her rude Cornish blood remains untamed.
Phrases used in connection with her, like "the forest of her hair" (p. 159),
reveal affinities with the wilderness that match the clamor in her heart.
Outdoors is where she commits adultery with Garnet, where she is attacked by the would-be rapist, and where she lives during the transforming
months between her abduction and her deliverance at the Oakeses' farm.

The green shawl she wears aboard *Bristol Maid* symbolizes her re-
pressed eroticism, green being the color of both the jungle and the sea. (J.R.
Dyce believes that green symbolizes fertility for White.[10]) Thus her datelin-
ing her first recorded diary entry, "*At sea*" (p. 69), grazes the same truth as
Captain Purdew's question to her, "Were you born at sea, perhaps?"

(p. 46). The idly put question lodges in our minds. The minerals and land formations of her birthplace owe more to the action of the nearby sea than to conditions prevailing inland. What is more, Cornwall's location at land's end and the letter beginning the name of the town nearest her girlhood home, Zennor, help make her a denizen of borders and margins. Nor do her years at stuffy Cheltenham, where she lives on the fringe of gentility, subdue her primitive energies. Ellen exposes the hidden depths of basic human drives. Referring to "the sacramental aspect of what could only appear a repellent and inhuman act" (p. 315), she draws obscure strength from eating human flesh. A dark, buried self comes to life among the Aboriginal men, who move her with their physical splendor. The deep animal impulses they awaken she comes to see as more human than savage: "I dun't believe a person is every really cured of what they was born with" (pp. 331-32), she tells Jack Chance. By sinking her acquired traits, she has allowed her essential nature to come forth. Her claim that the Aboriginals didn't mistreat her acknowledges the strange new causality that has shaped her life. Her journey into herself features the snake, symbol of evil and original sin in the Christian West. Eating roasted snake produces in her "an ecstasy such as she had never experienced before" (p. 265). During a ritual snake dance she gets so carried away that her clapping, thumping, and moaning heightens the frenzy of her black neighbors.

Treachery and deceit cut more deeply in *Fringe* than in *Eye.* So drab and tame in contrast to Elizabeth Hunter, Ellen outdoes her brilliant counterpart as her implication in the human calamity deepens. Never before has White traced the dark, sensuous mystery motivating his people to our common ancestry. Displaying his powers of vision at a new height, *Fringe* features malice, death, nightmare, and the violation of taboos, as impulse rides herd over moral precept. The darkness rolls in unwatched. Whereas Austin sails to the southern hemisphere to join his brother, Ellen, to whom the voyage offers no prospects besides those of tending to her husband, encounters herself—usually outdoors and wearing green, the color Austin finds so becoming to her. Veronica Brady claims that this primal encounter has social reverberations: "The novel's center of gravity is closer to that of the traditional novel, being about education in the art of living with others."[11] That some of these others are convicts and cannibals shows that, like Lewis Carroll's Alice, we rise by sinking. Danger excites Ellen. Like Voss, she fights isolation and fragmentation in order to discover herself both as an individual and as part of a group. She proceeds through immersion in the sensual, palpable world, not through denial. Housing both healthful foodstuffs and haunting premonitions, the teeming jungle is her element. Woman stands for passion which, bypassing rational controls, can destroy as well as gladden and fulfill. An Aboriginal stabs her rival to death; Oswald Dignam, the cabin boy, drowns while hunting for shellfish to feed his beloved Mrs. Roxburgh; Jack Chance murdered Mab in England when he found her with another man. Love's savagery strikes a responsive chord in Ellen. Her exposure to Garnet's lust, to that of her would-be rapist, to the cruelty of her native captors, and to the fury of the sea has taught her to suspend judgment. This anarchy touches something both vital and familiar within her, as did her sortie into cannibalism. To gainsay it, she sees, would be to deny her humanity. Guilt and crime keep dogging her. Infidelity, for which Jack slit Mab's throat, weighs on her conscience. Deepening her implication in sin, Mab's murder indirectly benefits her. Jack rescues her partly to repay a debt; having been helped to freedom by a woman after Mab's death, he feels obligated to the female sex.

Ellen feels her vague obligation directly. She will not only embrace but also love the murderer, perhaps with greatest heat when learning of his darkest deed—mounting Mab's corpse. Later she calls herself Mab and refers to her dead husband as Jack while delirious, indicating that she must soak herself in crime both physically and emotionally before her social reintegration can occur. Her newfound strength builds from both her character, i.e., what she is, and what she does. White has planned everything that happens to her. She wears green, the color of growing things, on the day of her rut with Garnet. Nothing about the event is casual or spontaneous. Before setting forth she is under a strain, looking "unnaturally drawn, her skin chalky, her lips thin" (p. 112). She can't pretend to pardon either herself or the adultery she has prearranged, and she is too honest to feign innocence. Even Merle senses her excitement as she lures Garnet into following her to the same spot where she had walked weeks before, looking for a place to lie down with him. White shows her, a practiced horsewoman, falling unhurt so that she can enjoy her tumble with Garnet: "The rider was not precisely thrown, but slithered free of saddle and stirrup, and landed somehow on one foot before falling spreadeagle on the miraculously soft leaf-mould" (p. 114). Both the fall and the tumble are stage managed. The soft rot on which she lands after parting company from her horse not ony protects her from injury; it is also the precise spot where she slept and had a sexual fantasy about Garnet during her first visit to the area. She is lying to Garnet when she claims to have jumped (p. 115) and then to have been thrown (p. 117) from the saddle. Even after talking to him for at least a minute, she neglects to cover her bosom, shaken free in the dismounting. He hits home when he asks her, after their tumble, "What have you done to us, Ellen?" (p. 117). Austin's greeting when she returns home also hits the mark: "You went riding. Well, I expect it has done you good. We all need our diversions, according to our different tempers" (p. 119). Ellen's temper, or humor, is hot, and her blood runs strong. She calls the tumble "an experience of sensuality she must have awaited all her life," and she pictures herself, during it, as both "this great, green ... obscene bird" and "the green, fathomless sea, tossing, threatening to swallow down the humanly manned ship which had ventured on her" (p. 116). Once again the female shows astonishing power to absorb and destroy.

She escapes neither the meaning of her act nor the green surge it sets into motion. The forest and the sea won't be denied. There is no escaping the impulses that drove her to Garnet; her voyage to the southern hemisphere carries her ever deeper into herself. She sees in Holly, a pretty emancipist servant girl at Dulcet, another embodiment of herself. Like her, Holly, who is named for a tree with sharp, pointed green leaves, rides Merle. Whereas she and Holly both get pregnant by Garnet, neither gives birth at Dulcet. Garnet has put the two women through the same paces, as if they were mares themselves. Just as he trains Merle so that Ellen can ride her, so he had already taught Holly how to ride the mare. A third woman, Maggie Aspinall, the wife of a Hobart physician, also rides Merle. Judging from a conversation that Ellen overhears, Maggie, too, belongs in Garnet's stable of lovers.

Ellen's instincts win out over the social training she received at Cheltenham. The more she suppresses the parallels between herself and Garnet's other two lovers, the more she plays herself false. Her leaving Dulcet for Hobart with her husband proves nothing. Rather than easing her sexual guilt, Hobart materializes at least three versions of it. She comes home one afternoon to find her alter ego, Maggie, awaiting her return. On another day she walks to Battery Point to shed her obsession with sex. Her head crammed with chaotic images, she turns into a forest clearing, where her guilty self-knowledge rises inexorably and hideously before her. Moments after discovering the first sign of her pregnancy, nausea, she confronts an image of her lust—a malicious old tramp dressed in green rags who leers at her through gapped teeth. The encounter parodies her earlier sexual bout with Garnet. The high winds (women in legend become pregnant from the wind) recall this earlier outing, when the winds also whipped and when brute lust also dominated the scene in a forest clearing. As Hawthorne showed in "Young Goodman Brown," to forsake the village for the wood is to give up the safeguards of civilization. The mad encounter in Hobart also strips Ellen of any rights she may have claimed to these defenses. She and her scruvy assailant share more than the lustfulness symbolized by their penchant for green garb. The assailant's resemblance to her father shows her that her sin is basic to her; she can no more run from the stranger than she can from herself. Only a third party can save her—suitably, her partner in adultery. But Garnet grants her no reprieve, even though he routs her attacker. One green-clad image of her sexuality has merely yielded to another. Because he confirms her guilt, Garnet distresses her more than the attacker does.

II

White equates the virile Garnet with guns, leather, and particularly horses. Captain Merivale remembers riding with him as a boy in chapter 1; he appears at Hobart's quay in chapter 3 with a horse-drawn buggy, in which he drives Ellen and Austin to Dulcet; his wife died after falling out of a gig he was driving; he is on horseback again when he routs the old reprobate in Hobart. His having decamped to Tasmania to avoid being charged, tried, and probably sentenced for forgery in England wipes out any moral difference between him and the nearby Port Arthur convicts, whom he calls "the scrapings from the streets of Dublin and London" (p. 99).

Ellen recoiled from her husband's blazing, if flawed, jewel of a brother even before meeting him. First she resented him for outshining Austin. She also saw herself as his fellow underdog and found the comparison unflattering. Whereas he has lost his place among the English gentry, she lacks the social credentials required to win one. These two unworthies resent being excluded. Each has already married an older person above his/her social situation. After the spouses die violently, each will couple with an ex-convict. Why shouldn't they have sex when they meet in a wild, green place? As early as their first meeting, the sight of his strong hands and thick, hairy wrists whetted her desire for freedom. Her rebellion against the restrictions imposed by her husband takes the form of sex. Within days of coming to Dulcet, she wanders off by herself to find a place to be alone with Garnet. Her sexual dream confirms the success of her reconnaissance mission. As further confirmation, the object of her dream materializes—on horseback; her dream lover has both invaded her unconscious and taken solid shape. Though evasive, her diary records her agitation. She refers to her husband with reserve and caution throughout, as Mr. R., while his randy brother is usually G.R. Her diary reveals more than she intends. Her longest recorded entry comes after meeting Garnet. Roused by his sexuality, she writes to compose herself. That White begins dating her entries in Dulcet prefigures her future disquiet: as soon as she meets Garnet, her days of inner peace are numbered.

Her career with horses also gauges her unrest. Horses shadow her sexuality, symbolizing instinct and passion. Garnet rides to each of his major confrontations with her. She also miscarried after falling from a horse in Gloucestershire. Hostile to order and sanity, the impulsiveness that horses represent tramples our civilized arrangements. While only Garnet turns up on a horse for the first forest meeting, both he and Ellen ride to the second. These incidents fall within a larger pattern. Ellen rode a "hairy . . . nag" (p. 98) in Cornwall because her work demanded it; in Cheltenham she rode for pleasure. Her visit to Tasmania restores purpose to her riding. After permitting Garnet to train Merle for her, when she could have invoked her husband's wish, made after her miscarriage, that she not ride, she uses the mare to take her to the spot she had chosen to have sex with Garnet. Impulse and instinct continue to express her character. Garnet kills Merle after the second woodland outing (as he killed his rich wife and wants to kill Ellen?) to protest Ellen's avoidance of him. Oswald, who will die for love of her, sounds like a horse when chewing an apple. Sex, death, and children have again fused symbolically, explaining to her the meaning of her life.

That meaning includes Garnet. Shortly after the first forest encounter she gives a pair of garnet earrings to Holly. But her act exorcises nothing. Her spelling out "G-A-R-N-u-r-d" (p. 182) associates her lover with the process of gathering and storing. Not only does his seed find a home in her body; it also claims her spirit. At the Oakes farm, she tries on a garnet silk dress that flatters her more than her widow's weeds. Analogously, she and Garnet suited each other admirably as lovers. As outcast and upstart, they shared the fate of not belonging which both angered them and enhanced their capacity for treachery and lust. Wearing the garnet dress betokens her acceptance of her own sin. She feels heat and light stirring within her as she caresses herself before a mirror. Despite the stillbirth of his son with Ellen, Garnet has created new life. The other survivor of the shipwreck, Pilcher, gives back a garnet ring he had stolen from her months before. Her throwing it into a flower bed again relates her lust and betrayal to fruitfulness. She doesn't need the ring; the garnet dress which reawakened her sexuality spells out her affinity to Garnet more vividly. By inviting the affinity she makes moral headway. She also adds to the renewal lacing the atmosphere. While her discarded ring nestles amid growing things, her hostess, Mrs. Lovell, has become pregnant.

Ellen's reawakened sexuality has attracted notice. Her social and natural selves join at her introduction, aboard the *Princess Charlotte*, to the London hardware merchant and widower Jevons. Perhaps distracted by the garnet dress, which makes her look "unwillingly resplendent" (p. 401), Jevons, who has already taken an interest in her, accidentally spills tea on Ellen. Her addressing him in her local idiom when he apologizes signals her acceptance of him as a prospective intimate. Though her words are commonplace, her diction lends them special meaning; she had never addressed either Garnet or (since her schooling at Cheltenham) Austin in her relaxed cradle tongue. The comic exchange with Jevons gives rise to compassion and solidarity. Responding in kind, he also invokes regional dialect. As he did with Basil Hunter, White may be using the exchange to ask whether people reveal more of themselves in buffoonery than in heroism or tears. Brady reads acceptance and fulfillment in the last reported dialogue in the novel: "The awkward farm girl she once was reaches out to console him and together they share a secret, their common humanity, their vulnerability and ridiculousness. There is thus a certain pathos but also a certain dignity about their acceptance of each other with which the action concludes."[12]

Ellen can help Jevons because, like him, she has lost a spouse. She has also achieved a dignified love with Jack Chance, Jevons's fellow Londoner. She and Jack shared a great deal. Each felt responsible for a mate's death, Ellen having accepted the blame for Austin's death after pulling on Aboriginal's spear from his neck. Each has two identities, Jack entering the novel at a corroboree as Ulappi the dancer, while Ellen wavers between her Gluyas and Roxburgh selves. Any comparisons between her and Jack, though, favor the runaway convict. (Like Forster, White harbors a sentimental affection for working class men, so long as they stay in their own place; obviously, the bush can be that place.) Jack eats more graciously than she. Whenever she tries to patronize him, she is reproached, as when she feigns interest in Mab and is told she resembles her. He shows more humanity than she by rejecting her idea to kill the old Aboriginal who blunders upon them near journey's end. What is most important, he makes her feel loved for what she is, rather than for what she might become. So free and generous is his love that she comes to trust him more than she does herself, knowing her capacity for deceit and treachery. In fact, the fear of endangering or corrupting him makes her want to protect him from herself.

The relationship between Ellen and Jack is opened and unforced. They talk, trek, and hunt for food; they play in a pond and climb a tree; after having furious sex, they abstain from lovemaking for days. Their abstinence worries neither. Need has created tenderness, affection, and trust between the unlikely pair. Jack's unburdening himself of deep, painful truths pertaining mostly to Mab has helped make Ellen feel unconditionally accepted. She feels closer to Jack than she ever felt to her husband; in fact, she later refers to him *as* her husband while delirious. Her soul has expanded. She comes to love him for the defects—the scarred back, mottled teeth, and smashed face—that once disgusted her. Such outgoings of the heart change her priorities. The wish to convince him of her love supplants her original goal of reaching Moreton Bay. They have grown so close that they dream the same dream at the same time; her identification with Mab in both dreams even links the dreamers to the thing being dreamt. Waking and dreaming have joined hands, erasing distinctions of both time and identity in a pure present: "It was all one by now, a continuous seamless tapestry, its details recurrent and interchangeable" (p. 312), she notes near the end of their time together. In line with the book's running contrast between nature and society, the discovery of civilization destroys this rough Eden of the heart; the attainment of her goal has destroyed the means by which that goal was attained. Jack's loss becomes her gain. He doesn't merely lose her; rather, he takes he to the place where he suffered most—the convict camp from which he escaped. For delivering her to this place of pain, he deserves her love.

Losing him jars her as much as returning to civilization. No sense of triumph crowns her return—she falls from her jungle paradise into a cowpat. The first word describing the return, uttered by Mrs. Oakes, to whose farm she has crawled, is "*Naked*" (p. 334); Ellen's own first utterance, "I will only want to sleep and forget" (p. 334), bespeaks her maimed rebirth. It also echoes both the novel's epigraph from Wordsworth and a phrase from *Eye*, "little acts of unpremeditated kindness" (p. 292). Smeared with dirt, blood, and excrement, she has forsaken the safeguards of the maternal wood for society—which fittingly, has materialized as a prison outpost. Like a baby, she cries, needs to be bathed, and is fed "a mess, soft, sweet, and bland" (p. 338) of eggs, bread, and warm milk. Like Wordsworth's infant in the *Intimations* ode, she can't express her vision. The truth underlying her evasions and distortions gains no release. Her new wisdom verging on madness, she either pains or bores others; Mrs. Oakes falls asleep during one of her recitations, while Lieutenant Cunningham, troubled by her eyes as much as by her words, finds her company chafing. People shun her painful incoherence, as their counterparts shunned Theodora Goodman's in *Aunt's Story* and Jackie's in *Voss*. Much of her anger is directed inward. Disowning her identity as Mrs. Roxburgh, she calls herself Mab, presumably to invite punishment for having failed Jack. This anger needs outlets or it will consume her. It finds a logical but inadequate target in her fellow castaway and survivor, Pilcher. Note that her answers to the questions put to her by the officers of the depot are cryptic and vague; her interrogators learn little from her about her ordeal. Despite their impatience with her, their questions are much gentler than those she asks Pilcher, her mirror image. She must learn to forgive herself. Their common struggles make her the last person who should browbeat him, yet she dismisses his story of his survival, "thinking that only a man could be so self-absorbed and boring" (p. 377), and the brutality of her questions about cannibalism rivals the evasiveness of her own words to him on the subject. Mr. Jevons will need a great deal of patience and tenderness to help her recover moral balance. Sensing her pain, the faded Mrs. Lovell tries to comfort her with what might be the noblest sentiment in all of White: "A woman can only look to the future. . . . However unimportant we are, it is only in unimportant ways. They will always depend on us because we are the source of renewal" (p. 382).

III

R.F. Brissenden notes "the possibility of salvation and love" [13] amid the dislocation and wreckage permeating the action. The possibility must be teased out. White uses bad weather to keynote this negativity. Until the time of the Aboriginal attack, rain is usually falling. Rain drenches Ellen and Austin the first time they go walking together in Cornwall; it is raining when they arrive in Tasmania; Ellen is rained on on the November afternoon when she fares forth in search of a love nest for herself and Garnet; sea mist and blowing rain soak her again on the deck of the *Bristol Maid*. The combination of rain, fog, and bad luck that runs the brig into a coral reef fits with the predominance of prisons in the novel. Reworking the blindness motif from *Eye*, White shows how people groping either in a fog or in the dark forest will meet grief. Prison permeates the novel. Ellen's captivity by the Aboriginals differs only in degree from the enslavement she knew at Cheltenham; if she hadn't viewed her marriage as a prison, she'd not have reached out in protest to Garnet. The note is sounded early, when the three characters comprising the prologue visit Delaney, an emancipist, on their way back from the wharf. (Delaney is one of the few people with a prison record that Ellen misses seeing.) Convicts still serving their sentences at Port Arthur and Moreton Bay dot the action, and civilization itself materializes as the fringe of a penal camp when Ellen leaves the bush.

But negation can coincide with fulfillment, as Eizabeth Hunter proved. The coincidence occurs when society's safeguards are stripped away. The unlikely Austin confronts "the moment when self-esteem is confronted by what may be pure being—or nothingness" (p. 208). He perceives the flimsiness of his life when he meets the steward Spurgeon at the edge of a spiny, wasted promontory, "where the land had almost become sea again" (p. 208). Spurgeon, another soul aware of his frailty and ephemerality, has contracted sea boils. White foreshadows the chance meeting between the two men carefully. Several days earlier Austin felt flooded with love for his wife while pins and needles were stinging the arm with which he had clasped her to his side. The meeting with Spurgeon also yokes pain to affirmation and insight. He tries to heal the steward's sea boils by rubbing them with a soap-and-sugar paste. This direct contact with suffering cheers him more than it does Spurgeon; the healer has been both healed and refreshed. Such moments refute those critics who have blamed White for standoffishness. Austin's exchange with Spurgeon underlies further growth and hope. When the natives later raid the band of castaways, nobody's blood snaps more than that of the reborn Austin Roxburgh. He lives more intensely than ever before during the minutes between the first fatality and his own.

White neither patronizes the natives nor portrays them as monsters. He describes their patterns of food-gathering and migration; he shows them building canoes, feasting, and making love. His rare judgment of them is indirect and favorable. Jack Chance finds them much better hosts than the prison officials whose cruelty drove him into the bush, and the cruelty with which they treat Ellen is no worse than that accorded His Majesty's more recent prisoners. Jack's proposition, "Man is unnatural and unjust" (p. 281), applies to all. White's refusal to belittle or condescend to the blacks squares with his other presentations of vice. An outgrowth of animal passions, vice can erupt at any time. Because it erupts so quickly, it can overtake virtue, the work of patience, imagination, and often denial. But it needn't always have the last word, and it *is* redeemable. The jet of energy that helped produce it is a blind, amoral force. If life is no literary conceit, neither is it a sty. The pregnancy that results from Ellen's sexual bout with Garnet on a bed of rotting vegetation shows life building from death, as will Ellen's rebirth both with Jack and, later, at the Oakes farm.

Renewal is always a presence. Just as the horses in the novel symbolize the surge of life, so the many birds evoke the ability of that surge to transcend itself; proper care will protect the surge from danger and defeat. The first meal that Jack, the professional birdcatcher, takes with Ellen in our presence consists of baked pigeon. Birds later build a nest on the communion table of Pilcher's makeshift chapel. But the effort of self-overcoming can fall short: the same birds that nest on Pilcher's communion table also foul his altar. One of the Lovell children carries a dead chick into Ellen's room. These references don't so much dissolve ambiguities as lend them warmth and point directions. The novel's whole mode of presentation sets forth a hostile universe. The outgoing voyage of *Bristol Maid* highlights images of fear and desolation: "Great clouts of dirty fog caught in the rigging before tearing free. The sea rolled, still revealing glints of a glaucous underbelly, but its surfaces were grey where not churned into a lather of white" (p. 44). White's refusal to understand and forgive can aggravate the grimness. Austin gets "a bash in the face" (p. 211) from an ocean wave while collecting the water needed to treat Spurgeon's sea boils. When the castaways reach land, White mocks them by treating them to an unexpected meal of roasted kangaroo before slaughtering them. Certain editorial intrusions—like "The scene lacked only the coachman and a footman to produce the hampers" (p. 235) and "Into action!" (p. 239) to describe Austin's elation within moments of his death—also smack of sadistic glee.

Other patterns formed by White's causal connections reveal uncanny psychological astuteness. The cranky Austin takes to his bed upon reaching Dulcet, the presence of his manly brother having rattled him. Yet he keeps prodding Ellen to be with Garnet. Is he offering her the chance to scale sexual heights she could never attain with him? This indirect offer is more than an expression of guilt or a loyalty test. Perhaps he shares some of the intuition that led Elizabeth Hunter to claim that she could smell a man's rankness on a woman after sex. Perhaps his insight disturbs him. He broaches the subject of leaving Dulcet with Ellen the morning after her sexual dream in the forest clearing. The very night when her dream becomes flesh several weeks later, he too has sex with her, even though he has just suffered a minor stroke. This wordless communication shows the characters in *Fringe* to be connected by lines of force both delicate and firm. Some of the connections come forth in dreams; the embarrassing moments Ellen skips in her diary surface when her conscious defenses aren't in place. White is yoking behavior to the unconscious. Like Austin's intuitive flashes and Ellen's apparently wayward visions, this inwardness grazes the subliminal forces that mold choice and thus form character.

The nineteenth-century diction in which the novel is couched conveys White's bold purpose inconsistently. Doris Grumbach finds chapter 1, the prologue, freighted by "a curiously dense, subjunctive and negative prose"[14] that strains the reader unduly. The ear can be strained as much as the patience. Combinations like "of a predominately literary nature" (p. 209) and "reflected fluctuating shapes" (p. 348) show that, in selecting an idiom that would establish the novel as a period piece, White sometimes overlooked the sounds of his words. Yet the same writer who ignores phonetics can snatch a grace beyond the scope of all but the best rhetoricians. Unfolding slowly and softly, the images in the following paragraph gain life through the counterpoint of fricatives within a rhythm dominated by stressed syllables: "Captain Purdew's dawn entered the galley without their noticing. It smudged their faces with grubby shadow and drew from the corners of darkness the cold grey smell of ash parted from the original coals" (p. 182). White can use word music to portray violence as well as calm; the storms, sexual encounters, and killings described in the book display a concentration hallucinatory in force. The dramatic edge of *Fringe* bruises and shocks. White can make words do whatever he asks of them. His inability to consistently make the right demands robs the book, his most interrelated and searching, of the control that distinguishes great literature.

12. Ways of Escape

REJECTING THE SOCIAL and moral realism often associated with English-language fiction, *The Twyborn Affair* (1979) turns from the external world to the one within. It also follows the modernist practice of presenting character as radically individual. Mixing dream and desire, it portrays the world as an outward reflection of the private ego. Life makes impressions in *Twyborn Affair*, as it did in Ford Madox Ford's *The Good Soldier*, another work whose main assumptions and approaches break with those of the British fictional tradition. Its main figure, like those of Ford's 1915 novel, half perceives and half invents what he construes as reality, including himself. *Twyborn Affair* discusses the nature and variety of love—sacred and profane, selfless and possessive. Perhaps White has never gotten closer to the anger, panic, and disgust troubling his heart. Facing his obsessions squarely, he neither holds back nor hides behind the star self-protectiveness of the Nobel Prize. Occasionally he resorts to an essayistic vocabulary; parentheses will make him forget rules of punctuation; the odd sentence will sprawl. On the whole, though, *The Twyborn Affair* displays a modest, unemphatic inventiveness rare in White. The proportion of dialogue to narration runs uncharacteristically high; and, as a comparison with the long, unbroken blocks of print in *Tree* or *Riders* will show, most of the paragraphs are agreeably short. This readability represents a stylistic breakthrough. For perhaps the only time in his novelistic career, White has combined simplicity of language with the sense of life as it is lived.

Seeing in White's relatively straightforward diction the drive to write more revealingly about himself, Nancy Schapiro calls *The Twyborn Affair* "an exploration of sexual, national, and human identities."[1] The terror underlying the exploration asserts itself in what happens to the explorer. Two constants in Eddie Twyborn's life are concealment and defection. The appearance of the Sydney couple Boyd and Joanie Golson drives Eddie, masquerading as a young wife, and his lover from St. Mayeul on the French Riviera in Part One. Others defect in Part Two. Kath Prowse, the wife of the manager of Bogong, a large sheep ranch in New South Wales, has already left her husband, and the ranch's owner will take several trips while he is Eddie's employer. In Part Three Eddie, now living as Mrs. Eadith Trist, cuts short two country weekend parties before walking away from his business. Now as both Anthea Scudamore Mortlock of "Dead Roses" and Dorothy Hunter de Lascabanes of *Eye* showed, defectors often feel insecure or threatened; they are uneasy wherever they find themselves. A series of defections infers self-escape; someone who constantly defects is either looking for an important quality he can't find in himself or fleeing an indwelling truth he can't cope with. The life portrayed in *Twyborn Affair* is so ambivalent that a running toward can both look and feel like a running away. Eddie's practice of looking at himself in a mirror doesn't help him discover his identity.

This fragmentation means that forward progress can't be made by moving backward, as happened in *Fringe*. The human landscape of *Twyborn Affair* is full of broken, blurred, or mixed signals. In Part I, Eudoxia and Angelos Vatatzes rent a "pseudo-villa" (p. 21) owned by a "demi-Anglaise" (p. 31). At Bogong, Eddie sees himself as both a "crypto-queen" (p. 143) and an "outcast-initiate" (p. 194); he is also the "pseudo-lover" (p. 255) of the wife of the ranch's owner, a "crypto-poet" (p. 238). Ambivalence follows him to London, where, as Eadith Trist, a "pseudo-man-cum-crypto-woman" (p. 298), he moves among the "crypto-rich" (p. 409). *Twyborn Affair* is also a book about borderlines and frontiers. Eddie prefers to walk the edge, rather than settling into a dreary inland sameness. His mother protested against uniformity by corking on a mustache, putting on her judge husband's checked trousers, and dancing with Joanie Golson at the fashionable Australia Hotel; Roderick Gravenor, a member of the peerage, crosses both social and legal barriers to help run Eadith Trist's brothel; his sister marries a man their father's age. Sameness has become so pervasive that Eddie wears a mask to protect his individuality; better to walk the edge disguised than be absorbed and nullified by the mass. Conformity threatens him everywhere. Not only are his parents called Eadie and Edward; their maid is also called Etty, and Eadith Trist's *chargée d'affaires* in Chelsea answers to Ada. The standardization of modern life has infected the family, the short hop from Etty to Ada reflecting the corruption of the home into a whorehouse.

This decay bespeaks a general moral malaise. The novel starts less than six months before the outbreak of World War I and ends in a bombing raid during World War II. Only a generation removed from their sturdy pioneer past, the Golsons and Twyborns, each of whose houses supplies a witness to the two wars, have felt death's hand; another Australian contemporary, Marcia Lushington, loses four infants. It is also fitting that Eadie, Joanie, and Eadith/Eddie live in London in the 1930s, as moribund a place in *Twyborn Affair* as it was in *Living and Dead*. Joanie and the alcoholic Eadie were lovers years before. Eddie, representing the new generation, is more complex, as his different lives show. His rebellion against conformity is more desperate, more stylized, and ultimately more self-defeating. He indulges in cross-dressing in each of the book's three sections; he crosses both generations (Angelos Vatatzes and Marcia Lushington) and social barriers (Don Prowse and Philip Thring) to gain a lover; he defies society with his tranvestism, his homosexuality, and his brothel-keeping. But he doth protest too much; his defiance is too studied and preplanned to stand as true rebellion. The Chelsea brothel succeeds because it suits the spirit of the day, rather than defying it. Like the most arrant profiteer or materialist, Eddie has sacrificed personal feelings to commercialism. His romantic drive to freedom in society has been crushed by the profit motive. Although set mostly in his brothel, the action of Part Three is chaste, formal, and confining. Whatever the brothel offers its visitors depends upon the calculation and control of the brothel-keeper. Because routine blocks spontaneity, Eddie's journey to self-fulfillment is one of denial and defeat.

Gratification, on the other hand, has always eluded him, in conformity as well as in rebellion. The theme of *Twyborn Affair* is conveyed by one of the novel's epigraphs, from White's fellow Australian David Malouf: "What else should our lives be but a series of beginnings, of painful settings out into the unknown, pushing off from the edge of consciousness into the mystery of what we have not yet become." As Eddie knows, a person needs a fixed, stable point from which to launch himself for any setting out. He also feels that he doesn't know himself well enough to try the unknown. At age twenty-five he says inwardly, "I would like to think myself morally justified in being true to what I am—if I knew what that is. I must discover" (p. 63). The rest of the novel treats his anguished quest. Although a person who doesn't know whether he'd rather be a man or a woman can serve as the butt of comedy, in White's hands this basic question of identity sends out tragic reverberations. Eddie's search is prompted less by cash, titles, and lust than by need. White heightens his private turmoil by aligning it twice with a public disaster—international war.

War is infectious. Part One takes place in the spring of 1914, when Europe was mobilizing for war; at the outset of Part Two Eddie has just been discharged from the army, where he served as a lieutenant and won a DSO; the action ends during the London blitz some twenty years later. Other dangers, doubts, and insecurities haunt Eddie: homosexuality, intergenerational sex, cross-dressing, ocean crossings, disguises, and masks.

Everyone feels homeless, disoriented, or trapped. Eddie's wish to belong pulls against his disaffection for prescibed social norms. His saying, "I arrive everywhere too early, or too late" (p. 299), defines the archetypal defector. Out of touch with himself, he is never where he wants to be. In his search for madder music he forfeits the pleasures of the here and now. His rating the refinements of sex higher than simple desire divides him from both his deepest needs and those he loves. A rich society woman praises Eadith Trist for her "originality and independence—in choosing the life . . . she wanted to lead" (p. 358). But Eadith feels more like a drone than a rebel. "Practical seriousness is what a whorehouse demands" (p. 427), she advises Ada Potter before giving up the house on Beckwith Street. Although she has remained fixated on sex, she can only know it vicariously. An anxious would-be lover is making no idle charge when he says, "You might have set yourself up as the patron saint of chastity" (p. 369).

Yet White also believes that the reluctance to try new ideas serves stagnancy, discourages diversity, and bridles independence. Progress doesn't come from the sane, reasonable person. Only the outcast presses for change, even if he suffers for it. His pain is familiar. Studying man in his sad prepolitical chains, *The Twyborn Affair* puts forth a dialectic in which suffering asserts itself as boldly as in the epigraph, from Gandhi, to *Happy Valley*, in Theodora Goodman's different lives, and in Hurtle Duffield's theophanies. Suffering is still the key both to consciousness and to the mystery of unity.

I

Eddie's pain also reflects White's tendency to resist comfortable answers to life's problems. In describing Eddie's drive to self-fulfillment as a self-denial, *Twyborn Affair* shows that strategies for shunning loss can produce results as dire as loss itself. Eddie's exile and self-alienation mirror the distress of the modern. His practice of arriving too early or too late makes him as much of a permanent outsider as Dorothy Hunter, who felt most Australian in France and vice versa, and Ellen Roxburgh, whose life consisted of adapting to other people's standards. Like these women, Eddie doesn't know whether he belongs in Europe or in Australia. Neither can he say if he'd rather wear skirts or trousers, even though he exhausts himself looking for an answer. Both his transvestism and his homosexuality create fresh opportunities for White to extend his investigation of the individual's place in modern society. *The Twyborn Affair* is full of new hopes and new risks. The divided social loyalties of Hurtle Duffield, Elizabeth Hunter, Ellen Roxburgh, and Mag Bosanquet of *Big Toys*, all of whom have risen to a higher social class since birth, have shifted ground and deepened. Besides testing himself at various social levels, Eddie crosses the sea three times, hurdles generations in search of love, and lives for many years as a woman. White's most fragmented and perhaps most tormented creation also writes in his diary, "Shall my will ever grow strong and free enough for me to face up to myself?" (p. 122). Wanting to know who he is and what he stands for, he feels responsible to his uniqueness. Yet he will show others only a thin slice of himself or face the world through a mask. He doesn't confront reality squarely; a crypto-world calls for a pseudo-self. Also, he can afford setback as a woman, since his female life, occurring in brackets, bypasses his male essence. Because the setback doesn't threaten his true self, it can be ignored. Yet playing the woman becomes more than a charade. The shadow has fused with the substance, making him a stranger to himself. Is he coming to terms with himself or running away? His puzzlement deepens. Does his extended drag act represent a self-betrayal or an inlet to growth, cheer, and self-acceptance? Appearance and reality have switched places. When this expert in disguises attends a masked ball in his street clothes, he may be hiding more than any of the costumed guests.

Torn between the urges to give and to preserve the self, he will reach for friendship but then pull away. Eventually the passion to conceal rules him; all of his relationships must occur behind a mask. Having ruled out vital contacts, he becomes increasingly self-absorbed: "I never set out to lose myself. Finding myself is more to the point" (p. 239), he says at Bogong of his failure to commit himself to another person. Even though his fellow stockhands come to accept this rich man's son, he can't throw himself into jackarooing any more than he can enjoy sex with Marcia. Were this self-consumed man able to relax, he would help his individuality emerge. But he subjects his emotions to such close scrutiny that he immobilizes himself.

One reason he can't help himself by helping others is his upbringing. Without belaboring the subject of early influences, we can say that his parents never showed him how to love. His mother never wanted children to begin with. Sinking further into alcoholic lesbianism, she paid more attention to her dogs than to him; the letters she writes during his childhood constantly refer to him as a burden and a nuisance. His father failed him for different reasons. Whereas Eadie Twyborn misdirected her love, the judge never knew how to express his. As in *Eye*, letters in *Twyborn Affair* include feeble, self-serving explanations for failing immediate family members in extremity. Judge Edward Twyborn won't leave Sydney to see his hospitalized son. After dismissing Eddie's fall from a horse as "bad news, though not as bad as it might have been" (p. 206), he rules out visiting his son because he respects Eddie's independence. (Australian men shrink from emotion throughout White; Stan Parker refuses to touch his

dog, Basil Hunter uses the theater to cage his feelings, and Judge Twyborn's makes his avoidance of Bogong sould like Eddie's idea.) Bizarre and
even perverse on the surface, Eddie's sexuality makes sense when viewed as
an ongoing internal process. Because he couldn't reach out to his parents as
a boy, he learned to do without love. This deprivation made him feel
underserving of tenderness, intimacy, and warmth. "He wondered
whether he could really exist without the sources of unhappiness. . . . He
knew that his body and his mind craved the everlasting torments" (p. 272),
he notes of himself at age twenty-eight or thirty.

Conflict even smudges his tie with Angelos Vatatzes, perhaps the hot-
test sexual relationship in all of White. "Why am I besotted on this elderly,
dotty, in many ways tiresome Greek?" he wonders while living as Angelos's wife. An answer springs to mind straightaway: "I can only think it's
because we have been made for each other, that our minds as well as our
bodies fit, every bump to every cranny, and quirk to quirk" (p. 23). He
might have added his determination to make the love bond work. Living
with Angelos satisfies two leading impulses: his need to exchange love with
a father figure and his craving for self-laceration. The latter claim exerts a
tighter grip. Decadence sets in whenever the few move too far away from
the many. The rightness of the many counts less than the strength emanating from their control of public opinion. Eddie lives with a man forty-three
years his senior to prevent being absorbed into modern life's dreary
sameness. But his use of sexual love as a form of social protest distorts love;
his wearing a mask, i.e., women's clothes and makeup, also pads the
impact of his self-assertion. Like any other decadent, he overrates style.
Before he can give or receive love, he must dress as a woman; or his lover
must be either a middle-aged woman or an elderly man, whose encroaching feebleness will soon end all displays of sexuality; or he must be
raped. This labored orchestration of feeling kills feeling. By midlife he is
acting as if he would like to destroy sexual love altogether by draining it of
warmth, smothering it inside a scenario, and selling it to the public.

Androgyny, a fount of strength in *The Solid Mandala*, brings shame,
denial, and fragmentation in *The Twyborn Affair*, Eddie's extended drag
acts clouding, rather than enhancing, his maleness. Pluralism can impair
dialectic. The person inclined to opposing values robs himself of a strong,
hard surface from which to launch himself. He can't define himself negatively. Eddie's world shrinks and pales in each of the novel's three parts. In
Part One he lives both in and through the body; Part Two shows him again
relating to the world physically but without the joy of his high noon with
Angelos; finally he is all spirit, having disassociated himself from sex in all
but the entrepreneurial sense. This estrangement, no new development,
was prefigured both by the ephemerality of his love tie with Angelos and by
the tie's powerful sexuality. Doxy and Angelos ignore the dilapidation of

their villa, lavishing themselves on each other's flesh, swathing themselves in music, and, revealingly, confusing verb tenses. Further denials of time include their ignoring both their huge age difference and the details of their prior existences; by tacit agreement, they say very little about their lives before they met. But their timeless world is at odds with reality, which explains why it shatters when time catches up with it in the form of Joanie Golson, who appears unexpectedly in St. Mayeul. (The encounter also rocks Joanie, who finds Eudoxia as desirable as she had found Eadie years before; a major proposition in the novel states that time resurrects as well as destroys.) Angelos fears that Joanie will take Eudoxia back to Australia, leaving him stranded. Eudoxia fears her as part of the past she both suppresses and craves. Neither party knows how much Joanie has inferred (does the former Joanie Sewell see well, runs the implied pun), but they can't afford to wait for an answer. Time has run out. They leave, i.e., defect from, St. Mayeul, and within days Angelos is dead.

The coincidence of Eudoxia's twenty-fifth birthday with her discovery of Joanie infers the inescapability of those finite values—change and time—which will plague Eddie in Part Two, where the revenant Joanie is again fled. The physical self that Eddie indulged in southern France he mortifies while jackarooing at Bogong, the Lushingtons' ranch in the Monaro district of New South Wales (setting also of *Happy Valley*). The physicality dominating Part Two occurs in Eddie's daily routine of manual labor, his falling from a horse, his plunge into an icy stream, and the sex he has with both Marcia Lushington and Don Prowse, Bogong's manager. This physicality generates a meaning that scares Eddie. As befits the outdoors setting of most of the unit, green, the color of fertility in White, [2] permeates Part Two. The fertility symbolism justifies itself: lambs are born, a local woman marries and gives birth, and Eddie fathers a son with Marcia. In keeping with his negativism, though, the baby dies and Eddie defects. Bogong offers everything he needs to renew himself. Yet he denies himself the joys of renewal and refreshment. Though he enjoys sex with Marcia more than he had planned, he downgrades both the act and the pleasure it gives. Whenever Marcia speaks lovingly to him, he answers with a slur. His inner demon has driven him to self-disparagement. He calls things by their ugliest names and searches out the most demeaning details to spoil his fun. Instead of basking in Marcia's charm, which, having roused him, a homosexual, must be impressive, he fixates on the bubbles forming in the gaps between her teeth and the skin tone which reminds him of raw scallop.

Eddie degrades Marcia because women threaten him. He can never think of his former fiancée, Marian Dibden, whom he jilted the night before their wedding, without conjuring up the image of an enclosed tennis court, symbolic of gentility's constraints; Waldo Brown's first sortie

into polite society in *Mandala* also occurred at a tennis party. Yet Eddie's
ties with men rattle him as much as those with women. As Eudoxia, he
continually thought about leaving Angelos. He does leave the stormy,
middle-aged Don Prowse, but only after having sex with him. Sobbing and
reeking of whisky, Don rapes him in a barn. Their "breathing in some kind
of harmony" (p. 285) afterward suggests Eddie's complicity; if he didn't
actively provoke Don, he instinctively accepted him. A week later he
mounts Don, but this consummation, rather than bringing the two men
together, divides them permanently. As Ellen did with Garnet Roxburgh in
Fringe, he turns from Don after seeing his instincts overcome his reason; he
won't accept the meaning of his act. No sooner has he risen from Don than
he tells him he is leaving Bogong the next day.

He remains in flight. The many comparisons between brothel-keeping
and running a convent show that, as Eadith Trist, bawd of Beckwith Street,
he has renounced flesh for spirit. Eddie doesn't know whether his identity
as Eadith represents discovery or escape from self. The futility accompanying Eadith's longstanding love for her patron, Lord Roderick Gravenor,
sets a new limit in self-denial; Rod makes a deeper psychic impact than
Don Prowse did. Rod's two names also invoke the truth, familiar in White,
that sexual passion can be deathly. This truth applies as keenly to Eadith as
to anybody in the novel. She has learned that masks and disguises can take
on a reality never intended by their wearers. Anybody who wears a mask
or a disguise will eventually come to resemble it; nor will he be able to
detach himself from it. Eadith's substitution of aesthetic for moral principles has cost her dearly. She can't love Rod physically because to do so
would disclose her sexual identity. Rod is thus denied mental and physical
knowledge of the person he loves. What is more, he can never know that
Eadith's sacrifice surpasses his own: "She must struggle back to the lover
she had failed, and would continue failing, because of the importance his
illusions held for both of them" (p. 411). Normally grounded in trust and
openness, love for her demands falsehood. She must forgo the physical
consummation which normally confirms love, for Rod's sake as well as her
own. In her laborious quest to scale new erotic heights, she has forteited
those mundane joys which strengthen and console the most conventional,
unimaginative suburbanite. She has mastered only the technique of illusion. Her house and her facade possess her fully.

Nor can she escape the shadow of sexual abnormality or depravity.
She drifts into prostitution slowly but inevitably, the Chelsea whorehouse
standing as an emblem of London, where she has chosen to live. The sex
she has ruled out for herself fascinates her as an intellectual exercise.
Before setting up as a bawd, she worked for a florist, tending and vending
the phallus-like blooms. Australian practicality, which White contrasts
throughout with the ineffectuality of European tradition and culture, helps

her change careers and then prosper. Her business grows; she moves to larger quarters, adds new girls, makes capital improvements, and wins the patronage of society's upper crust. But if her expertise brings Eadith aesthetic accomplishment, power, fame, and money, it continues to leave her empty; fantasy and the elaborate scenarios needed to maintain it choke vitality. Like Genet's Madame Irma in *The Balcony* (1956), she maintains the formality of her revels. Because any show of spontaneity threatens this control, the favors she peddles are curiously sexless; the more perverse those favors, the more deliberate their planning and packaging. And she, as impresario and director of the charade, is the most sexless of all. White's reference to her "over-organized, airless house" (p. 420) refers both to her strict supervision and to her appearing to her charges as an abbess, an artist, and a sergeant major. The hidden peephole fitted to each "cell" (p. 329) of her house also makes her an all-seeing God. (White's reference to the "steely tonsure" and "monastic scalp" [p. 428] of Eddie at the end, just before he is bombed to death, suggests, in another key, the deathliness of joining the human to the divine.) Brothel-keeping dwarfs and deprives her while appearing to elevate her. The path between her brothel and some of England's most exclusive homes is well worn, as the titled and the powerful visit Beckwith street, invite her to their salons and weekend house parties, and elevate her into an institution. She succeeds so wildly with England's *haute monde* because, while she shares its values, her Australianness helps her from being taken in completely. Thanks in part to this outsider's objectivity, her house consorts with, rather than defying, the decadence and brutality of the day.

But, as always, her success is a function of personal failure. Unable to escape the shackles of self, she takes no instinctive stand, reducing human sexuality to a system of effects carefully arranged to win a clientele. She has lost track of who she is and what she wants. Hers is the art of abstraction (like that of White, another Anglicized homosexual artist from Australia who has gained honors but not the warmth of feeling accepted for himself?). The drabness of her everyday routine shows how her lonely rebellion has failed: whatever sleep she can grab (she is insomniac) comes when she is alone; she goes walking alone at dawn, when the demands of her job relax, wearing the flowing, out-of-date clothes most helpful to her impersonation. Her world is a poor show. Rosemary Dinnage has related her self-defeating routine to her name: "She is abbess, headmistress, a neuter. . . . She is *triste;* and arranges trysts, unattainable for herself, between aristocrats and her stable of hand-picked and disciplined whores."[3] Eadith's last name (echoing, incidentally, the name of Tristan, who, like her, discovered forbidden love the path to death in a foreign land) also invites variations on the word "trust." Her house is a trust in the sense of being a large, solid business supported by powerful patrons and backers. It has achieved its eminence because of its foundation in trust: its guests don't have to worry about robbery, police raids, or venereal disease. On the other hand, this sad trysting place relies upon illusion and deception. Eadith's expertise rules out trust, especially self-trust. "Mrs. Trist represents the ultimate sadness of a confused sexual identity,"[4] says Schapiro, and her argument can be borne out. When a divided psychosexuality like Eadith's is further addled by self-imposed restraints, sadness must result. What is more, the distrust she engenders spreads outward. Rod Gravenor never knows how close his explanation of their mutual frustration comes to the truth: "You never trust me, do you? or believe me, Eadith darling" (p. 405). Her invocation of her business in her answer shows how adept she has become at concealment. Trust is a luxury she can't afford.

To her surprise, the chance to lower her defenses does come. She accidentally meets her mother, perhaps the only person in the world with whom she can risk being herself. Their reunion takes place on a bench adjoining the church where Eadie, now old and widowed, came to pray. She and Eadith scribble notes to each other on the flyleaf of a prayer book. What they want to communicate is too desperate for speech; White says of Eadith, "she couldn't have trusted her lips" (p. 422) to convey her meaning to her mother. The first words spoken after the written exchange—significantly, by Eadie—create a harmony Eadith has never known. For the first time her mother has given her tenderness and support. Such is the power of love that her lifetime of deprivation takes only a minute to dispel. After Eadith identifies herself as Eadie's daughter, in response to being asked if she is Eadie's son, Eddie, Eadie says, "I am so glad. I've always wanted a daughter" (p. 423). Eadith takes heart that her mother has seen through her disguise; the recognition proclaims Eadith's existence as solid and abiding. Moreover, this existence has been welcomed on its own terms. Eadith has finally been accepted for herself.

She can now risk taking the next step. Buoyed by her new self-confidence, Eadith becomes Eddie. The supremely male activity of warfare aids the change, as it did twenty-five years before. Having earned both a commission and a DSO in World War I, he also puts on men's clothes for the first time in years during the London blitz. The bomb that kills him seems like a pessimist's practical joke. Grim and wrenching, *The Twyborn Affair* begins in displacement and ends in death. That the bomb which kills Eddie also severs his hand from his arm amounts to a divine, or authorial, rebuke; the man who always reached for the perverse and the outrageous has his wrist slapped by a flying shard of concrete when he tries to be himself. Earlier versions of his punishment lend symbolic force to his wrist-severing; it is almost as if White is refining a narrative element to which his writer's instinct led him. Getting his hand caught in a cheese press when he was a boy gave Dick Gluyas, Ellen's father in *Fringe*, a gnarled yellow horn in place of a thumbnail; in *Twyborn Affair* Don Prowse has a blue thumbnail and Greg Lushington a purple one; reaching into dangerous corners may have also torn a hole in the index finger of Eadith's glove (as it did to the glove of Eden Standish in *The Living and the Dead*).

The glove symbolism adds to the book's pessimism. Eddie's accomplished artistry as a bawd has turned his into a living death. Yet when he steps outside the brothel to test himself anew, he dies violently. Death awaits him whichever way he turns. This bleak, puzzling resolution bespeaks tired technique. White uses the bombing not to force a confrontation or to provoke a revelation, but to bilk Eddie of his chance. The references to holocaust and apocalypse in the novel's closing pages play White's vision false. Eadie may have to return to Australia with the mistaken belief that her child has reverted to his usual practice of defecting. At her age she can't realistically hope to see Eddie again; nor will she know what happened to him, or why. In mitigation, though, Eddie did find what he wanted and even plucked up the nerve to pursue it. He ignored falling bombs to face his mother dressed and barbered as a man. Eadie seems to have intuited his purpose, too, waiting for him in her room rather than following a "kindly maid" (p. 430) to her hotel's bomb shelter. In reuniting with Eadith, she recovered her own lost, vital past. If she has been cheated of her supreme fulfillment—receiving Eadith as Eddie—her discovery of the child she hasn't seen in twenty years has helped heal the wounds caused by her husband's death. Not only has she glimpsed her private paradise but, by loving her child for the first time, she has also experienced it directly. White should have trusted her and Eddie to wrest meaning from their union, which needed no borrowed glory from public occasions.

II

Plenty of evidence can be brought forth to support G.A. Wilkes's claim that *Twyborn Affair* is "as brilliantly and delicately executed as anything Patrick White has written."[5] Deft scene-shifting varies both mood and tempo as the action swings from the French Riviera to New South Wales before ending in London. But this variety would fall flat if it weren't refreshed by descriptive vitality. The rhythm and control of White's language engages our hearts in addition to winning our respect. Properties radiate from the things and people he describes, rather than just sitting passively in them, suggesting that mind inhabits all, even rocks and chairs. Particularly memorable are his descriptions of the enigmatic outback. The Monaro is a huge, wild, unpredictable place. Stiff, bristly green plants alternate with feathery pastel blooms fragrant with soft mystery. Days of fierce heat give way to freezing nights. These sharp alternations reflect the contradictions White sees in the Australian national character. Curly Golson, Joanie's merchant husband, embodies what Kenneth Minogue calls the "no-nonsense empiricism" governing Australia: "Australians are constitutionally suspicious of anything high flown, anything that strays from the observable facts of nature."[6] Bored with art, religion, and intellectuality, Curly feels most comfortable around familiar possessions, like his brushes and his tweeds. He spends his European vacation dozing, reading English-language newspapers, and going to the races, rather than visiting cathedrals and art galleries. Yet his wife underrates him when she refers to his "native crudity" (p. 54). This boyish, stolid colonial will act decently and sensibly in a crisis, even though he lacks Old World polish. Other Australians, mostly women, let European culture and tradition cow them. The old colonial cringe works full throttle on Joanie Golson, as it did on Alfreda Courtney in *Vivisector;* the greater the Australian exile's social ambitions, the more burdensome she will find her colonial background. Joanie is immobilized by her fear of committing a social gaffe, and the more complex and ambivalent Eddie, who lives as a woman in Europe, prefers to suppress his nature rather than look uncouth.

This confusion is foreshadowed in the book's first sentence, a question Eudoxia/Eadith will ask herself many times: "Which road this afternoon, Madam?" (p. 11). The developing action lends resonance to the question. Not until the start of Part Two do readers learn that Doxy was a Twyborn, and even if they had suspected that she was Eadie's child, they still believed her to have been female. Only in Angelos's dying words at the end of Part One is Doxy identified as a man: "I have had from you, dear boy, the only happiness I've ever known" (p. 126), Angelos tells Doxy in front of their landlady. The Twyborn affair has been unfolding right before the reader's eyes but without his knowledge, adding, in the process, the art of misdirection to White's store of literary skills. The magician's sleight-of-hand also touches Part Two, which, like Part Three of *The Solid Mandala*, begins on an ocean liner bound for Australia, with many new characters on board. But White has introduced another surprise by rousing expectations he knows he will not fulfill. The ocean setting has led us to look for the Golsons, who had booked passage on a liner to flee the dangers of a Europe girding for war; but several years have passed, the war that frightened the Golsons is over, and the homeward-bound Australian is Eddie. Eddie will profit, however briefly, from time's ability to resurrect as it destroys. The news of his father's death, conveyed, appropriately, at an English country house party, an image of decadence for White, helps Eddie's manhood to resurface. Shaken by the sad news, Eadith cuts the weekend party short and returns to London. She has not fled the past, having already blundered into Joanie Golson, who is now fat, old, and nearly blind, just days before the party. Eadith sees in her mother's ex-lover the leading themes of her own life—homosexuality, encroaching age, and the denial of her Australian past as an attribute of loneliness—and she finds herself able to face them squarely.

White seems to suffer as much as Eadith does from her earlier struggles both to reenter time and to accept herself. The malice unearthed by these struggles contradicts Wilkes's belief that *Twyborn Affair* is "one of his [White's] most compassionate books."[7] The novel lacks good will, openness of mind, and carefree humor. It hardly recounts an experience without referring to it with disdain or revulsion. Experience that can't be described as nasty or brutal seems to bore White. Although he shows different forms of ugliness in close detail, he dismisses the reunion of Eadie and Eadith in a blanket, passive summary: "Eadith visited her mother the following afternoon, and then regularly. They had many delightful conversations, others more disquieting" (p. 424). The first kiss that mother and child have exchanged in twenty years he describes as the foraging of pigs: "Mother and daughter nuzzled at each other's cheeks; they might have been foraging for some elusive truffle" (p. 425). Women are portrayed scurvily in the book. Recurring from *Aunt's Story* and later works is an obsession with women's mustaches. Some of his descriptions imply that it is normal for a woman to be mustachioed: Joanie Golson "fell to dabbling where the mustache would have been" (p. 15), and she later notices Eudoxia perspiring "just where a mustache would have been" (p. 85). White doesn't know when to stop. The mustaches on Theodora Goodman and Dulcie Feinstein Saporta were thematic, expressing the vitality of the women's male qualities. However, like Eadie's mustache of burnt cork, Marcia Lushington's "too heavy Caucasian mustache" (p. 215) is only a blot which White, in his drive to denigrate, searches for on the upper lips of Doxy and Joanie as well.

This drive runs perhaps deeper in *Twyborn Affair* than in White's other novels. If the teeth of a minor character are "only very slightly buckled" (p. 134), they hardly merit a mention, other than giving White a chance to demean. The English upper classes (to which the girl with the slightly buckled teeth belongs) face heavy attack for their alleged sexual misconduct, which they will sometimes lavish on people of a different race. Trying to temper his manufactured moral outrage with a deadpan tone, White merely apes Evelyn Waugh in his summary of an English socialite's disgrace: "Cecily had been forced to leave the country for a while after an affair with an entire negro band ending in the death of a drummer and exposure of a drug ring" (p. 337). Later, a brigadier general (whose priest brother is one of Eadith's best customers) dies atop a black prostitute. White enjoys invoking the death penalty for sexual misconduct. An aristocrat recalls "poor darling Daddy dying of a drawn-out bout with unconfessed syph" (p. 347), and one of Eadith's whores, a religious girl who attends mass and confession daily, is murdered by a priest. Still another whore falls under a train at Clapman Junction, a respectable suburb when the death took place; perhaps White killed her both to give the lie to suburban respectability and to punish her for going where she didn't belong. The contradiction marring his angry justice fits with the disgust for human purpose he registers throughout the action.

This disgust spoils *Twyborn Affair*'s third part. White's description of sex in works like *Vivisector* and *Fringe* have an externality their clawing voracity never dispels. In sexual matters White is always the rapt outsider, torn between attraction and revulsion. William Walsh justifiably objects, in an otherwise friendly review, to "a certain flawed condition . . . which allows flourishes of melodrama"[8] in the novel. What White intends as comic turns out to be melodramatic in the sense that bad melodrama dwarfs and vulgarizes what it sets out to heighten. Because of his unsure comic sense, the scenes in Beckwith Street are too scattered, tasteless, and disconcerting to sustain dramatic tension. In particular, the anecdotes about Eadith's fillies disclose a squeamishness parading as a desire to shock. A clubfooted Irish girl specializing in chains and whips tells Eadith, "Some gentlemen . . . come in their pants at the sight of me in me surgical boot" (p. 332). An anecdote about an ageing prostitute begins: "Maisie had been let live in the attic of a house belonging to a rich benevolent queer, who was in the habit of siphoning off some of her rougher trade" (p. 362). Also, the problems Eadith must deal with inside her house look prearranged and predictable because of their range in mood and severity. One of her whores suffers from body odor, while another tries to give herself an abortion with a knitting needle; a third and fourth, the darkest and fairest-skinned members of the stable, fall in love and grow possessive.

White the craftsman knows that such clumsy strokes impair the broader moral effects of serious fiction. Yet he also writes from his deepest self, where such moral insights means little. Both the wild coincidences, like Eadith's three chance discoveries of her mother in London, and the sad artistic comedown of the brothel scenes stem from White's closeness to his materials. *The Twyborn Affair* needs distancing. Ironically, this fictional warning about the dangers of masks and disguises suffers for want of a mediating interface. Like Eddie, White served as a military officer and worked as a jackaroo in New South Wales after living in Europe; while he was writing about Doxy's romantic career with Angelos, he, too, was living with a Greek gentleman in his sixties; he may also have found, like Eadith, that the art he had intended as a pathway into life instead shut out life. A particularly painful moment in the novel that cries out with pain comes in White's giving the first and shortest-lived of the Lushington's dead infant sons his own birthday, 28 May 1912. One of the novel's epigraphs, from the photographer Diane Arbus, reads, "Sometimes you'll see someone with nothing on but a bandaid"; Eddie Twyborn's last words are, "Fetch me a bandaid, Ada" (p. 430). *The Twyborn Affair* neither asks easy questions nor relaxes into a cozy narrative mode. White comes to us covered only by a bandaid in order to establish the truth. Any artist who gives so much of himself deserves to have his faults excused. The mistakes in *Twyborn Affair* were not only worth making but would also be worth repeating. Destroying and creating himself simultaneously, White both extends artistic frontiers and enhances our knowledge of the human psyche. Rarely has fragmentation been portrayed with such brutal intensity as in this novel. But while we flinch from the portrayal, we also marvel at it. White's savage imagination, ignoring civilized constraints, is nonetheless a civilizing force. High, grand, and subtle, his sources of inspiration are larger than life, not twisted or neurotic. They spring from imaginative breadth, daring, and intense dedication.

Conclusion:
Courting the Ineffable

ANY FINAL assessment of Patrick White's art must deal with Leonie Kramer's objection to his "strict supervision" of narrative flow, character deployment, and dialogue: "The spontaneous overflow of life that is so characteristic of Dickens and Dostoyevsky . . . is notably absent in White. . . . There is a deliberation which suggests that each step is carefully planned, and that the whole action is moving towards a predetermined end. Curiously, that end, when it comes, might not seem so inevitable as one would expect, nor as appropriate as that of the more conventionally planned, yet also more casually narrated novel."[1]

Kramer's brilliant disclaimer neglects the strong sense of subtext in White's work—the many unarticulated turns of emotion and changes of mind that comprise our inner worlds yet never get translated into observable behavior. "Everything important, alas, can only be experienced alone" (*Twyborn Affair*, p. 80) notes Eudoxia Vatatzes in one of those passages that have made readers wonder whether White is a novelist. Identity precedes belonging; a person must be something before he/she can be part of something else. Listening to the private voices of his characters, White records buried experience—the poems we might have written and the lovers we might have embraced. Kramer's insight into the apparent clash between his idea and enactment counts more to White's credit than to his detriment. He has been widely attacked for both randomness and oversupervision (but not in the same essay, other than Kramer's).

Brian Davies's statement, "The sensed power is behind the novels rather than being present in them,"[2] implies that White is not working up to the full range of his talent. White does give the contradictory impressions of slacking and pushing too hard. Nor can the impressions be discounted. Carefully developed novels like *Voss* and *Riders* call to mind the truth that the best literature has a reality that reality itself lacks. Yet their self-insistence undermines the truth they purport to convey. Just as life's greatest goods, like health and happiness, are best enjoyed unconsciously, so do great books leave much unsaid, substituting analogy for direct statement. White can't be engaging and profound at the same time. Trying too hard, he worries his ideas, and his scenes look contrived for the sake of producing a preordained effect.

Yet literature is supposed to lend form to life. Like Kramer, we look for conclusiveness at the end of a novel. Art arranges and simplifies its materials for the purpose of describing the artist's feelings both about the world and about himself. White defies our preconceptions about narrative art because he leaves in the discontinuities and contradictions; "Truth is more often ugliness than beauty" (*Twyborn Affair*, p. 344), says Eadith Trist. White has set out to convey as truthfully as possible an enigma, and enigmas disregard those aesthetic paradigms we have been trained to lean on to make sense of a narrative. His refusal to mediate or lend form to the experiences he recounts gives the impression that he has confused literature with life; i.e., he has frustrated our craving for form. The surprise or accident that bespeaks life's vibrancy can undermine a novel, which is expected to be balanced, integrated, and self-correcting. White's work posits a mystery no human formulas can explain—a network of essences that informs the gross material world and makes everything redeemable. The spiritual truths coursing through the world of daily experiences are always a presence if not a force. Those two epigraphs to *The Solid Mandala*—"There is another world, but it is in this one" and "It is not outside, it is inside: wholly within"—undergird White's metaphysics.

But they ignore his doubt and unrest. The ideal rarely reveals itself in actuality. Having come to consciousness in World War I and to manhood in World War II, he knows conflict firsthand. The dark gods speak to him as loudly as the white ones do; ugliness stirs him as deeply as beauty. This self-division has made him shake an angry fist at the universe. His most vivid impulses are pessimistic, but even his pessimism, while spiritually necessary, he finds intellectually suspect. Although his despair offends his mind as deeply as it moves his soul, his psyche also rejects truths that his mind affirms. Whereas he can rationally accept the truth that life makes no absolute statements, he recoils from it emotionally and spiritually, his notion of the ideal having imposed a standard he can't compromise. The same ugliness that offers redemption makes him wince; Theodora Goodman goes mad, Himmelfarb suffers and dies, and the once-beautiful Elizabeth Hunter retains the mental clarity to see herself dried and twisted by age. Yet all purposeful activity sacrifices some feature of human life that will impress many as all important. White's saints of failure have a tragic sense of life. Perceiving existential shadows, they seek deeper rewards than are promised by wealth, property, and social rank. In recounting their tragedies White is dealing with his own ambivalence while also taking on the difficult and the mysterious in the world at large. His risks include writing about themes he can't perceive clearly enough either to control or to know; in *Fringe*, Ellen and Jack Chance dream the same dream simultaneously, and Theodora Goodman wonders about "the way you can sometimes grasp experience before it is undergone" (*Aunt's Story*, p. 80). This preoccupation with freeing onself from time's constraints typifies White. In 1980 he discussed the problem of trying to shape the impalpable: "What do I believe? I'm accused of not making it explicit. How to be explicit about an overreaching grandeur, a daily wrestling match with an opponent whose limbs never become material. . . . Whose essence is contained less in what is said than in the silences."[3]

His work shows what happens to those who, like him, court the ineffable. The intense person perceives reality more keenly than the rest of us, but his solitary brooding also sets him so far apart from us that he can't come back. Committing oneself to the mystery of unity causes madness; Sophocles's sphinx, Shakespeare's Fool, and Melville's Pip all spoke in riddles because they dared not express their visions directly. White's Doll Quigley and Arthur Brown come to grief, having neglected the division between the human and the divine, that no man's land that entices Eddie Twyborn. One must stand close enough to the fire to be warmed, but not so close as to be burned—expecially if one is only wearing a bandaid. On the other hand, the hearts of those who withdraw from the flames remain frozen; the shallow and the complacent can never perceive the truth. How to decode the ultimate? Perhaps the laborious licking of a postage stamp by a Vic Moriarty (*Happy Valley*) or a Boo Hollingrake (*Vivisector*), the music of Chabrier, which sounds through *Twyborn Affair*, or the discordancies of White's sometimes ugly, disintegrating syntax holds a clue.

Such intimations should suffice. The very elements comprising reality unleash doom. Fire burns the Hôtel du Midi, the Armstrongs' Glastonbury, and Himmelfarb's shack; breathing Sydney's rank air undermines Alf Dubbo's already weak lungs and hastens his death; Nance Lightfoot breaks up on the rocks and earth near Hurtle Duffield's shack; Oswald Dignam drowns in a snarling sea. These depredations achieve a resonance that jars our basic assumptions about life as well as about literature. We find ourselves upset over having these assumptions shaken and over being denied safe alternatives to take their place. The dread that grazes our spines constitutes a moral prod; we must make our way in a landscape rife with pain and ugliness. This landscape recalls Marianne Moore's statement in "Poetry" about "imaginary gardens with real toads in them." But the gleams it gives out also foster the intellectual independence and individualism to sift the ethereal from the gross, even if the job must be done amid shadows, echoes, and silhouettes.

Notes

CHAPTER 1

1. "Patrick White," in *In the Making*, ed. Craig McGregor (Melbourne: Nelson, 1969), pp. 219-20.

2. Peter Shrubb, "Patrick White: Chaos Accepted," *Quadrant* 12 (May-June 1968): 8.

3. McGregor, ed., *In the Making*, p. 220.

4. "A Conversation with Patrick White," *Southerly* 33 (1973): 139.

5. Katherine England, "God the Vivisector," *Adelaide Advertiser*, 24 October 1970, p. 16; Zulfikar Ghose, "The One Comprehensive Vision," *Texas Studies in Literature and Language* (hereinafter cited as *TSLL*) 21 (Summer 1979): 264-65.

6. R.F. Brissenden, *Patrick White* (London: Longmans, Green, 1966), p. 19.

7. J.R. Dyce, *Patrick White as Playwright* (St. Lucia [Brisbane]: University of Queensland Press, 1974), p. 51.

8. Harry Heseltine, "Patrick White's Style," *Quadrant* 7 (Winter 1963): 61-74.

9. McGregor, ed., *In the Making*, p. 220.

10. Veronica Brady, "*A Fringe of Leaves*: Civilization by the Skin of Our Own Teeth," *Southerly* 37 (June 1977): 125.

11. "White Will Give Away Nobel Prize Money," *Canberra Times*, 20 October 1973, p. 3; "Patrick White Gives Away $80,000," *Sydney Morning Herald*, 20 October 1973, p. l; Perth *West Australian*, 20 October 1973, p. 4.

12. See Peter Beatson, *The Eye in the Mandala* (London: Elek, 1976), p. 48.

13. *Diane Arbus*, ed. Doon Arbus and Marvin Israel (Millerton, N.Y.: Aperture, 1973), p. 3.

14. Beatson, *Eye in Mandala*, p. 106.

15. Ibid., p. 48.

16. Ibid., p. 9.

17. R.F. Brissenden, "*The Vivisector*: Art and Science," in *The Australian Experience*, ed. W.S. Ramson (Canberra: Australian National University Press, 1974), pp. 311-12.

18. Beatson, *Eye in Mandala*, p. 167.

19. G.A. Wilkes, "Patrick White's *The Tree of Man*," in *Ten Essays on Patrick White*, ed. G.A. Wilkes (Sydney: Angus and Robertson, 1970), p. 3l.

20. Dorothy Green, "*Voss*: Stubborn Music," in Ramson, ed., *Australian Experience*, p. 287.

21. Patrick White, "The Prodigal Son," *Australian Letters* 1 (April 1958): 39.

22. "Patrick White's Nightmare," [Sydney] *Observer*, 22 February 1958, p. 19.

23. Rodney Mather, "Patrick White and Lawrence: A Contrast," *Critical Review* (Melbourne) 13 (1970): 48.

24. Leonie Kramer, "*The Tree of Man*: An Essay in Skepticism," in Ramson, ed., *Australian Experience*, p. 273.

25. Beatson, *Eye in Mandala*, p. 1.

26. Brian Kiernan, *Images of Society and Nature* (Melbourne: Oxford University Press, 1971), p. 134.

27. Kramer, "Essay in Skepticism," p. 281.

28. Alan Lawson, "Meaning and Experience: A Review-Essay on Some Recurrent Problems in Patrick White Criticism," *TSLL* 21 (Summer 1979): 291.

29. "New Novels," *Sydney Morning Herald*, 1 April 1939, p. 20; A.D. Hope, "The Bunyip Stages a Comeback," ibid., 16 June 1956, p. 15; Roy Campbell, "Foggy Weather over Leichhardt," *Sydney Daily Telegraph*, 15 February 1958 p. 18; "Patrick White's Nightmare," [Sydney] *Observer*, 22 February 1958, p. 19.

30. William Walsh, *Patrick White's Fiction* (Sydney: George Allen and Unwin, 1977), p. 25; George Steiner, "Books: Down Under," *New Yorker*, 23 May 1977, p. 132.

31. Thelma Herring, "Odyssey of a Spinster: A Study of *The Aunt's Story*," in Wilkes, ed., *Ten Essays*, p. 3; Kiernan, *Images*, p. 147.

32. Herring, "Odyssey," pp. 4, 25; Mather, "White and Lawrence," p. 37.

33. Hope, "Bunyip," p. 15.

34. Neil Jillett, "Patrick White Returns to Sarsaparilla," [Melbourne] *Age*, 28 May 1966, p. 21.

35. Heseltine, "White's Style," p. 61.

36. Beatson, *Eye in Mandala*, p. 135.

37. See also *Riders in the Chariot*, p. 119, and *The Vivisector*, p. 43.

38. Angus Wilson, "The Lives of the Saints of Sarsaparilla," *London Observer*, 29 October 1961, p. 30; Kevon Kemp, "The Season in Sydney," *Bulletin*, 1 June 1963, p. 32; Roger Covell, "Patrick White's Plays," *Quadrant* 8 (April-May 1964): 11.

39. White, "Prodigal Son," p. 37.

40. Russel Ward, *The History of Australia: The Twentieth Century* (New York: Harper and Row, 1978), p. 208.

41. "There is very little that Australians do that does not have a certain sporty element about it, summed up in the national motto of 'Have a go.' It gives them a friendly directness that often cuts through the Gordian rituals of much European intercourse, the sort of rituals that enforce social distance" (Kenneth Minogue, "Material Benefits," *TLS*, 9 April 1976, p. 19).

42. White, "Prodigal Son," p. 37.

43. Jack Lindsay, "The Alienated Australian Intellectual," *Meanjin* 22 (March 1963): 58.

44. "The exaltation of the 'average' . . . made me panic most," said White of his return to Australia in 1948 after having lived abroad for many years ("Prodigal Son," p. 39).

45. Ibid., pp. 39-40.

46. McGregor, ed., *In the Making*, p. 220.

CHAPTER 2

1. Elisabeth Riddell, "The Whites: Patrick, Pastoralists and Polo Ponies," *Bulletin* 8 (January 1980): 44-49.

2. Patrick White, *The Ploughman and Other Poems* (Sydney: Beacon Press, 1935), n.p.

3. "New Novels," *Sydney Morning Herald*, 1 April 1939, p. 20.

4. Barry Argyle, *Patrick White* (Edinburgh: Oliver and Boyd, 1967), p. 7

5. Brissenden, *White*, pp. 16-17.

6. Argyle, *White*, p. 18.

7. Marjorie Bernard, "The Four Novels of Patrick White," *Meanjin* 15 (June 1956): 158.

8. Robert K. Johnson, "Patrick White and Theodora Goodman: Two Views of Reality," *Explorations* 6 (1979): 14.

9. Edmond Marin La Meslée, *The New Australia, 1883*, trans. and ed. Russel Ward (London: Heinemann, 1973), p. 17.

CHAPTER 3

1. Susan White, the novelist's only sibling and his junior by two years, died in the 1950s. She had acted in some of her brother's early plays in Sydney in the 1930s. A copy of *Thirteen Poems* (12 sheets, stapled and tied, printed and numbered on rectos only) is owned by the University of Sydney's Fisher Library, catalog no. RB 1630.19.

2. White, "Prodigal Son," p. 38; Patrick White, "Flaws in the Glass, Sketches for a Self-Portrait," *The Bulletin: Centenary Issue*, 29 January 1980, pp. 148, 151.

3. "A Conversation with Patrick White," p. 133.

4. White, "Prodigal Son," p. 38.

5. Herring, "Odyssey," p. 7.

6. Patricia A. Morley, *The Mystery of Unity: Theme and Technique in the Novels of Patrick White* (Toronto: McGill-Queens University Press, 1972), p. 49.

7. McGregor, ed., *In the Making*, p. 219.

8. Bernard, "Four Novels," p. 161.

9. Ibid., p. 161.

CHAPTER 4

1. "A Patrick White Chronology," *TSLL* 21 (Summer 1979): 304.

2. Johnson, "White and Goodman," pp. 14-15.

3. Cecil Hadgraft, "The Theme of Revelation in Patrick White's Novels," *Southerly* 37 (March 1977): 35.

4. Veronica Brady, "The Novelist and the Reign of Necessity: Patrick White

and Simone Weil," in *Patrick White: A Critical Symposium*, ed. R[on]. Shepard and K[irpal]. Singh (Adelaide: Centre for Research in the New Literatures in English, 1978), p. 111.

5. Peter Hastings, "The Erratic Brilliance of Patrick White," *Sydney Sunday Telegraph*, 1 March 1959, p. 98.

6. Herring, "Odyssey," pp. 12-13.

7. Ibid., p. 12; Hadgraft, "Theme of Revelation," p. 36; discussing the symbolism of Holstius's name, White said, "I liked the suggestion of *Holz* (wood) for a sturdy, though non-existent character" ("A Conversation with Patrick White," p. 141). The wooden body of Moraïtis's cello and of the pine trees growing near the intellectual George Goodman's library must have helped convince White to connect wood with transcendence and overcoming.

8. Beatson, *Eye in Mandala*, p. 137.

9. Shrubb, "White: Chaos Accepted," p. 9.

CHAPTER 5

1. Vincent Buckley, "Patrick White and His Epic," in *Australian Literary Criticism*, ed. Grahame Johnston (Melbourne: Oxford University Press, 1962), p. 188. The article first appeared in *Twentieth Century* 12 (1958): 239-52.

2. White, "Prodigal Son," p. 39.

3. W.D. Ashcroft, "More than One Horizon," in Shepard and Singh, eds., *White: A Critical Symposium*, p. 128.

4. Wilkes, "White's *Tree of Man*," p. 23.

5. "A Conversation with Patrick White," p. 136.

6. Buckley, "White and His Epic," p. 195.

7. Kramer, "*The Tree of Man*: An Essay in Skepticism," p. 268.

8. Manfred Mackenzie, "Apocalypse in Patrick White's *The Tree of Man*," *Meanjin* 25 (December 1966): 409.

9. Ibid., p. 411.

CHAPTER 6

1. Kiernan, *Images*, p. 113.

2. Geoffrey Dutton, "The Novels of Patrick White," *Critique* 6 (Winter 1963-64): 16.

3. Kylie Tennant, "Poetic Symbolism in novel by Patrick White," *Sydney Morning Herald*, 8 February 1958, p. 12; Alan Nicholls, "Miles Franklin Award Goes to White's Novel, Voss," [Melbourne] *Age*, 20 April 1958, p. 12.

4. Alan Moorehead, *Cooper's Creek* (New York: Harper, 1963), p. 24.

5. H.J. Oliver, "Patrick White's Significant Journey," *Southerly* 19 (1958): 46: Marcel Aurosseau, "The Writer in Relation to History: The Identity of Voss," in *On Native Grounds*, ed. C.B. Christesen (Sydney,: Angus and Robertson, 1968), pp. 456-67.

6. Brian Davies, "An Australian Engima: Conversation with Patrick White," *Melbourne University Magazine* (Spring 1962), p. 71.

7. Ibid., p. 71.

8. "A Conversation with Patrick White," p. 138.

9. "Patrick White's Nightmare," [Sydney] *Observer*, 22 February 1958, p. 20.

10. Kiernan, *Images*, p. 120.

11. Beatson, *Eye in Mandala*, p. 16.

12. G.A. Wilkes, "A Reading of *Voss*," in Wilkes, ed., *Ten Essays*, p. 138.

13. John B. Beston, "Voss's Proposal and Laura's Acceptance Letter: The Struggle for Dominance in *Voss*," *Quadrant* 16 (July-August 1972): 28.

14. Ibid., p. 27.

15. Argyle, *White*, p. 45.

16. "A Conversation with Patrick White," p. 138.

17. Green, "*Voss*," p. 303.

18. Ibid.

CHAPTER 7

1. David Bradley, "Australia through the Looking-Glass: Patrick White's Latest Novel," *Overland* 23 (April 1962): 43.

2. "A Conversation with Patrick White," p. 137. For insight into the religious beliefs and practices of White's forebears, see J.S. Ryan, "The Faith of His Fathers: Another Source for Patrick White's Mysticism," *Notes and Furphies: Bulletin of the Association for the Study of Australian Literature* 5 (October 1980): 16-19.

3. Morley, *Mystery of Unity*, p. 154.

4. Edgar L. Chapman, "The Mandala Design of Patrick White's *Riders in the Chariot*," *TSLL* 21 (Summer 1979): 186-202.

5. Argyle, *White*, p. 48.

6. Morley, *Mystery of Unity*, p. 158.

7. "A Conversation with Patrick White," p. 137.

8. White, "Prodigal Son," p. 38.

9. Robert F. Whitman, "The Dream Plays of Patrick White," *TSLL* 21 (Summer 1979): 257.

10. Colin Roderick, "*Riders in the Chariot*: An Exposition," *Southerly* 22 (1962): 72.

11. Argyle, *White*, p. 48.

12. John Colmer, "Duality in Patrick White," in Shepherd and Singh, eds., *White: Critical Symposium*, p. 73.

CHAPTER 8

1. McGregor, ed., *In the Making*, p. 220.

2. White, "Flaws in the Glass," pp. 151, 148.

3. D.T. Suzuki, *Zen Buddhism*, ed. William Barrett (Garden City, N.Y.: Doubleday, 1956), p. 216.

4. A.P. Riemer, "Visions of the Mandala in *The Tree of Man*," in Wilkes, ed., *Ten Essays*, p. 187.

5. Hadgraft, "Theme of Revelation," p. 40.

6. Paul M. St. Pierre, "Coterminous Beginnings," in Shepherd and Singh, eds., *White: Critical Symposium*, pp. 101-2.

7. G.A. Wilkes, "An Approach to Patrick White's *Solid Mandala*," *Southerly* 29 (1969): 110.

CHAPTER 9

1. Sir James George Frazer, *The Golden Bough*, 3rd ed. (New York: Macmillan, 1935), II, 376-87.
2. John Docker, "Patrick White and Romanticism: *The Vivisector*," *Southerly* 33 (March 1973): 51.
3. Robert S. Baker, "Romantic Onanism in *The Vivisector*," *TSLL* 21 (Summer 1979): 214.
4. Richard N. Coe, "The Artist and the Grocer: Patrick White's 'The Vivisector,'" *Meanjin* 29 (December 1970): 529.
5. Walsh, *White's Fiction*, p. 107.
6. "A Conversation with Patrick White," p. 142.
7. James Joyce, *A Portrait of the Artist as a Young Man* (New York: Viking, 1956), p. 171.
8. Baker, "Romantic Onanism," p. 206.
9. Beatson, *Eye in Mandala*, p. 55.
10. D.J. O'Hearn, "A Vision and a Model of Creativity," [Melbourne] *Age*, 31 October 1970, p. 16.
11. Docker, "White and Romanticism," p. 49.
12. William J. Scheick, "Gothic Grace and Rainbow Aesthetic," *TSLL* 21 (Summer 1979): 143.
13. Morley, *Mystery of Unity*, p. 222.
14. Adrian Mitchell, "Eventually White's Language: Words and More than Words," in Shepard and Singh, eds., *White: Critical Symposium*, p. 7.

CHAPTER 10

1. Riddell, "The Whites," p. 44.
2. Suzuki, in Barnett, ed., *Zen Buddhism*, p. 292.
3. Manfred Mackenzie, "'Dark Birds of Light': *The Eye of the Storm* as Swansong," *Southern Review* 10 (November 1977): 276.
4. Veronica Brady, "The Eye of the Storm," *Westerly* 4 (December 1973): 60.
5. *Ibid.*, p. 61.
6. Brian Kiernan, "True Smell of Mortality in New White Novel," [Melbourne] *Age*, 6 October 1973, p. 13.
7. Brady "Eye of the Storm," p. 64.

CHAPTER 11

1. For an explanation, with bibliographical references, of the misfortunes of Mrs. Fraser and the crewmates of the shipwrecked brig *Stirling Castle*, see Randolph Stow, "In the Boundless Garden," *TLS*, 10 September 1976, p. 1097, and Steiner, "Books: Down Under," pp. 131-32.

2. "A Conversation with Patrick White," p. 139.

3. Geoffrey Blainey, *The Tyranny of Distance* (Melbourne: Macmillan, 1968), explains how distance has helped shape both Australian history and the Australian self-image.

4. Brian Kiernan, *Patrick White* (New York: St. Martin's, 1980), p. 125.

5. William Hay, *The Escape of the Notorious Sir William Heans* (1919; rpt. Melbourne: Melbourne University Press, 1955), p. 3.

6. White, "Prodigal Son," p. 38.

7. Manly Johnson, "Patrick White: *A Fringe of Leaves,*" in Shepherd and Singh, eds., *White: Critical Symposium*, pp. 87-98, discusses the influence of Virgil upon White's treatment of rural and forest settings in the novel.

8. See Geoffrey Blainey, *The Rush That Never Ended: A History of Australian Mining* (Melbourne: Melbourne University Press, 1964), chs. 11 and 12.

9. John Fowles, *Islands*, photographs by Fay Godwin (Boston: Little, Brown, 1976), p. 61.

10. Dyce, *White as Playwright*, p. 103.

11. Brady, "A Fringe of Leaves," p. 135.

12. Ibid., p. 129.

13. R.F. Brissenden, "On the Edge of the Empire: Some Thoughts on Recent Australian Fiction," *Sewanee Review* 87 (Winter 1979): 150.

14. Doris Grumbach, " 'Fringe of Leaves': Noble Effort from a Nobel Prize Winner," *Los Angeles Times Book Review*, 9 January 1977, p. 1.

CHAPTER 12

1. Nancy Schapiro, "Mysteries of Sensual Identity," *St. Louis Post-Dispatch*, 30 March 1980, p. 4C.

2. Dyce, *White as Playwright*, p. 103.

3. Rosemary Dinnage, "Her Life as a Man," *New York Review of Books*, 17 April 1980, p. 25.

4. Schapiro, "Mysteries," p. 4C.

5. G.A. Wilkes, "White Has Not Yet Begun to Write," *Weekend Australian Magazine*, 10-11 November 1979, p. 12.

6. Minogue, "Material Benefits," p. 419.

7. Wilkes, "White Has Not Yet Begun to Write." p. 12.

8. William Walsh, "Centres of the Self," *TLS*, 30 November 1979, p. 77.

CONCLUSION

1. Kramer, "*The Tree of Man*," p. 269.

2. Davies, "Australian Enigma: Conversation with Patrick White," p. 69.

3. White, "Flaws in the Glass," p. 151.

Index